YA   8/16/05
GRAPHIC NOVEL   12.99
FAN

Fantastic Four

FANTASTIC 4

Adaptation by Mike Carey
Based on the Motion Picture Screenplay by Mark Frost and Michael France
Pencils: Dan Jurgens
Inks: Sandu Florea
Colors: SotoColor's J. Rauch
Letters: V.C.'s Mike Sellers
Assistant Editor: Nicole Wiley
Editor: John Barber
Consulting Editor: Ralph Macchio
Assistant Managing Editor: Amy Vandevender

FANTASTIC FOUR #5 (July 1962)
Writer: Stan Lee
Penciler: Jack Kirby
Inker: Joe Sinnott
Letters: Art Simek
Color Reconstruction: Digital Chameleon

FANTASTIC FOUR #190 (January 1978)
Writer/Editor: Marv Wolfman
Layouts: Sal Buscema
Finishes: Tony Dezuniga
Colors: Glynis Wein
Letters: Joe Rosen
Color Reconstruction: Jerron Quality Color

FANTASTIC FOUR #60 (October 2002)
Writer: Mark Waid
Penciler: Mark Wieringo
Inker: Karl Kesel
Colors: Paul Mounts
Letters: Richard Starkings & Comicraft's
Albert Deschesne
Editor: Tom Brevoort

Senior Editor, Special Projects: Jeff Youngquist
Assistant Editor: Jennifer Grünwald
Director of Sales: David Gabriel
Book Designer: Carrie Beadle
Creative Director: Tom Marvelli

Editor in Chief: Joe Quesada
Publisher: Dan Buckley

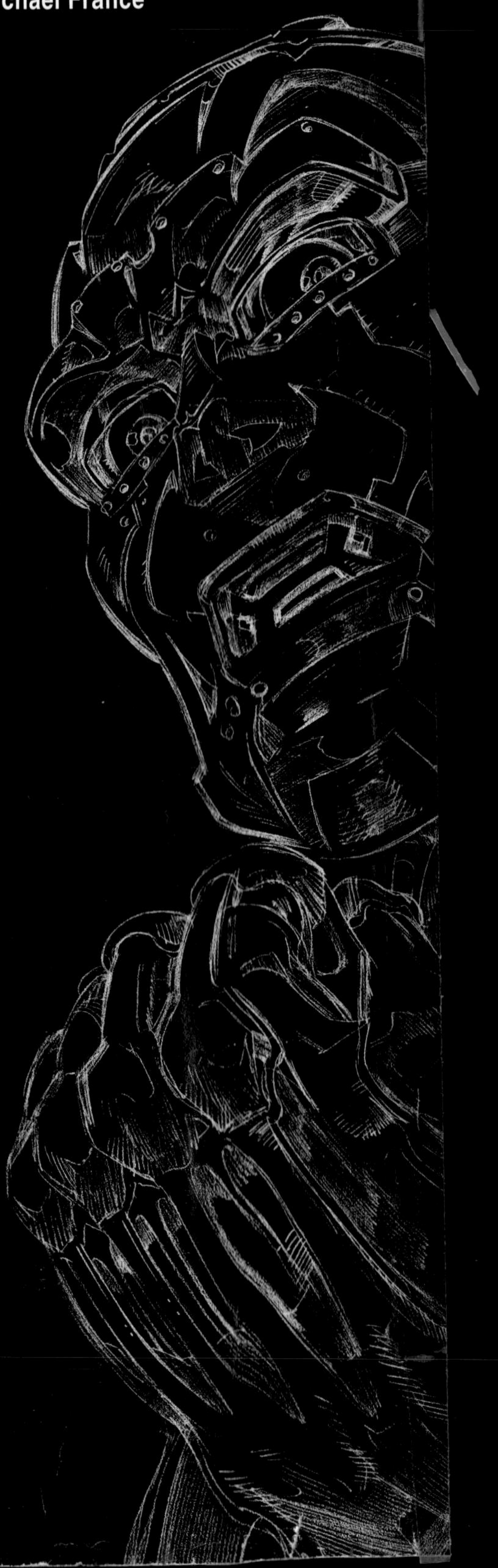

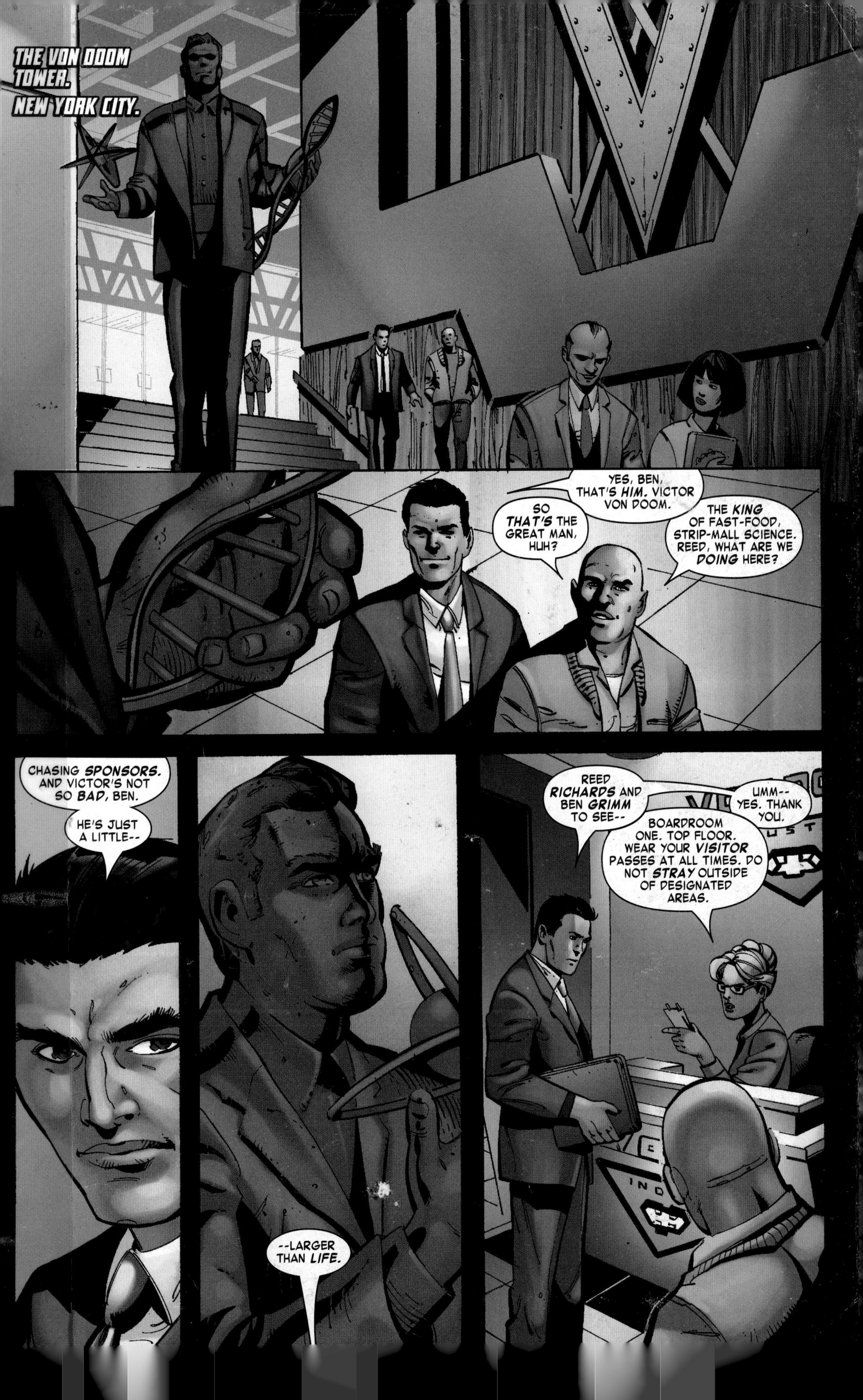
THE VON DOOM TOWER.
NEW YORK CITY.
SO THAT'S THE GREAT MAN, HUH?
YES, BEN, THAT'S HIM. VICTOR VON DOOM.
THE KING OF FAST-FOOD, STRIP-MALL SCIENCE. REED, WHAT ARE WE DOING HERE?
CHASING SPONSORS. AND VICTOR'S NOT SO BAD, BEN.
HE'S JUST A LITTLE--
--LARGER THAN LIFE.
REED RICHARDS AND BEN GRIMM TO SEE--
BOARDROOM ONE. TOP FLOOR. WEAR YOUR VISITOR PASSES AT ALL TIMES. DO NOT STRAY OUTSIDE OF DESIGNATED AREAS.
UMM-- YES. THANK YOU.

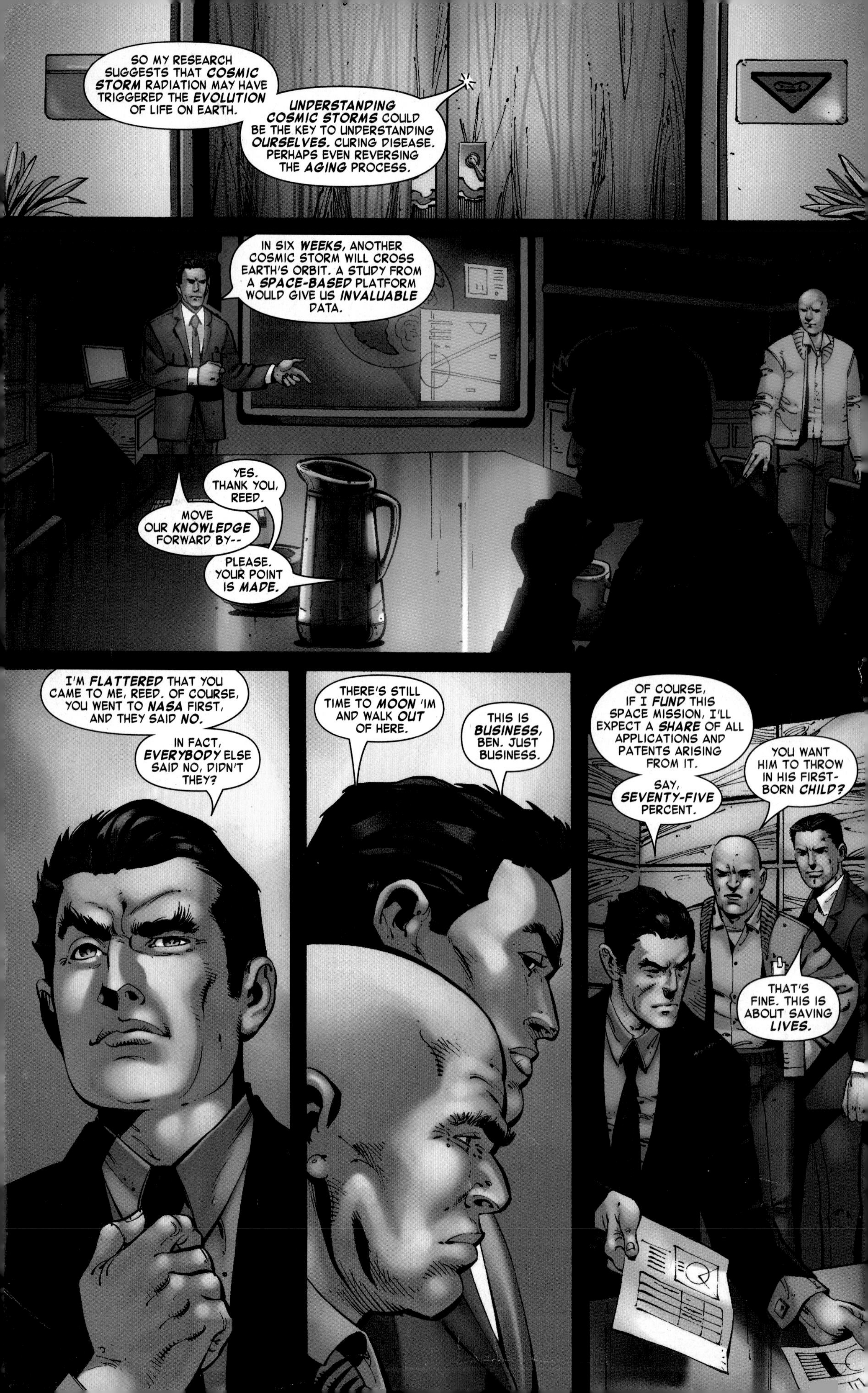
SO MY RESEARCH SUGGESTS THAT COSMIC STORM RADIATION MAY HAVE TRIGGERED THE EVOLUTION OF LIFE ON EARTH.
UNDERSTANDING COSMIC STORMS COULD BE THE KEY TO UNDERSTANDING OURSELVES. CURING DISEASE. PERHAPS EVEN REVERSING THE AGING PROCESS.
IN SIX WEEKS, ANOTHER COSMIC STORM WILL CROSS EARTH'S ORBIT. A STUDY FROM A SPACE-BASED PLATFORM WOULD GIVE US INVALUABLE DATA.
MOVE OUR KNOWLEDGE FORWARD BY--
YES. THANK YOU, REED.
PLEASE. YOUR POINT IS MADE.
I'M FLATTERED THAT YOU CAME TO ME, REED. OF COURSE, YOU WENT TO NASA FIRST, AND THEY SAID NO.
IN FACT, EVERYBODY ELSE SAID NO, DIDN'T THEY?
THERE'S STILL TIME TO MOON 'IM AND WALK OUT OF HERE.
THIS IS BUSINESS, BEN. JUST BUSINESS.
OF COURSE, IF I FUND THIS SPACE MISSION, I'LL EXPECT A SHARE OF ALL APPLICATIONS AND PATENTS ARISING FROM IT.
SAY, SEVENTY-FIVE PERCENT.
YOU WANT HIM TO THROW IN HIS FIRST-BORN CHILD?
THAT'S FINE. THIS IS ABOUT SAVING LIVES.

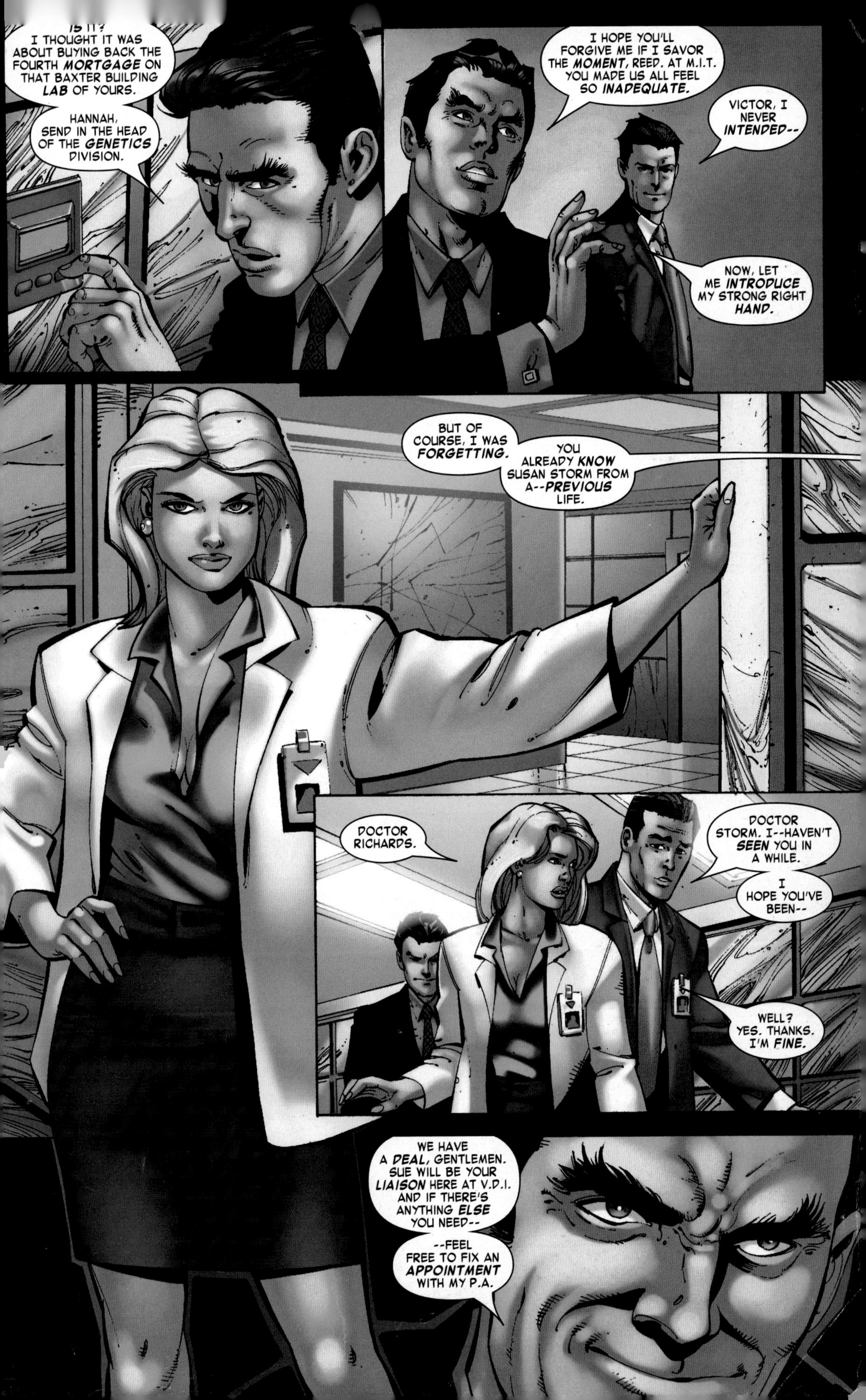
IS IT? I THOUGHT IT WAS ABOUT BUYING BACK THE FOURTH MORTGAGE ON THAT BAXTER BUILDING LAB OF YOURS.
HANNAH, SEND IN THE HEAD OF THE GENETICS DIVISION.
I HOPE YOU'LL FORGIVE ME IF I SAVOR THE MOMENT, REED. AT M.I.T. YOU MADE US ALL FEEL SO INADEQUATE.
VICTOR, I NEVER INTENDED--
NOW, LET ME INTRODUCE MY STRONG RIGHT HAND.
BUT OF COURSE, I WAS FORGETTING.
YOU ALREADY KNOW SUSAN STORM FROM A--PREVIOUS LIFE.
DOCTOR RICHARDS.
DOCTOR STORM. I--HAVEN'T SEEN YOU IN A WHILE.
I HOPE YOU'VE BEEN--
WELL? YES. THANKS. I'M FINE.
WE HAVE A DEAL, GENTLEMEN. SUE WILL BE YOUR LIAISON HERE AT V.D.I. AND IF THERE'S ANYTHING ELSE YOU NEED--
--FEEL FREE TO FIX AN APPOINTMENT WITH MY P.A.

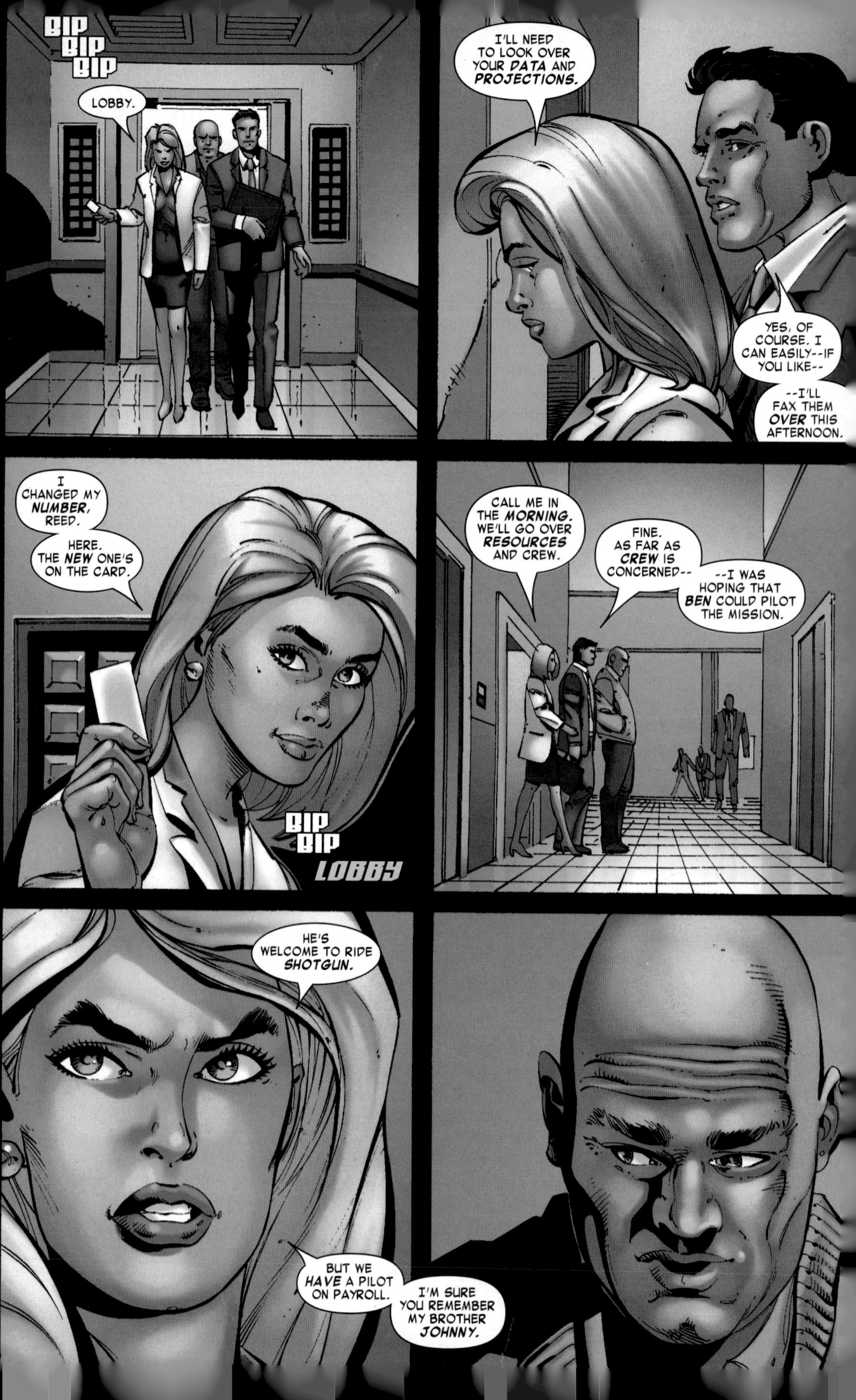
BIP BIP BIP
LOBBY.
I'LL NEED TO LOOK OVER YOUR DATA AND PROJECTIONS.
YES, OF COURSE. I CAN EASILY--IF YOU LIKE--
--I'LL FAX THEM OVER THIS AFTERNOON.
I CHANGED MY NUMBER, REED.
HERE. THE NEW ONE'S ON THE CARD.
BIP BIP
LOBBY
CALL ME IN THE MORNING. WE'LL GO OVER RESOURCES AND CREW.
FINE. AS FAR AS CREW IS CONCERNED--
--I WAS HOPING THAT BEN COULD PILOT THE MISSION.
HE'S WELCOME TO RIDE SHOTGUN.
BUT WE HAVE A PILOT ON PAYROLL.
I'M SURE YOU REMEMBER MY BROTHER JOHNNY.

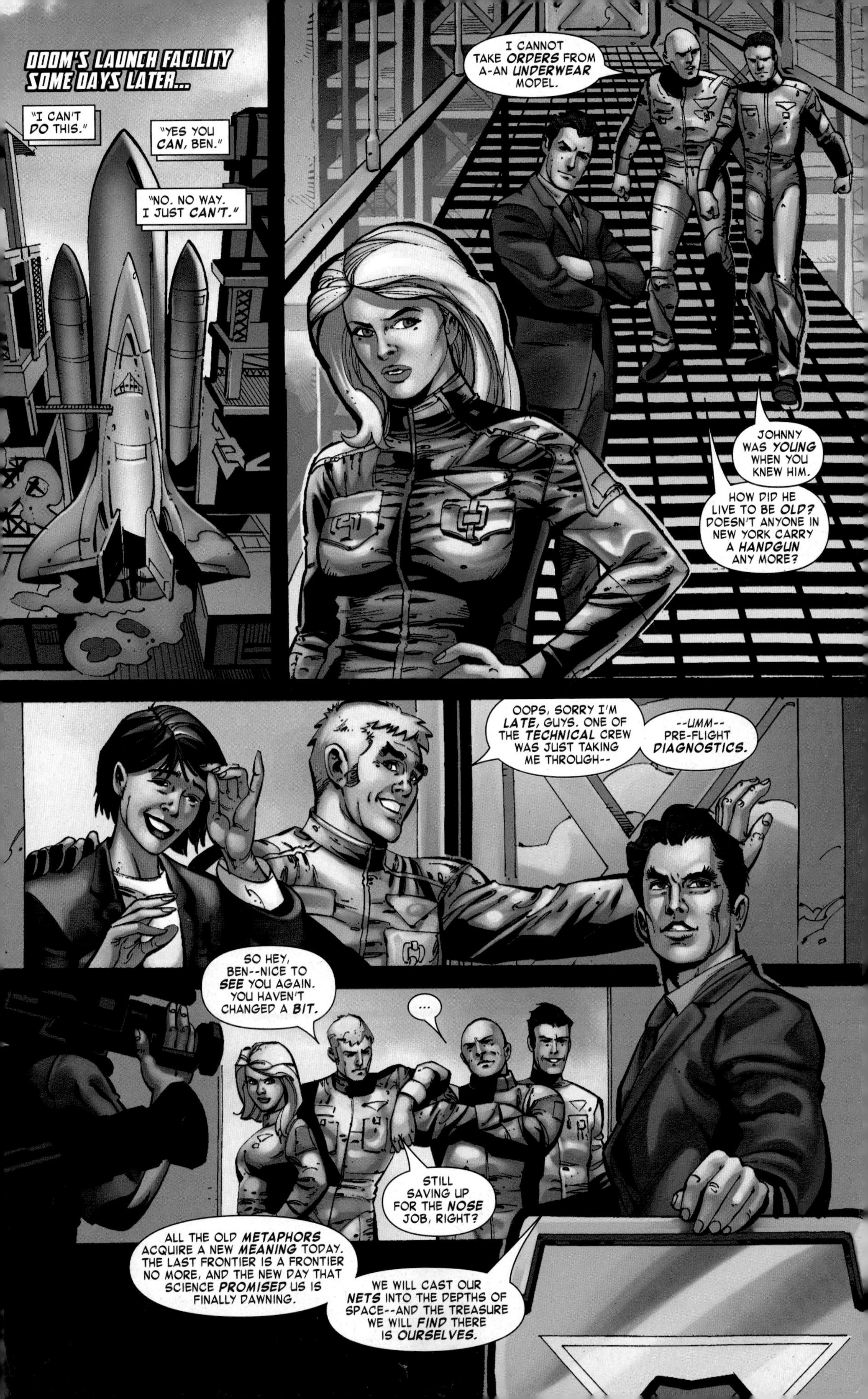
DOOM'S LAUNCH FACILITY SOME DAYS LATER...
"I CAN'T DO THIS."
"YES YOU CAN, BEN."
"NO. NO WAY. I JUST CAN'T."
I CANNOT TAKE ORDERS FROM A-AN UNDERWEAR MODEL.
JOHNNY WAS YOUNG WHEN YOU KNEW HIM.
HOW DID HE LIVE TO BE OLD? DOESN'T ANYONE IN NEW YORK CARRY A HANDGUN ANY MORE?
OOPS, SORRY I'M LATE, GUYS. ONE OF THE TECHNICAL CREW WAS JUST TAKING ME THROUGH--
--UMM-- PRE-FLIGHT DIAGNOSTICS.
SO HEY, BEN--NICE TO SEE YOU AGAIN. YOU HAVEN'T CHANGED A BIT.
...
STILL SAVING UP FOR THE NOSE JOB, RIGHT?
ALL THE OLD METAPHORS ACQUIRE A NEW MEANING TODAY. THE LAST FRONTIER IS A FRONTIER NO MORE, AND THE NEW DAY THAT SCIENCE PROMISED US IS FINALLY DAWNING.
WE WILL CAST OUR NETS INTO THE DEPTHS OF SPACE--AND THE TREASURE WE WILL FIND THERE IS OURSELVES.

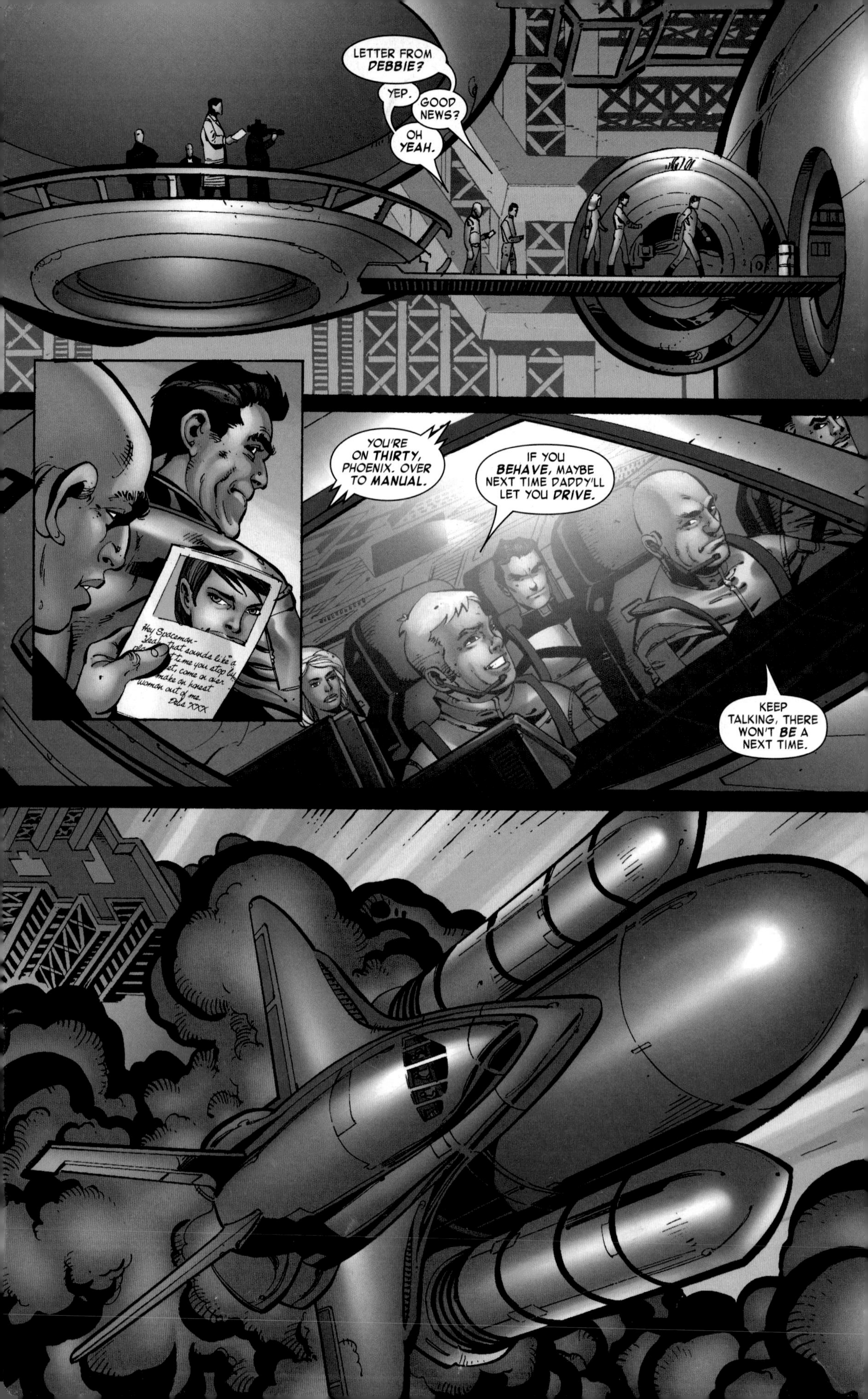
LETTER FROM DEBBIE?
YEP.
GOOD NEWS?
OH YEAH.
YOU'RE ON THIRTY, PHOENIX. OVER TO MANUAL.
IF YOU BEHAVE, MAYBE NEXT TIME DADDY'LL LET YOU DRIVE.
KEEP TALKING, THERE WON'T BE A NEXT TIME.

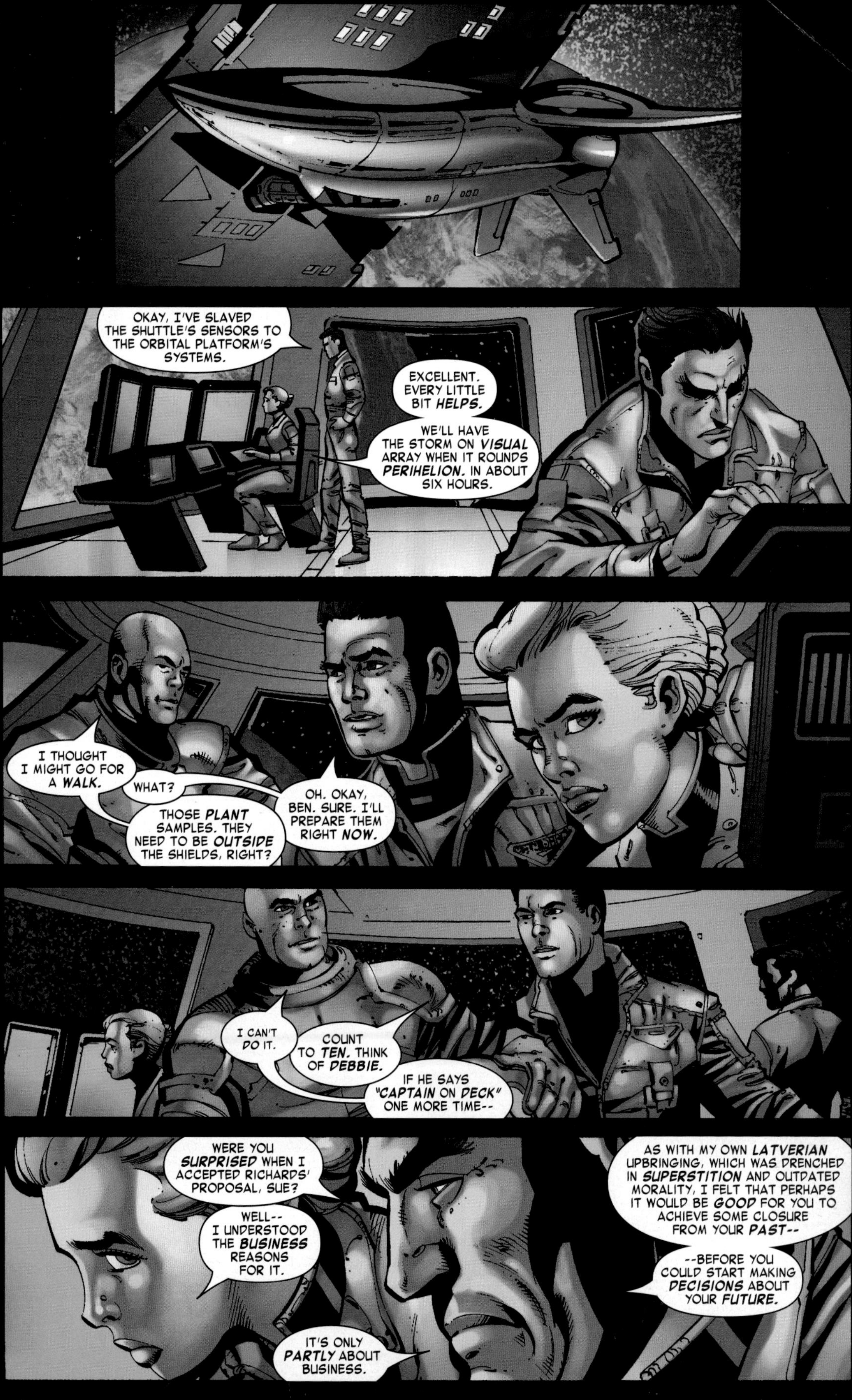

OKAY, I'VE SLAVED THE SHUTTLE'S SENSORS TO THE ORBITAL PLATFORM'S SYSTEMS.
EXCELLENT. EVERY LITTLE BIT HELPS.
WE'LL HAVE THE STORM ON VISUAL ARRAY WHEN IT ROUNDS PERIHELION. IN ABOUT SIX HOURS.
I THOUGHT I MIGHT GO FOR A WALK.
WHAT?
THOSE PLANT SAMPLES. THEY NEED TO BE OUTSIDE THE SHIELDS, RIGHT?
OH. OKAY, BEN. SURE. I'LL PREPARE THEM RIGHT NOW.
I CAN'T DO IT.
COUNT TO TEN. THINK OF DEBBIE.
IF HE SAYS "CAPTAIN ON DECK" ONE MORE TIME--
WERE YOU SURPRISED WHEN I ACCEPTED RICHARDS' PROPOSAL, SUE?
WELL-- I UNDERSTOOD THE BUSINESS REASONS FOR IT.
IT'S ONLY PARTLY ABOUT BUSINESS.
AS WITH MY OWN LATVERIAN UPBRINGING, WHICH WAS DRENCHED IN SUPERSTITION AND OUTDATED MORALITY, I FELT THAT PERHAPS IT WOULD BE GOOD FOR YOU TO ACHIEVE SOME CLOSURE FROM YOUR PAST--
--BEFORE YOU COULD START MAKING DECISIONS ABOUT YOUR FUTURE.

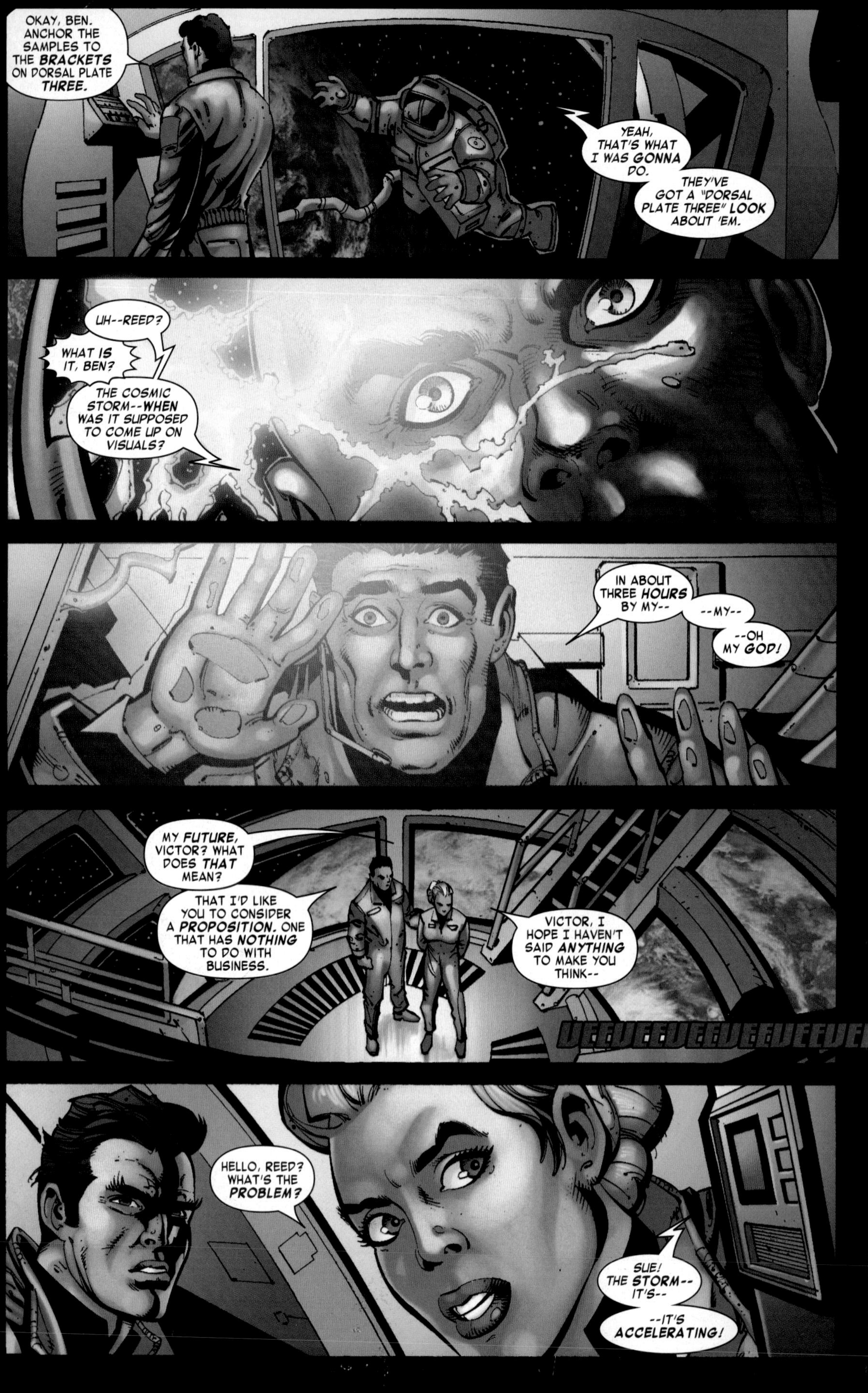

OKAY, BEN. ANCHOR THE SAMPLES TO THE BRACKETS ON DORSAL PLATE THREE.
YEAH, THAT'S WHAT I WAS GONNA DO.
THEY'VE GOT A "DORSAL PLATE THREE" LOOK ABOUT 'EM.
UH--REED?
WHAT IS IT, BEN?
THE COSMIC STORM--WHEN WAS IT SUPPOSED TO COME UP ON VISUALS?
IN ABOUT THREE HOURS BY MY--
--MY--
--OH MY GOD!
MY FUTURE, VICTOR? WHAT DOES THAT MEAN?
THAT I'D LIKE YOU TO CONSIDER A PROPOSITION. ONE THAT HAS NOTHING TO DO WITH BUSINESS.
VICTOR, I HOPE I HAVEN'T SAID ANYTHING TO MAKE YOU THINK--
VEEVEEVEEVEEVEEVEEVEI
HELLO, REED? WHAT'S THE PROBLEM?
SUE! THE STORM--IT'S--
--IT'S ACCELERATING!

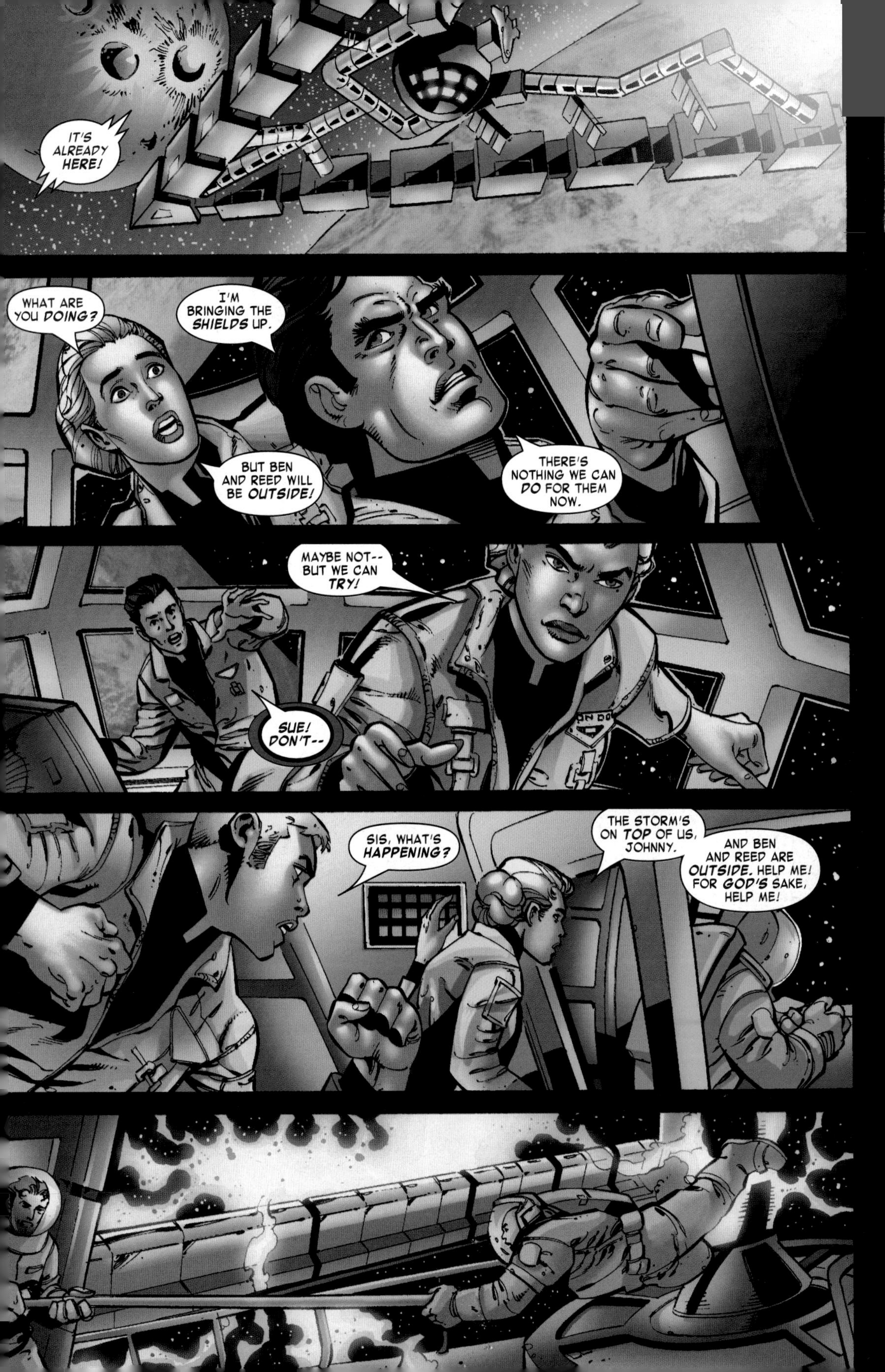
IT'S ALREADY HERE!
WHAT ARE YOU DOING?
I'M BRINGING THE SHIELDS UP.
BUT BEN AND REED WILL BE OUTSIDE!
THERE'S NOTHING WE CAN DO FOR THEM NOW.
MAYBE NOT-- BUT WE CAN TRY!
SUE! DON'T--
SIS, WHAT'S HAPPENING?
THE STORM'S ON TOP OF US, JOHNNY.
AND BEN AND REED ARE OUTSIDE. HELP ME! FOR GOD'S SAKE, HELP ME!

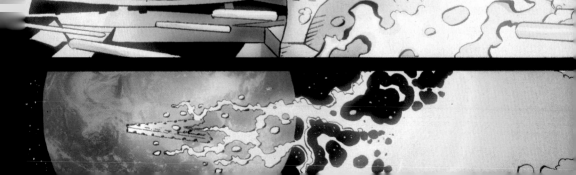

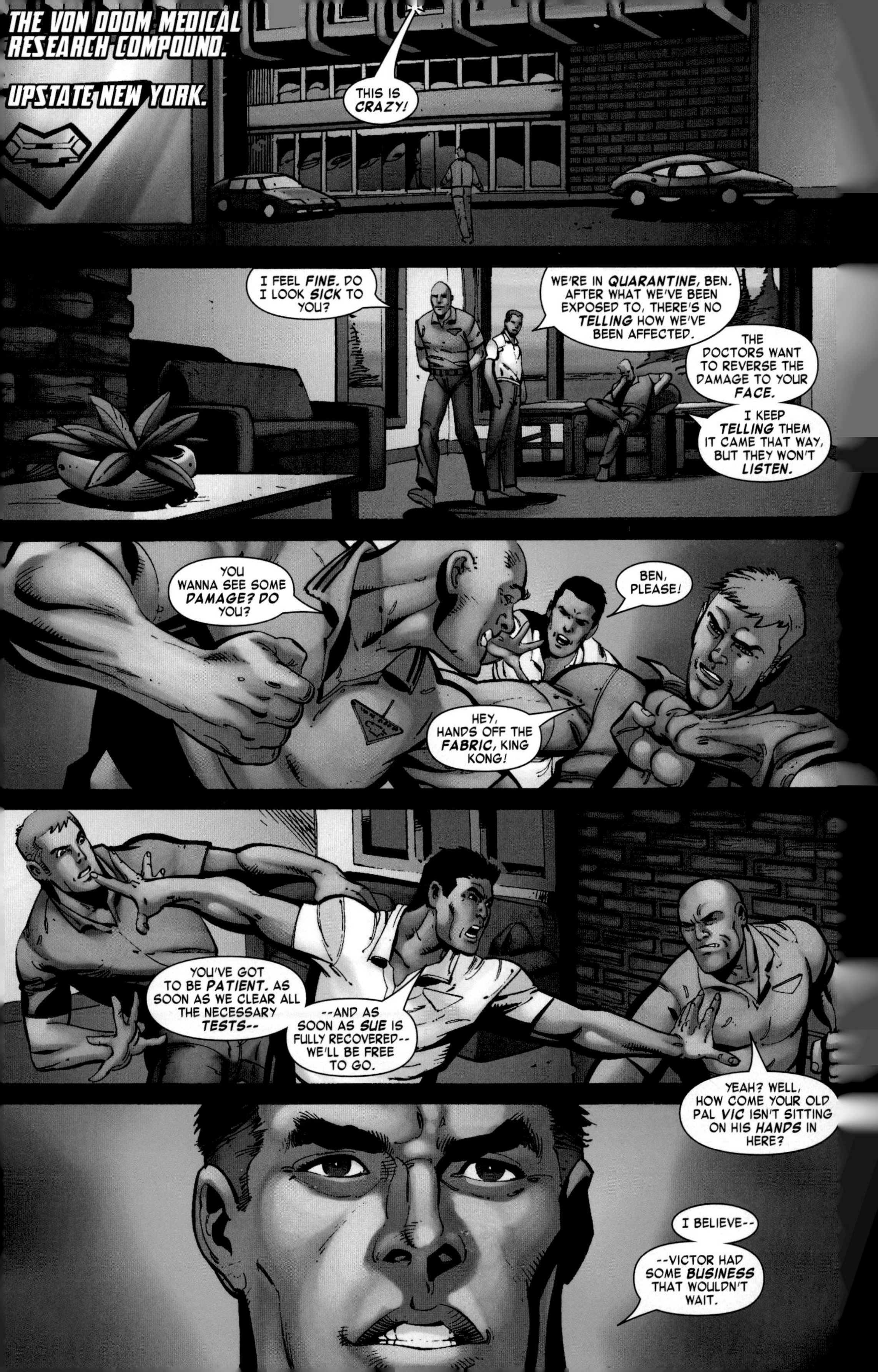
THE VON DOOM MEDICAL RESEARCH COMPOUND.
UPSTATE NEW YORK.
THIS IS CRAZY!
I FEEL FINE. DO I LOOK SICK TO YOU?
WE'RE IN QUARANTINE, BEN. AFTER WHAT WE'VE BEEN EXPOSED TO, THERE'S NO TELLING HOW WE'VE BEEN AFFECTED.
THE DOCTORS WANT TO REVERSE THE DAMAGE TO YOUR FACE.
I KEEP TELLING THEM IT CAME THAT WAY, BUT THEY WON'T LISTEN.
YOU WANNA SEE SOME DAMAGE? DO YOU?
BEN, PLEASE!
HEY, HANDS OFF THE FABRIC, KING KONG!
YOU'VE GOT TO BE PATIENT. AS SOON AS WE CLEAR ALL THE NECESSARY TESTS--
--AND AS SOON AS SUE IS FULLY RECOVERED--WE'LL BE FREE TO GO.
YEAH? WELL, HOW COME YOUR OLD PAL VIC ISN'T SITTING ON HIS HANDS IN HERE?
I BELIEVE--
--VICTOR HAD SOME BUSINESS THAT WOULDN'T WAIT.

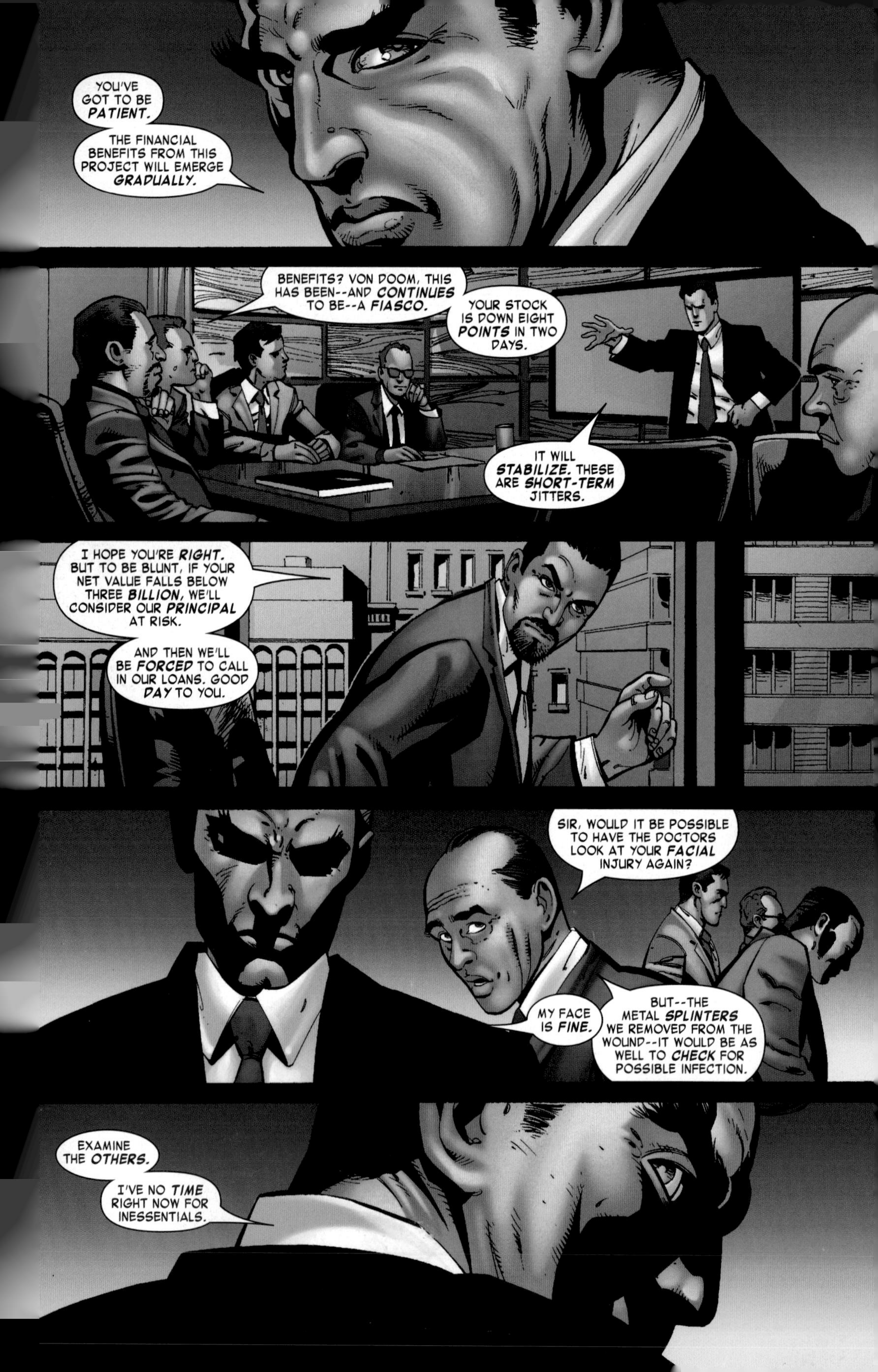
YOU'VE GOT TO BE PATIENT.
THE FINANCIAL BENEFITS FROM THIS PROJECT WILL EMERGE GRADUALLY.
BENEFITS? VON DOOM, THIS HAS BEEN--AND CONTINUES TO BE--A FIASCO.
YOUR STOCK IS DOWN EIGHT POINTS IN TWO DAYS.
IT WILL STABILIZE. THESE ARE SHORT-TERM JITTERS.
I HOPE YOU'RE RIGHT. BUT TO BE BLUNT, IF YOUR NET VALUE FALLS BELOW THREE BILLION, WE'LL CONSIDER OUR PRINCIPAL AT RISK.
AND THEN WE'LL BE FORCED TO CALL IN OUR LOANS. GOOD DAY TO YOU.
SIR, WOULD IT BE POSSIBLE TO HAVE THE DOCTORS LOOK AT YOUR FACIAL INJURY AGAIN?
MY FACE IS FINE.
BUT--THE METAL SPLINTERS WE REMOVED FROM THE WOUND--IT WOULD BE AS WELL TO CHECK FOR POSSIBLE INFECTION.
EXAMINE THE OTHERS.
I'VE NO TIME RIGHT NOW FOR INESSENTIALS.

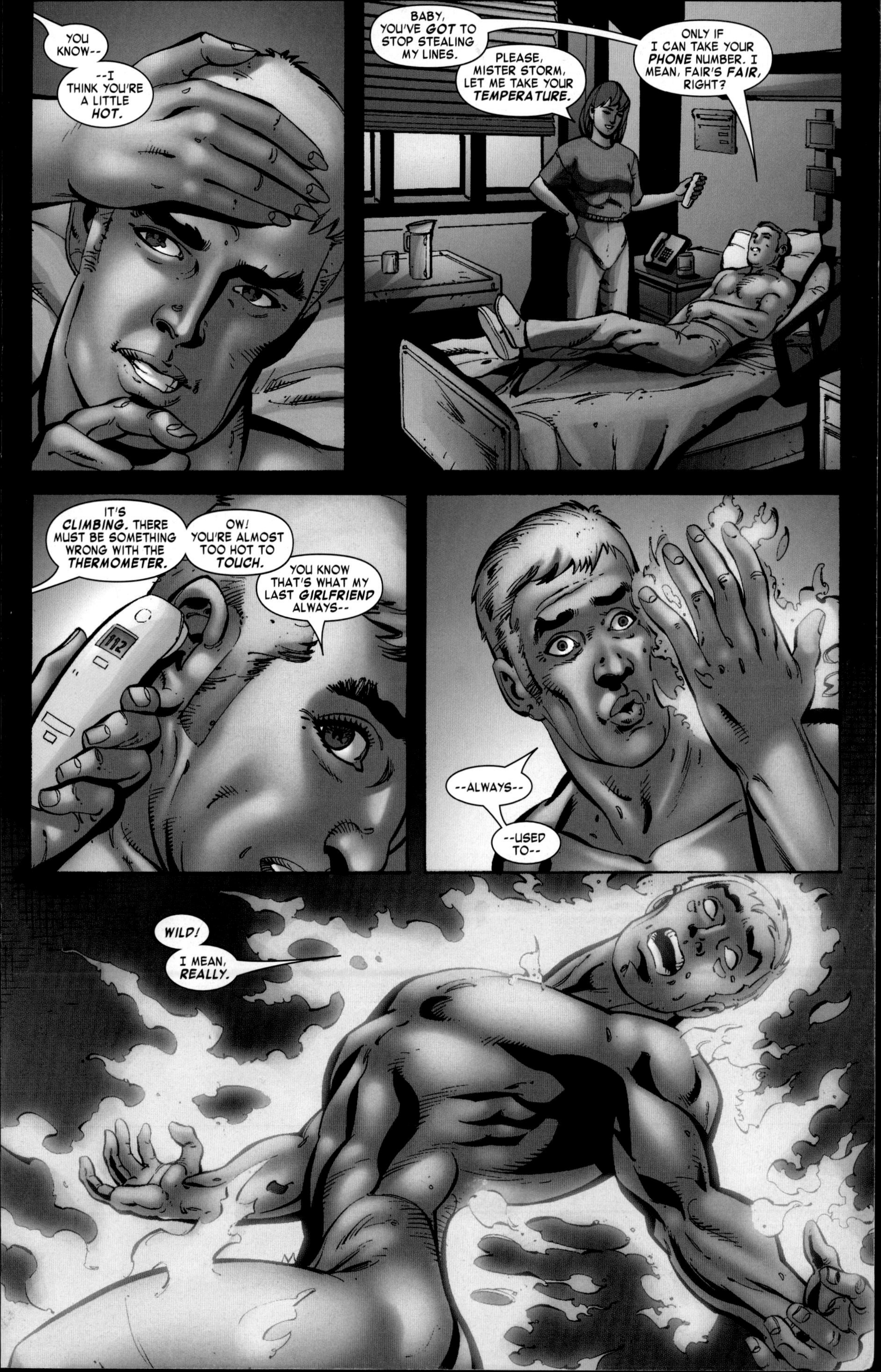
YOU KNOW--
--I THINK YOU'RE A LITTLE *HOT*.
BABY, YOU'VE *GOT* TO STOP STEALING MY LINES.
PLEASE, MISTER STORM, LET ME TAKE YOUR *TEMPERATURE*.
ONLY IF I CAN TAKE YOUR *PHONE* NUMBER. I MEAN, FAIR'S *FAIR*, RIGHT?
IT'S *CLIMBING*. THERE MUST BE SOMETHING WRONG WITH THE *THERMOMETER*.
OW! YOU'RE ALMOST TOO HOT TO *TOUCH*.
YOU KNOW THAT'S WHAT MY LAST *GIRLFRIEND* ALWAYS--
112
--ALWAYS--
--USED TO--
WILD!
I MEAN, *REALLY*.

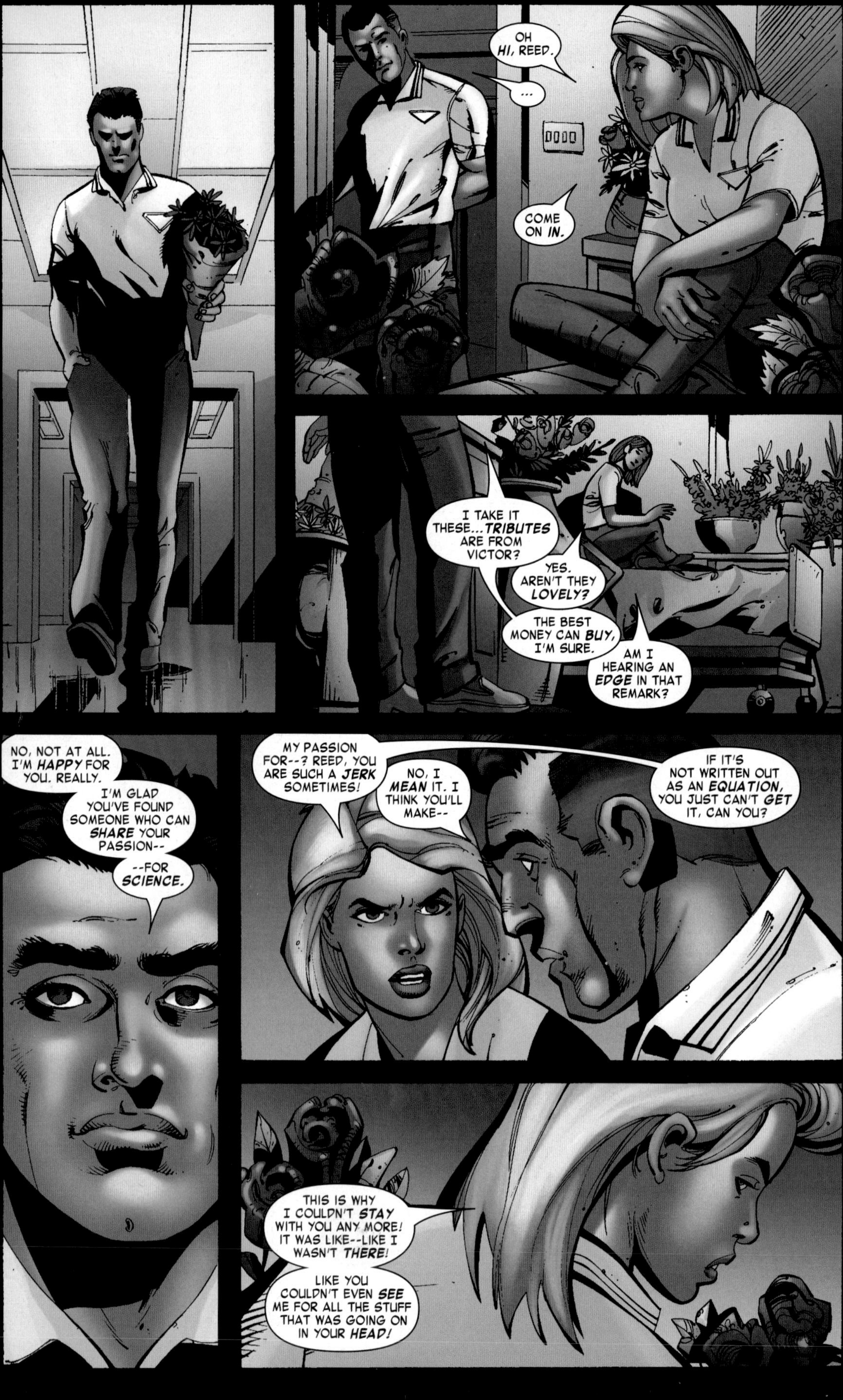

OH HI, REED.
...
COME ON IN.
I TAKE IT THESE...TRIBUTES ARE FROM VICTOR?
YES. AREN'T THEY LOVELY?
THE BEST MONEY CAN BUY, I'M SURE.
AM I HEARING AN EDGE IN THAT REMARK?
NO, NOT AT ALL. I'M HAPPY FOR YOU. REALLY.
I'M GLAD YOU'VE FOUND SOMEONE WHO CAN SHARE YOUR PASSION--
--FOR SCIENCE.
MY PASSION FOR--? REED, YOU ARE SUCH A JERK SOMETIMES!
NO, I MEAN IT. I THINK YOU'LL MAKE--
IF IT'S NOT WRITTEN OUT AS AN EQUATION, YOU JUST CAN'T GET IT, CAN YOU?
THIS IS WHY I COULDN'T STAY WITH YOU ANY MORE! IT WAS LIKE--LIKE I WASN'T THERE!
LIKE YOU COULDN'T EVEN SEE ME FOR ALL THE STUFF THAT WAS GOING ON IN YOUR HEAD!

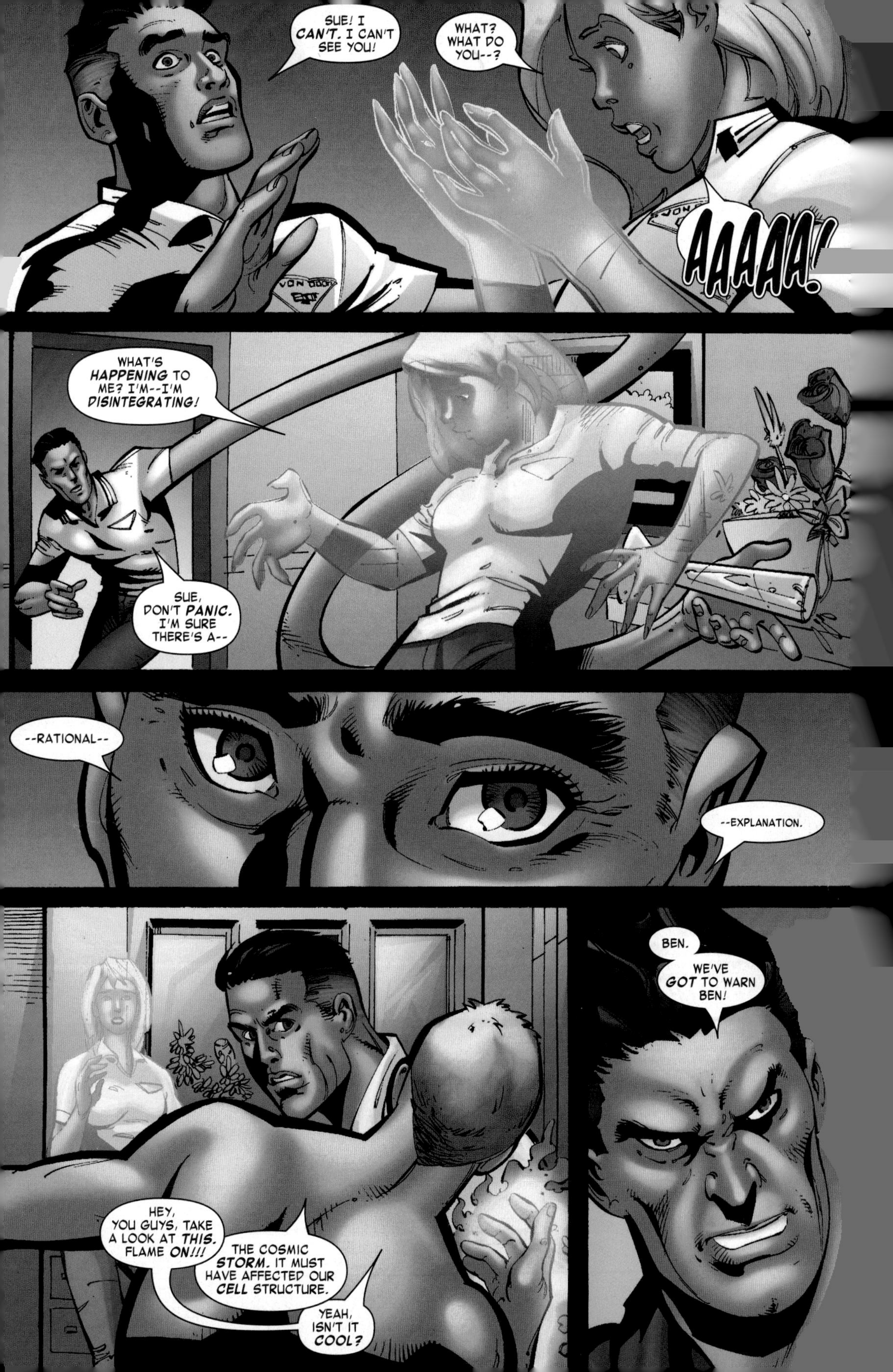
SUE! I CAN'T. I CAN'T SEE YOU!
WHAT? WHAT DO YOU--?
AAAAA!
WHAT'S HAPPENING TO ME? I'M--I'M DISINTEGRATING!
SUE, DON'T PANIC. I'M SURE THERE'S A--
--RATIONAL--
--EXPLANATION.
HEY, YOU GUYS, TAKE A LOOK AT THIS. FLAME ON!!!
THE COSMIC STORM. IT MUST HAVE AFFECTED OUR CELL STRUCTURE.
YEAH, ISN'T IT COOL?
BEN.
WE'VE GOT TO WARN BEN!

HHHHH
KKHHH

BEN? ARE YOU *IN* THERE?

OPEN THE DOOR. I NEED TO *TALK* TO YOU!

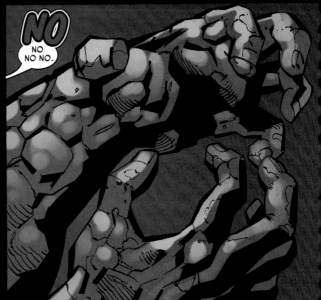

NO

NO NO NO.

ALL RIGHT. THERE'S *ANOTHER* WAY TO DO THIS.

I COULD *BURN* THE DOOR DOWN.

DON'T BE *RIDICULOUS*, JOHNNY.

NO, SERIOUSLY--

NOW THAT'S JUST-- *UNSETTLING*.

SO, YOU-- UH--YOU THINK HE MAY HAVE *GOTTEN* THE NEWS ALREADY?

REED, WHERE WILL HE *GO*?

THAT'S AN *EASY* ONE.

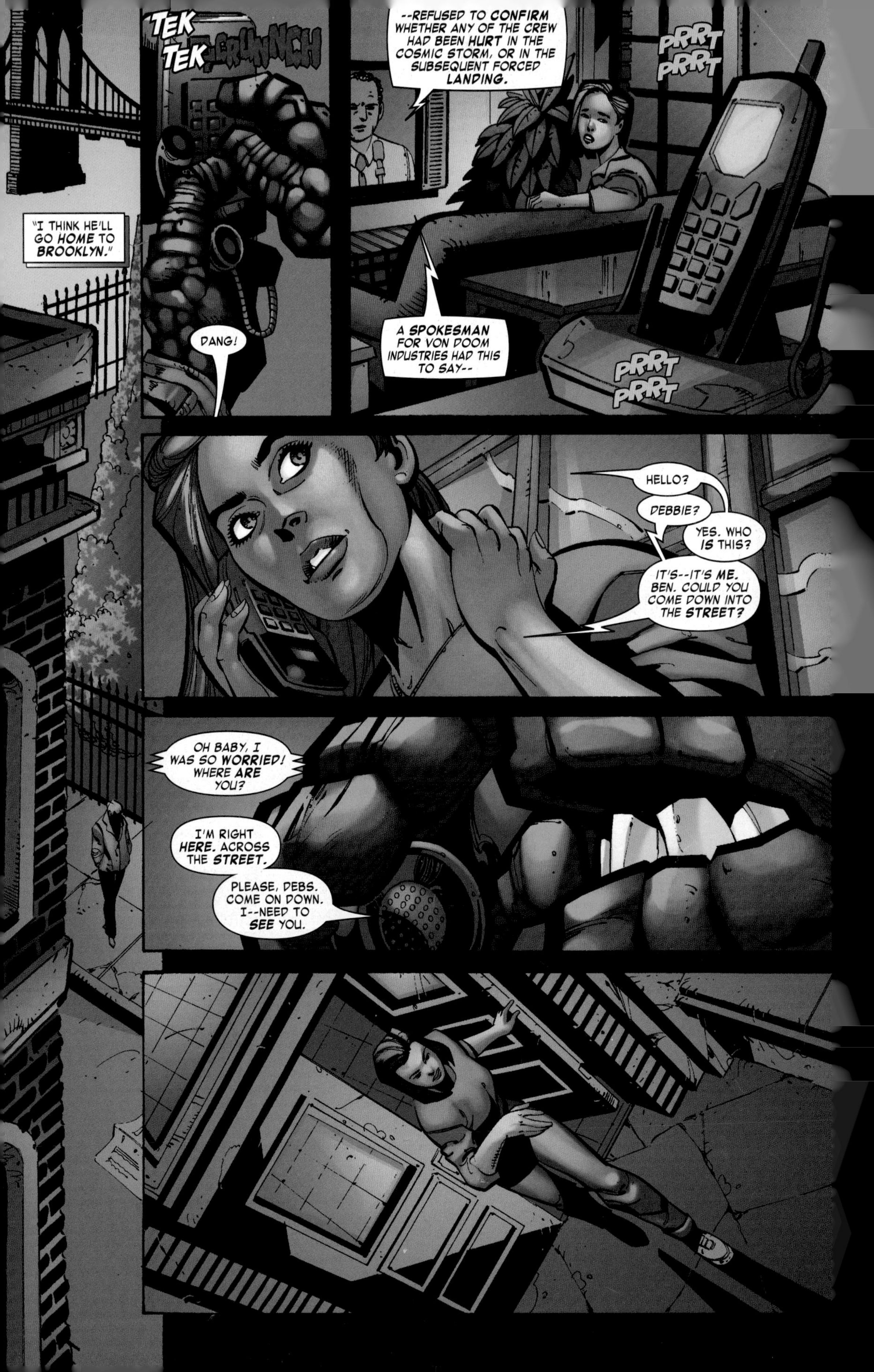
"I THINK HE'LL GO HOME TO BROOKLYN."
TEK TEK
CRUNNCH
DANG!
--REFUSED TO CONFIRM WHETHER ANY OF THE CREW HAD BEEN HURT IN THE COSMIC STORM, OR IN THE SUBSEQUENT FORCED LANDING.
A SPOKESMAN FOR VON DOOM INDUSTRIES HAD THIS TO SAY--
PRRT PRRT
PRRT PRRT
HELLO?
DEBBIE?
YES. WHO IS THIS?
IT'S--IT'S ME. BEN. COULD YOU COME DOWN INTO THE STREET?
OH BABY, I WAS SO WORRIED! WHERE ARE YOU?
I'M RIGHT HERE. ACROSS THE STREET.
PLEASE, DEBS. COME ON DOWN. I--NEED TO SEE YOU.

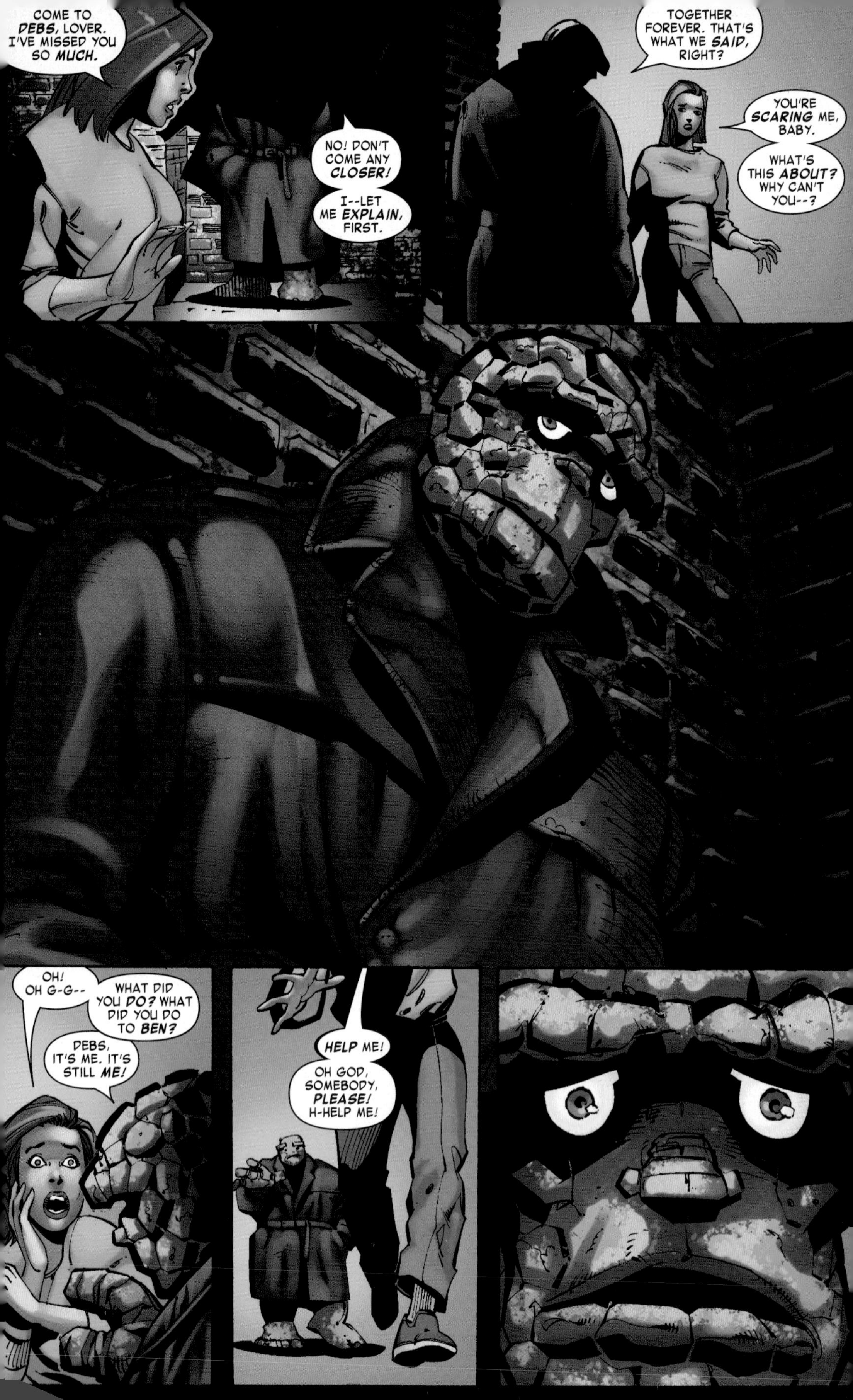
COME TO DEBS, LOVER. I'VE MISSED YOU SO MUCH.
NO! DON'T COME ANY CLOSER!
I--LET ME EXPLAIN, FIRST.
TOGETHER FOREVER. THAT'S WHAT WE SAID, RIGHT?
YOU'RE SCARING ME, BABY.
WHAT'S THIS ABOUT? WHY CAN'T YOU--?
OH! OH G-G--
WHAT DID YOU DO? WHAT DID YOU DO TO BEN?
DEBS, IT'S ME. IT'S STILL ME!
HELP ME!
OH GOD, SOMEBODY, PLEASE! H-HELP ME!

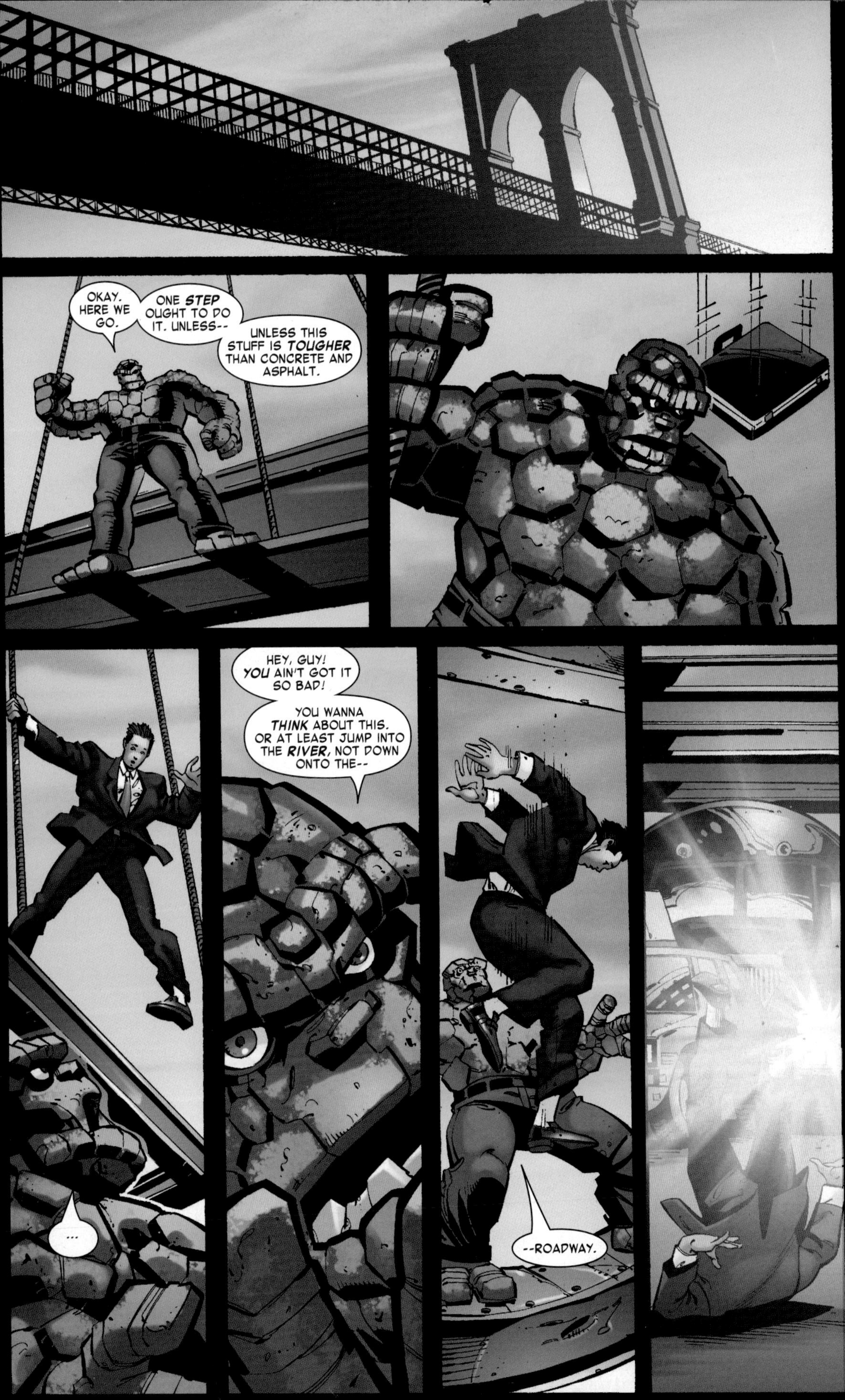
OKAY. HERE WE GO.
ONE STEP OUGHT TO DO IT. UNLESS--
UNLESS THIS STUFF IS TOUGHER THAN CONCRETE AND ASPHALT.
...
HEY, GUY! YOU AIN'T GOT IT SO BAD!
YOU WANNA THINK ABOUT THIS. OR AT LEAST JUMP INTO THE RIVER, NOT DOWN ONTO THE--
--ROADWAY.

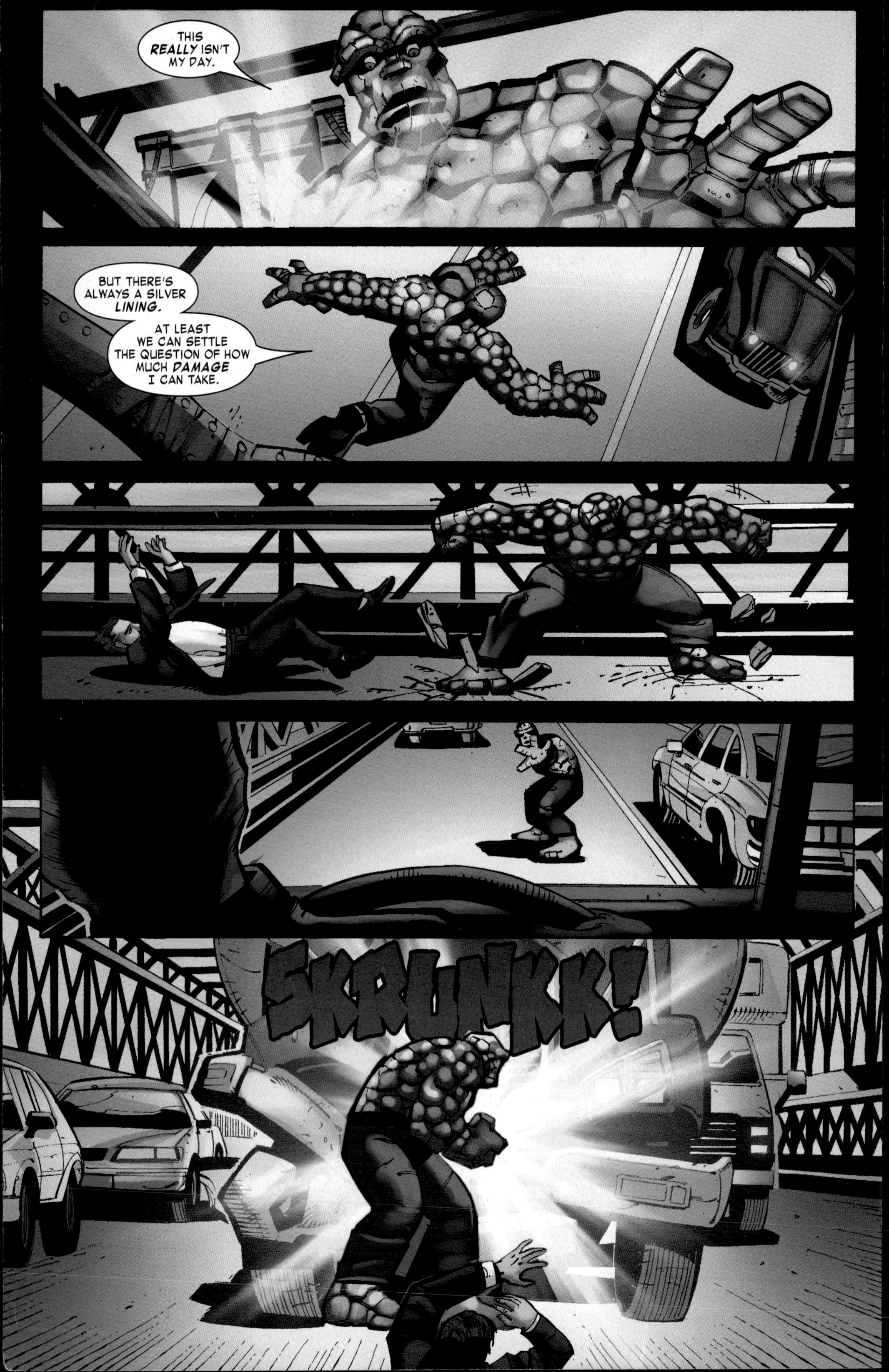
THIS REALLY ISN'T MY DAY.
BUT THERE'S ALWAYS A SILVER LINING.
AT LEAST WE CAN SETTLE THE QUESTION OF HOW MUCH DAMAGE I CAN TAKE.
SKRUNKK!

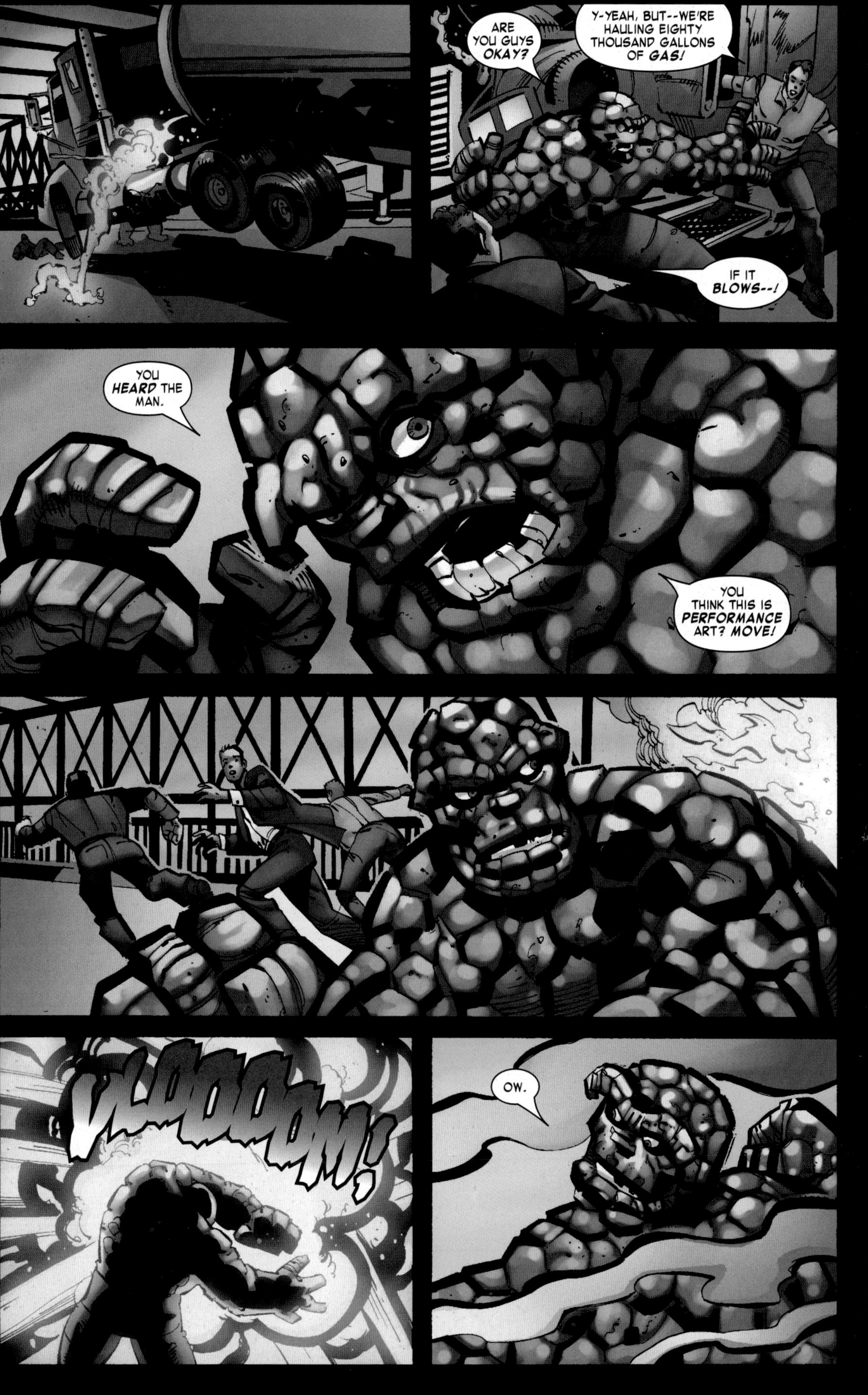
ARE YOU GUYS OKAY?
Y-YEAH, BUT--WE'RE HAULING EIGHTY THOUSAND GALLONS OF GAS!
IF IT BLOWS--!
YOU HEARD THE MAN.
YOU THINK THIS IS PERFORMANCE ART? MOVE!
VLOOOOM!
OW.

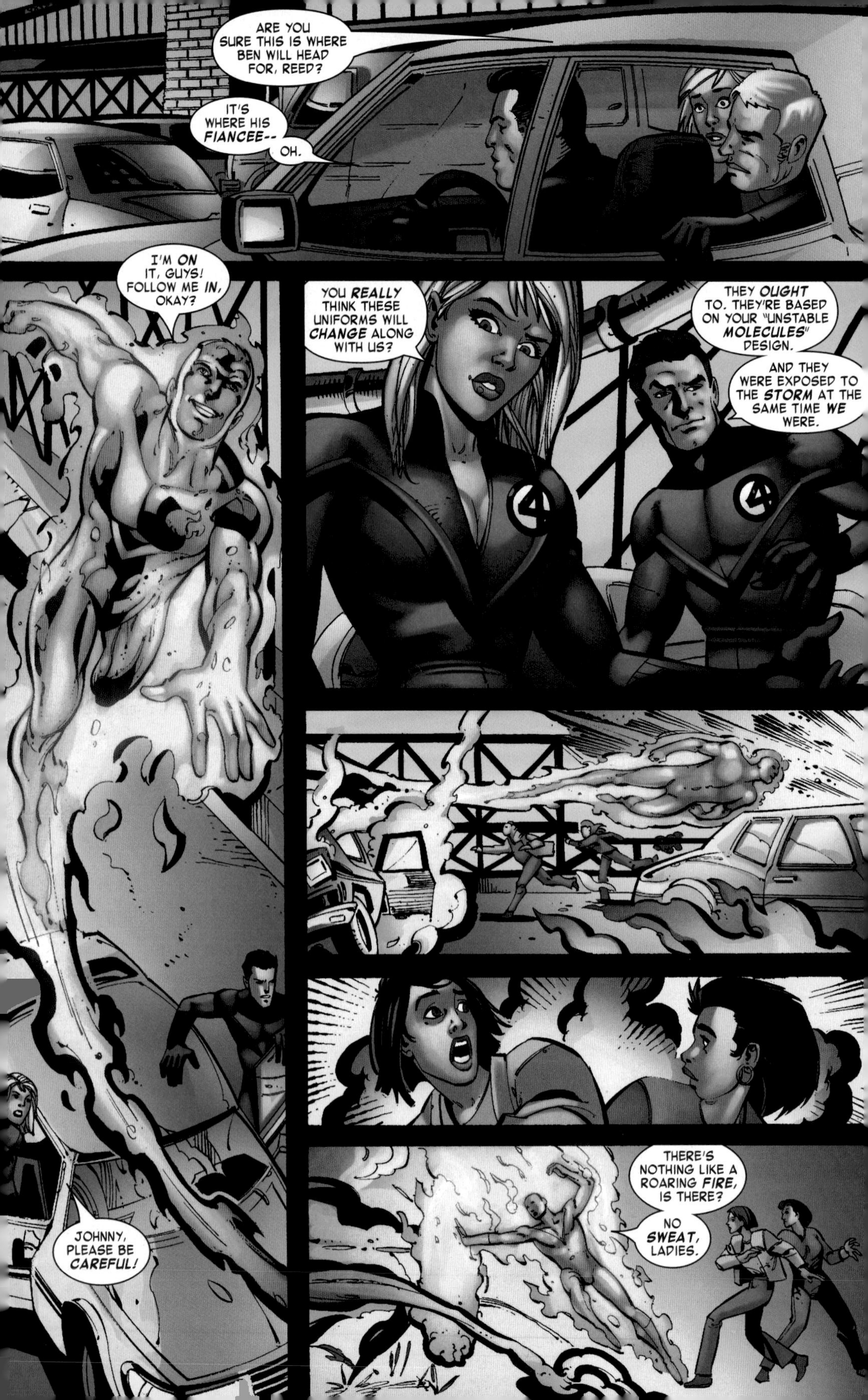
ARE YOU SURE THIS IS WHERE BEN WILL HEAD FOR, REED?
IT'S WHERE HIS FIANCEE--
OH.
I'M ON IT, GUYS! FOLLOW ME IN, OKAY?
YOU REALLY THINK THESE UNIFORMS WILL CHANGE ALONG WITH US?
THEY OUGHT TO. THEY'RE BASED ON YOUR "UNSTABLE MOLECULES" DESIGN.
AND THEY WERE EXPOSED TO THE STORM AT THE SAME TIME WE WERE.
THERE'S NOTHING LIKE A ROARING FIRE, IS THERE?
NO SWEAT, LADIES.
JOHNNY, PLEASE BE CAREFUL!

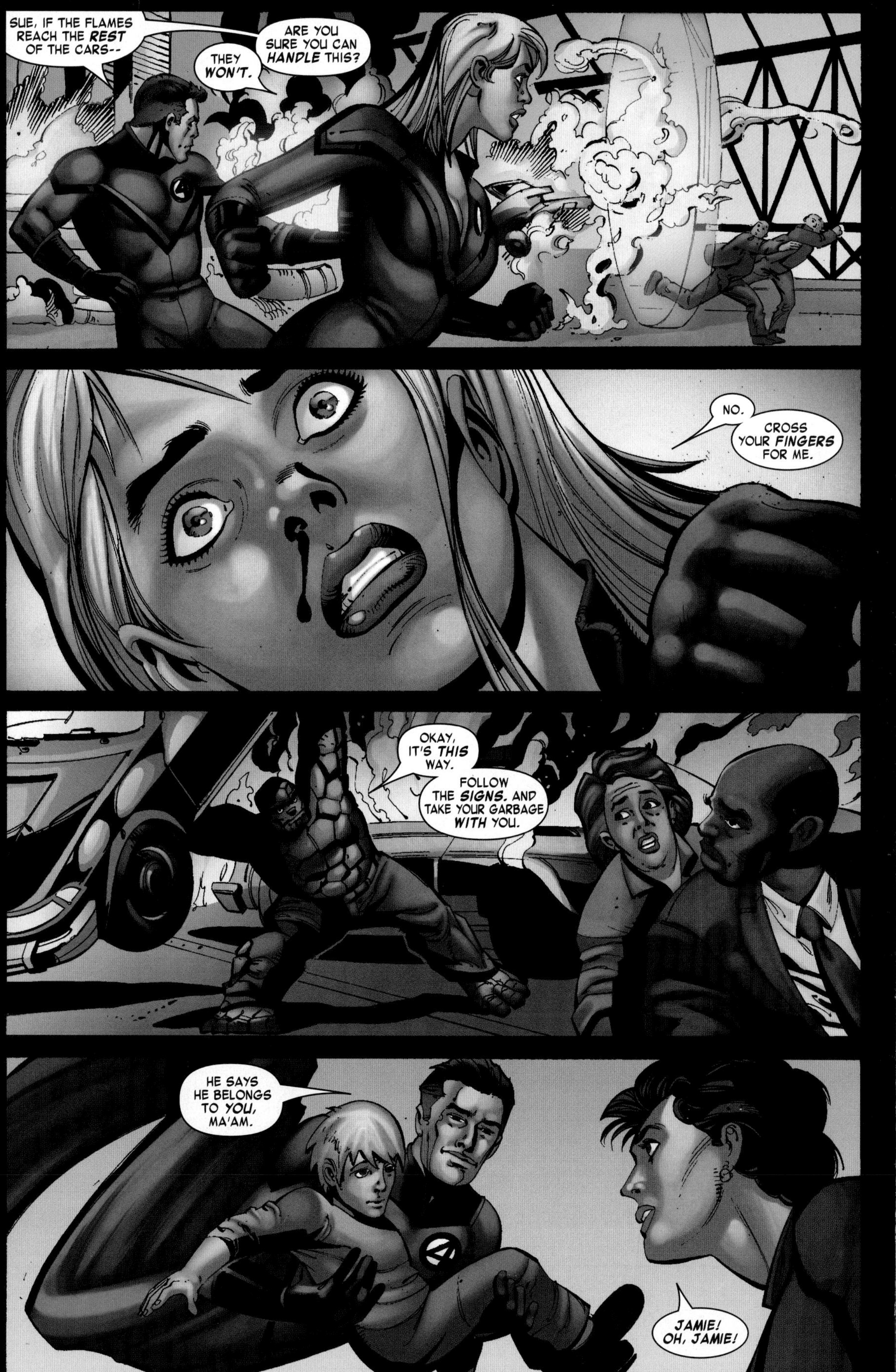
SUE, IF THE FLAMES REACH THE REST OF THE CARS--
THEY WON'T.
ARE YOU SURE YOU CAN HANDLE THIS?
NO.
CROSS YOUR FINGERS FOR ME.
OKAY, IT'S THIS WAY.
FOLLOW THE SIGNS. AND TAKE YOUR GARBAGE WITH YOU.
HE SAYS HE BELONGS TO YOU, MA'AM.
JAMIE! OH, JAMIE!

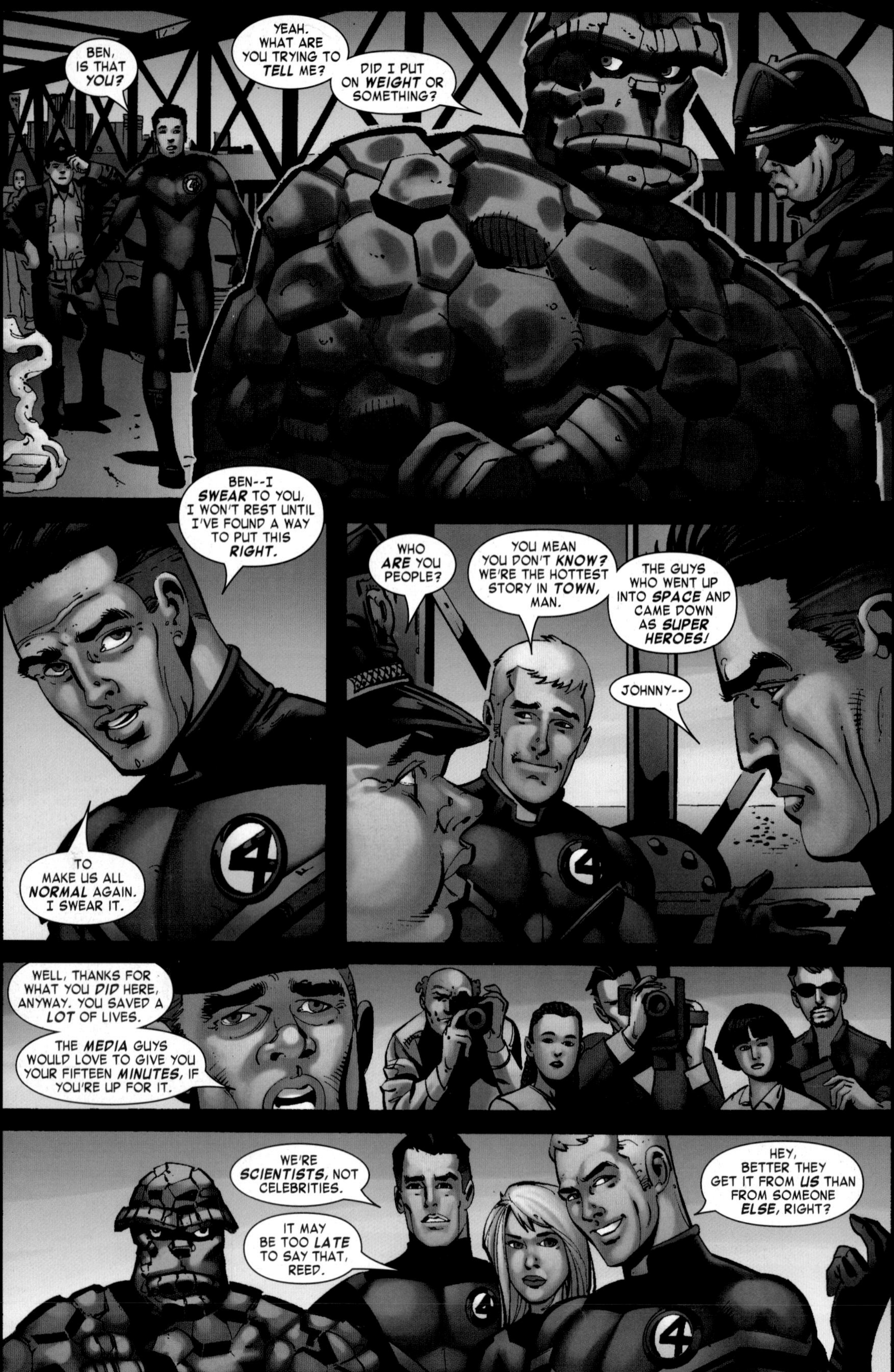
BEN, IS THAT YOU?
YEAH. WHAT ARE YOU TRYING TO TELL ME?
DID I PUT ON WEIGHT OR SOMETHING?
BEN--I SWEAR TO YOU, I WON'T REST UNTIL I'VE FOUND A WAY TO PUT THIS RIGHT.
TO MAKE US ALL NORMAL AGAIN. I SWEAR IT.
WHO ARE YOU PEOPLE?
YOU MEAN YOU DON'T KNOW? WE'RE THE HOTTEST STORY IN TOWN, MAN.
THE GUYS WHO WENT UP INTO SPACE AND CAME DOWN AS SUPER HEROES!
JOHNNY--
WELL, THANKS FOR WHAT YOU DID HERE, ANYWAY. YOU SAVED A LOT OF LIVES.
THE MEDIA GUYS WOULD LOVE TO GIVE YOU YOUR FIFTEEN MINUTES, IF YOU'RE UP FOR IT.
WE'RE SCIENTISTS, NOT CELEBRITIES.
IT MAY BE TOO LATE TO SAY THAT, REED.
HEY, BETTER THEY GET IT FROM US THAN FROM SOMEONE ELSE, RIGHT?

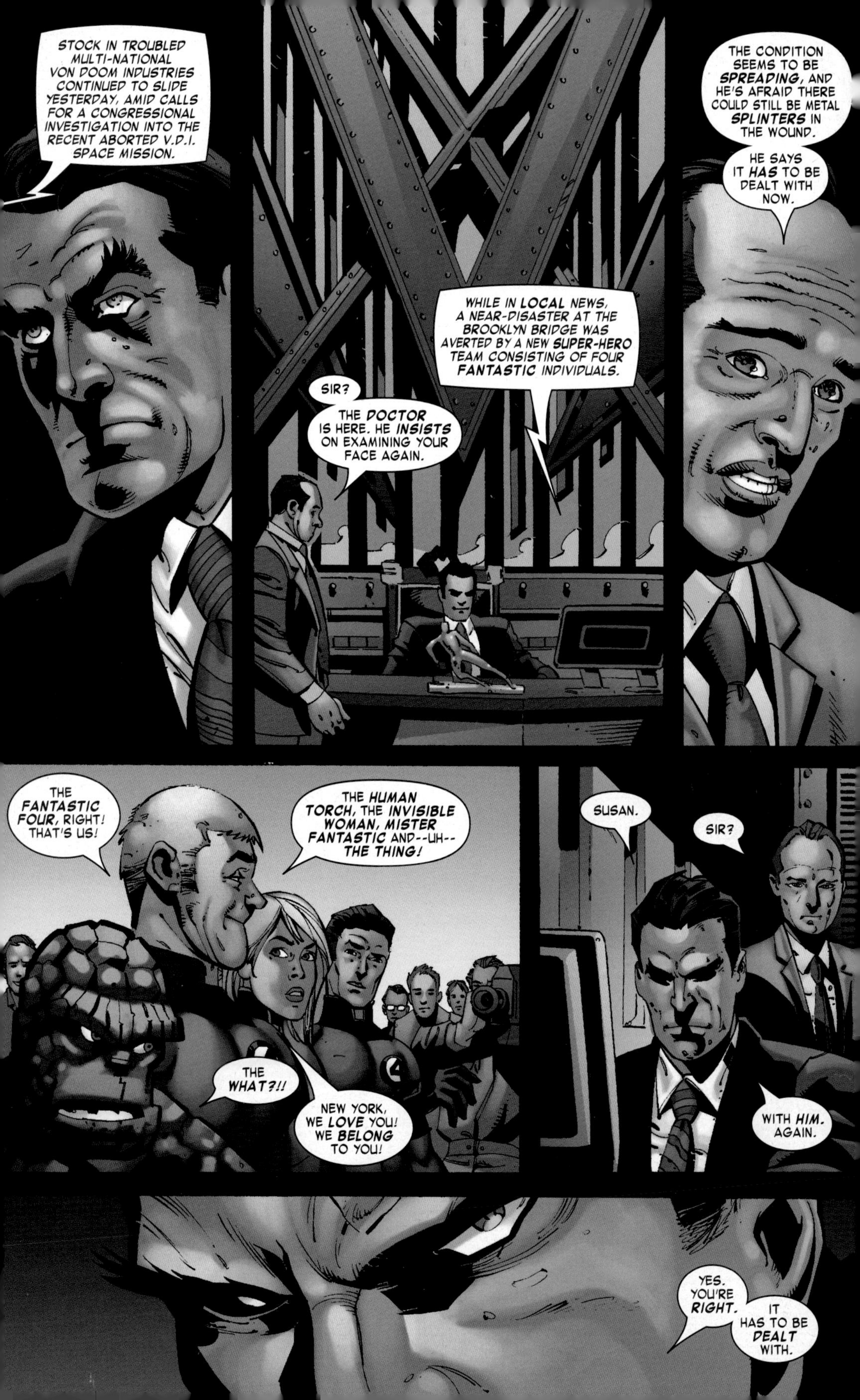
STOCK IN TROUBLED MULTI-NATIONAL VON DOOM INDUSTRIES CONTINUED TO SLIDE YESTERDAY, AMID CALLS FOR A CONGRESSIONAL INVESTIGATION INTO THE RECENT ABORTED V.D.I. SPACE MISSION.
WHILE IN LOCAL NEWS, A NEAR-DISASTER AT THE BROOKLYN BRIDGE WAS AVERTED BY A NEW SUPER-HERO TEAM CONSISTING OF FOUR FANTASTIC INDIVIDUALS.
SIR?
THE DOCTOR IS HERE. HE INSISTS ON EXAMINING YOUR FACE AGAIN.
THE CONDITION SEEMS TO BE SPREADING, AND HE'S AFRAID THERE COULD STILL BE METAL SPLINTERS IN THE WOUND.
HE SAYS IT HAS TO BE DEALT WITH NOW.
THE FANTASTIC FOUR, RIGHT! THAT'S US!
THE HUMAN TORCH, THE INVISIBLE WOMAN, MISTER FANTASTIC AND--UH-- THE THING!
THE WHAT?!!
NEW YORK, WE LOVE YOU! WE BELONG TO YOU!
SUSAN.
SIR?
WITH HIM. AGAIN.
YES. YOU'RE RIGHT.
IT HAS TO BE DEALT WITH.

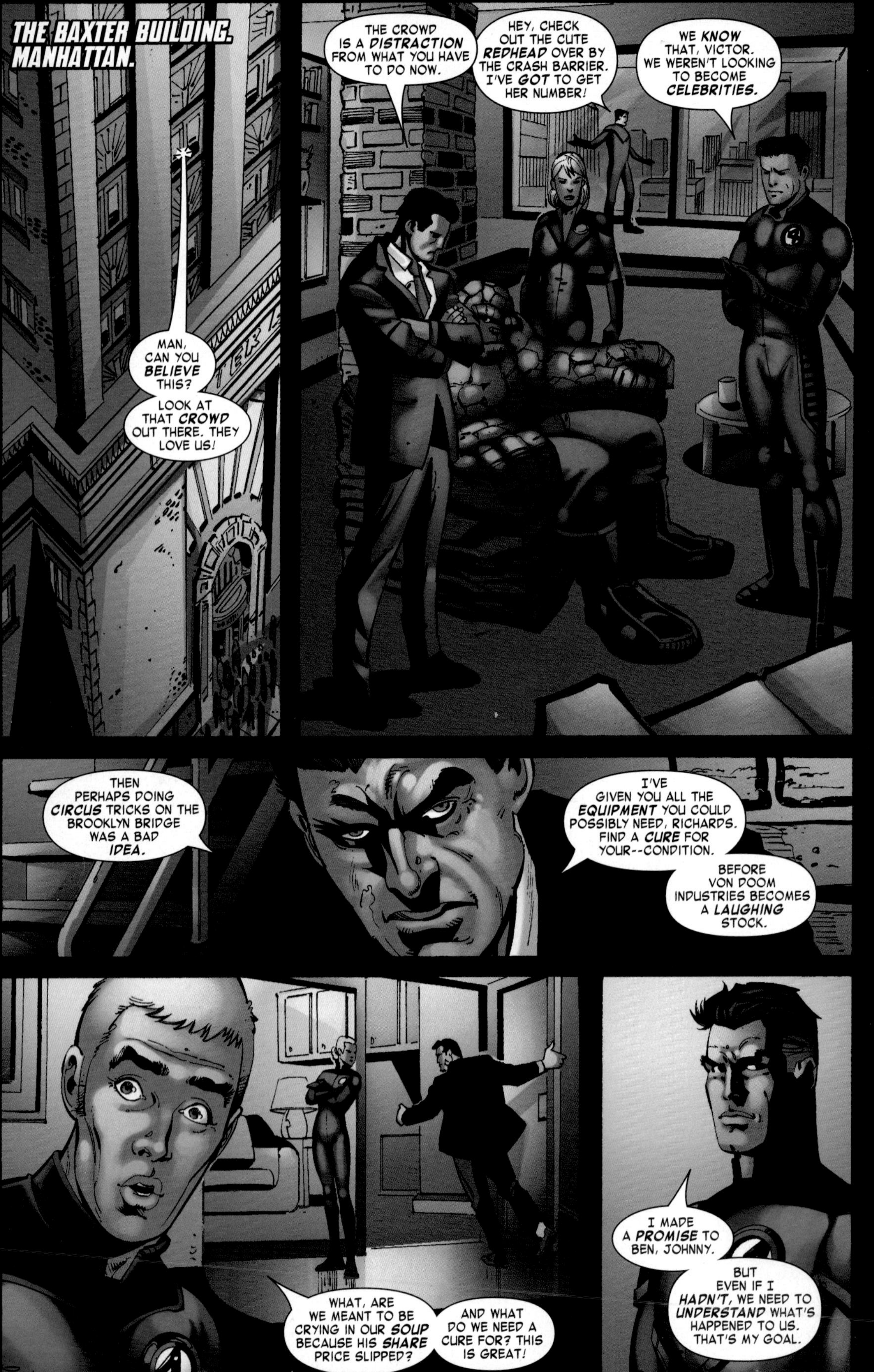
THE BAXTER BUILDING. MANHATTAN.
MAN, CAN YOU BELIEVE THIS?
LOOK AT THAT CROWD OUT THERE. THEY LOVE US!
THE CROWD IS A DISTRACTION FROM WHAT YOU HAVE TO DO NOW.
HEY, CHECK OUT THE CUTE REDHEAD OVER BY THE CRASH BARRIER. I'VE GOT TO GET HER NUMBER!
WE KNOW THAT, VICTOR. WE WEREN'T LOOKING TO BECOME CELEBRITIES.
THEN PERHAPS DOING CIRCUS TRICKS ON THE BROOKLYN BRIDGE WAS A BAD IDEA.
I'VE GIVEN YOU ALL THE EQUIPMENT YOU COULD POSSIBLY NEED, RICHARDS. FIND A CURE FOR YOUR--CONDITION.
BEFORE VON DOOM INDUSTRIES BECOMES A LAUGHING STOCK.
WHAT, ARE WE MEANT TO BE CRYING IN OUR SOUP BECAUSE HIS SHARE PRICE SLIPPED?
AND WHAT DO WE NEED A CURE FOR? THIS IS GREAT!
I MADE A PROMISE TO BEN, JOHNNY.
BUT EVEN IF I HADN'T, WE NEED TO UNDERSTAND WHAT'S HAPPENED TO US. THAT'S MY GOAL.

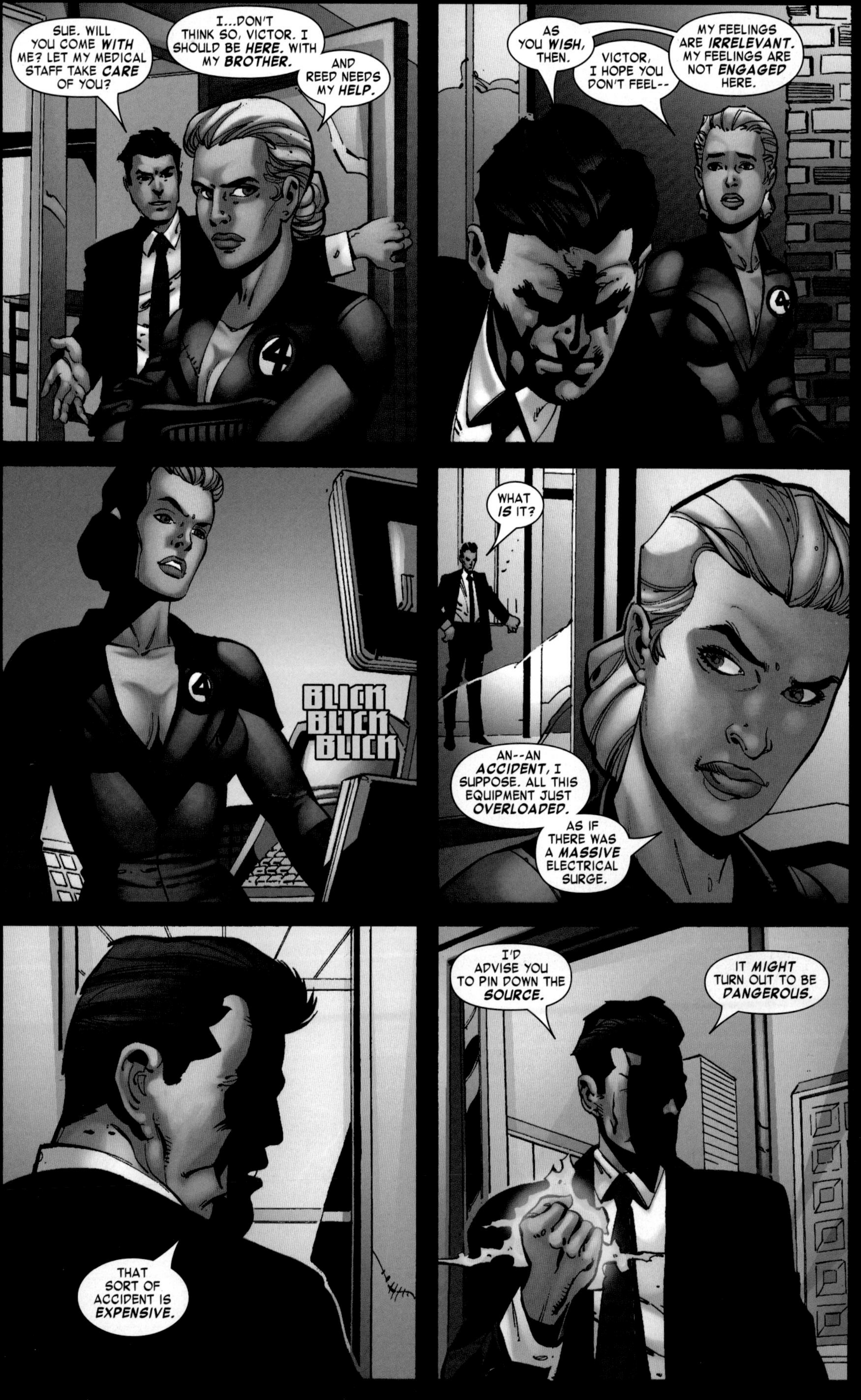
SUE. WILL YOU COME WITH ME? LET MY MEDICAL STAFF TAKE CARE OF YOU?
I...DON'T THINK SO, VICTOR. I SHOULD BE HERE. WITH MY BROTHER.
AND REED NEEDS MY HELP.
AS YOU WISH, THEN.
VICTOR, I HOPE YOU DON'T FEEL--
MY FEELINGS ARE IRRELEVANT. MY FEELINGS ARE NOT ENGAGED HERE.
BLICK BLICK BLICK
WHAT IS IT?
AN--AN ACCIDENT, I SUPPOSE. ALL THIS EQUIPMENT JUST OVERLOADED.
AS IF THERE WAS A MASSIVE ELECTRICAL SURGE.
THAT SORT OF ACCIDENT IS EXPENSIVE.
I'D ADVISE YOU TO PIN DOWN THE SOURCE.
IT MIGHT TURN OUT TO BE DANGEROUS.

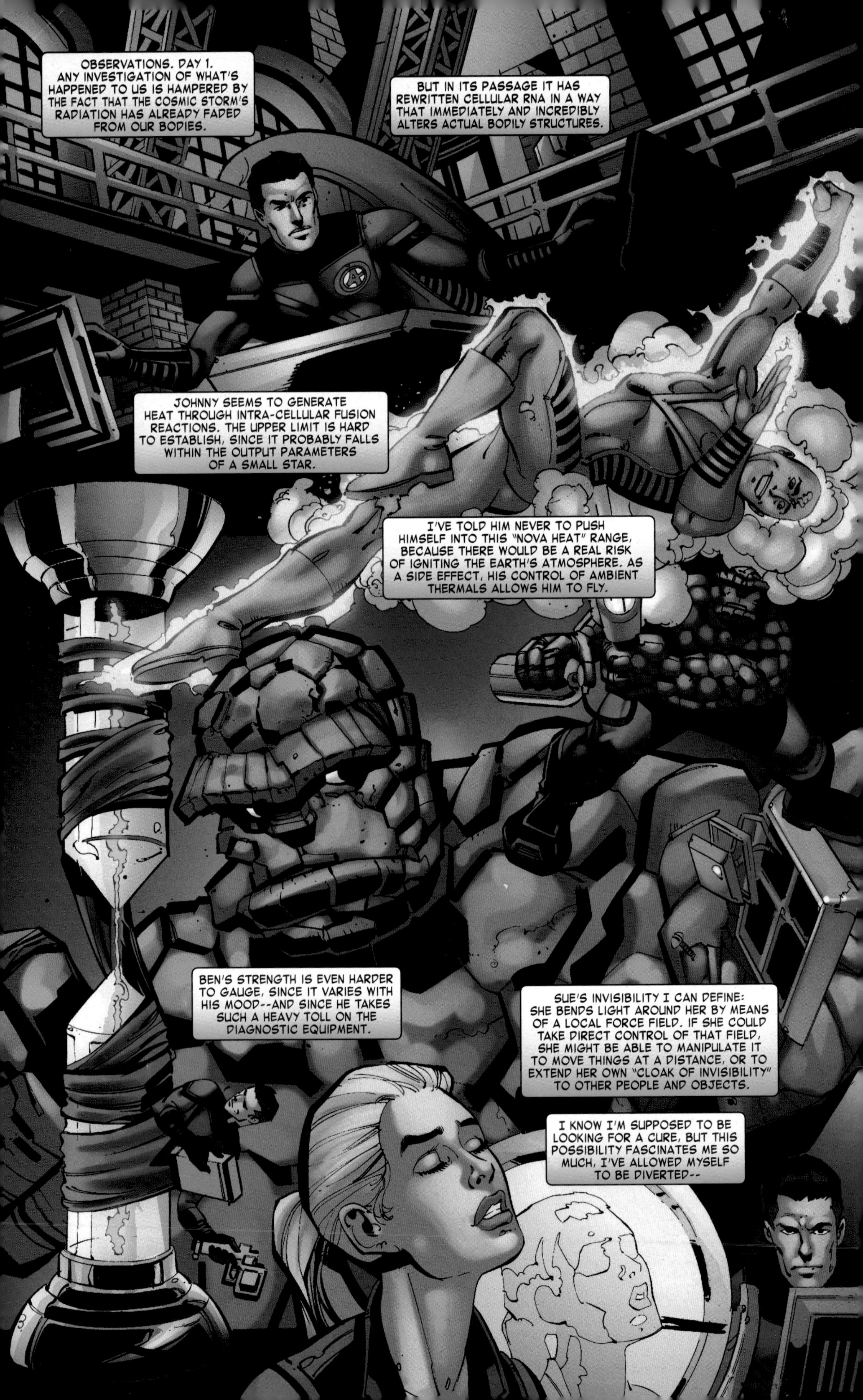
OBSERVATIONS. DAY 1. ANY INVESTIGATION OF WHAT'S HAPPENED TO US IS HAMPERED BY THE FACT THAT THE COSMIC STORM'S RADIATION HAS ALREADY FADED FROM OUR BODIES.
BUT IN ITS PASSAGE IT HAS REWRITTEN CELLULAR RNA IN A WAY THAT IMMEDIATELY AND INCREDIBLY ALTERS ACTUAL BODILY STRUCTURES.
JOHNNY SEEMS TO GENERATE HEAT THROUGH INTRA-CELLULAR FUSION REACTIONS. THE UPPER LIMIT IS HARD TO ESTABLISH, SINCE IT PROBABLY FALLS WITHIN THE OUTPUT PARAMETERS OF A SMALL STAR.
I'VE TOLD HIM NEVER TO PUSH HIMSELF INTO THIS "NOVA HEAT" RANGE, BECAUSE THERE WOULD BE A REAL RISK OF IGNITING THE EARTH'S ATMOSPHERE. AS A SIDE EFFECT, HIS CONTROL OF AMBIENT THERMALS ALLOWS HIM TO FLY.
BEN'S STRENGTH IS EVEN HARDER TO GAUGE, SINCE IT VARIES WITH HIS MOOD--AND SINCE HE TAKES SUCH A HEAVY TOLL ON THE DIAGNOSTIC EQUIPMENT.
SUE'S INVISIBILITY I CAN DEFINE: SHE BENDS LIGHT AROUND HER BY MEANS OF A LOCAL FORCE FIELD. IF SHE COULD TAKE DIRECT CONTROL OF THAT FIELD, SHE MIGHT BE ABLE TO MANIPULATE IT TO MOVE THINGS AT A DISTANCE, OR TO EXTEND HER OWN "CLOAK OF INVISIBILITY" TO OTHER PEOPLE AND OBJECTS.
I KNOW I'M SUPPOSED TO BE LOOKING FOR A CURE, BUT THIS POSSIBILITY FASCINATES ME SO MUCH, I'VE ALLOWED MYSELF TO BE DIVERTED--

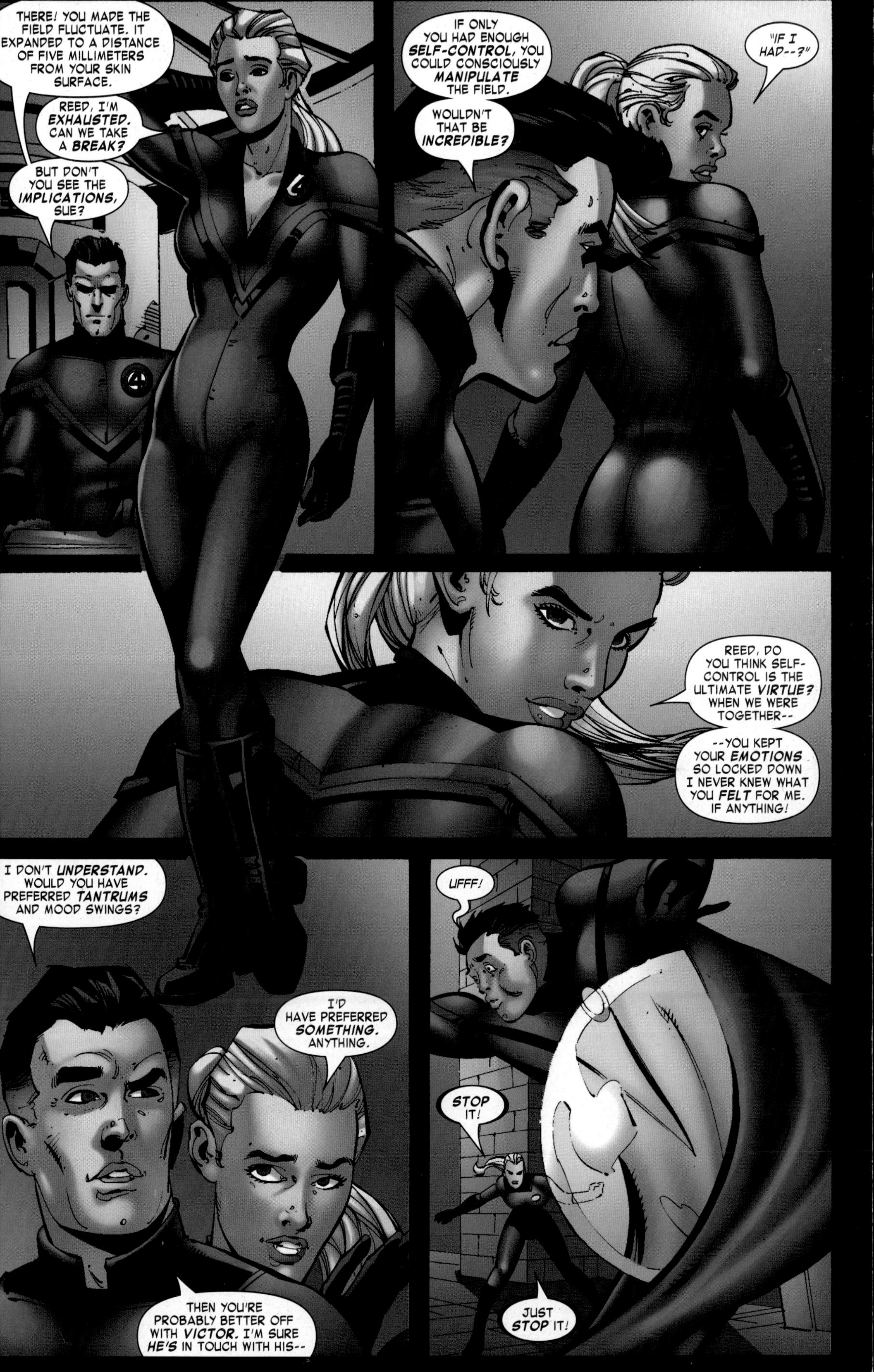
THERE! YOU MADE THE FIELD FLUCTUATE. IT EXPANDED TO A DISTANCE OF FIVE MILLIMETERS FROM YOUR SKIN SURFACE.
REED, I'M EXHAUSTED. CAN WE TAKE A BREAK?
BUT DON'T YOU SEE THE IMPLICATIONS, SUE?
IF ONLY YOU HAD ENOUGH SELF-CONTROL, YOU COULD CONSCIOUSLY MANIPULATE THE FIELD.
WOULDN'T THAT BE INCREDIBLE?
"IF I HAD--?"
REED, DO YOU THINK SELF-CONTROL IS THE ULTIMATE VIRTUE? WHEN WE WERE TOGETHER--
--YOU KEPT YOUR EMOTIONS SO LOCKED DOWN I NEVER KNEW WHAT YOU FELT FOR ME. IF ANYTHING!
I DON'T UNDERSTAND. WOULD YOU HAVE PREFERRED TANTRUMS AND MOOD SWINGS?
I'D HAVE PREFERRED SOMETHING. ANYTHING.
THEN YOU'RE PROBABLY BETTER OFF WITH VICTOR. I'M SURE HE'S IN TOUCH WITH HIS--
UFFF!
STOP IT!
JUST STOP IT!

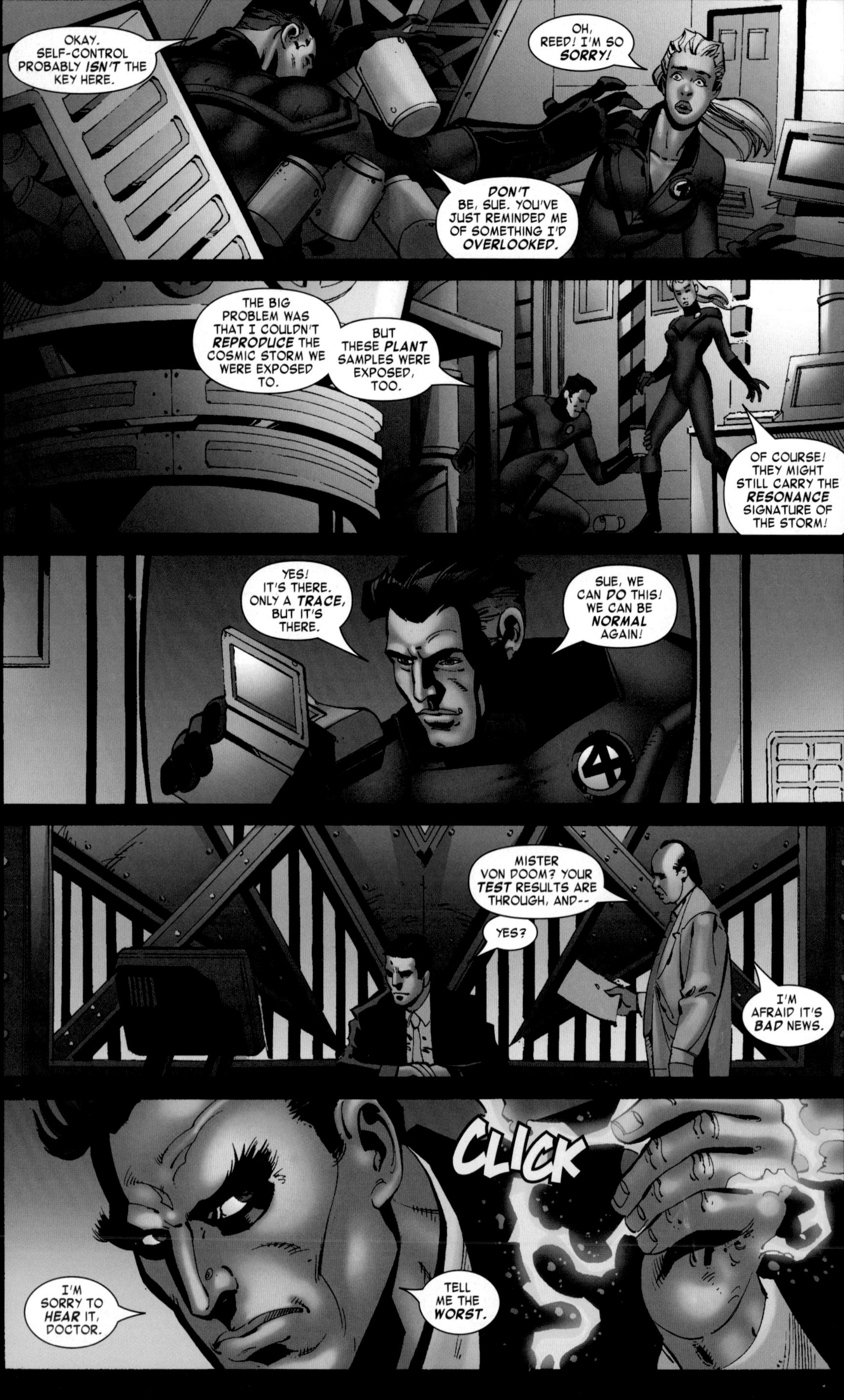
OKAY. SELF-CONTROL PROBABLY ISN'T THE KEY HERE.
OH, REED! I'M SO SORRY!
DON'T BE, SUE. YOU'VE JUST REMINDED ME OF SOMETHING I'D OVERLOOKED.
THE BIG PROBLEM WAS THAT I COULDN'T REPRODUCE THE COSMIC STORM WE WERE EXPOSED TO.
BUT THESE PLANT SAMPLES WERE EXPOSED, TOO.
OF COURSE! THEY MIGHT STILL CARRY THE RESONANCE SIGNATURE OF THE STORM!
YES! IT'S THERE. ONLY A TRACE, BUT IT'S THERE.
SUE, WE CAN DO THIS! WE CAN BE NORMAL AGAIN!
MISTER VON DOOM? YOUR TEST RESULTS ARE THROUGH, AND--
YES?
I'M AFRAID IT'S BAD NEWS.
CLICK
I'M SORRY TO HEAR IT, DOCTOR.
TELL ME THE WORST.

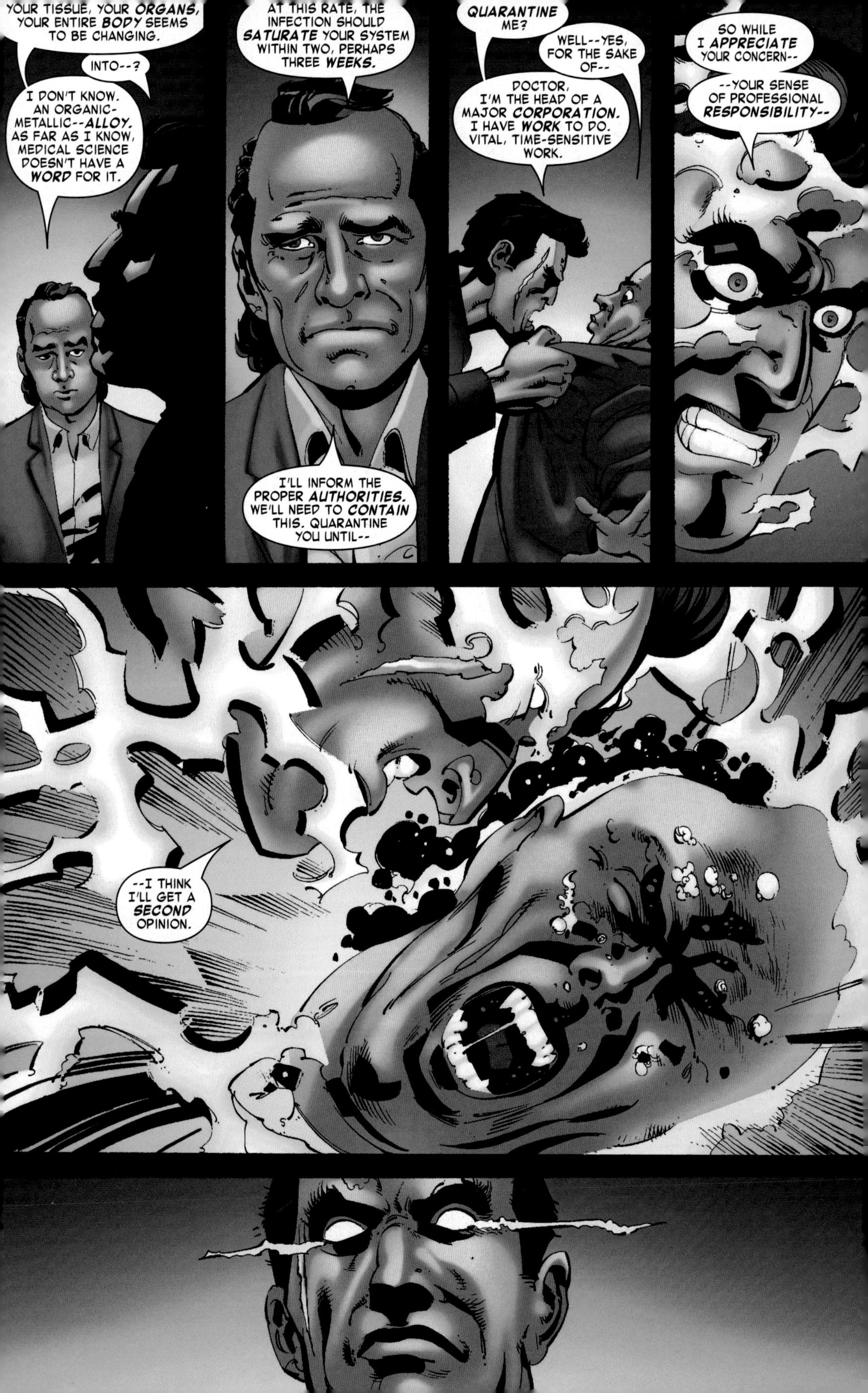
YOUR TISSUE, YOUR ORGANS, YOUR ENTIRE BODY SEEMS TO BE CHANGING.
INTO--?
I DON'T KNOW. AN ORGANIC-METALLIC--ALLOY. AS FAR AS I KNOW, MEDICAL SCIENCE DOESN'T HAVE A WORD FOR IT.
AT THIS RATE, THE INFECTION SHOULD SATURATE YOUR SYSTEM WITHIN TWO, PERHAPS THREE WEEKS.
I'LL INFORM THE PROPER AUTHORITIES. WE'LL NEED TO CONTAIN THIS. QUARANTINE YOU UNTIL--
QUARANTINE ME?
WELL--YES, FOR THE SAKE OF--
DOCTOR, I'M THE HEAD OF A MAJOR CORPORATION. I HAVE WORK TO DO. VITAL, TIME-SENSITIVE WORK.
SO WHILE I APPRECIATE YOUR CONCERN--
--YOUR SENSE OF PROFESSIONAL RESPONSIBILITY--
--I THINK I'LL GET A SECOND OPINION.

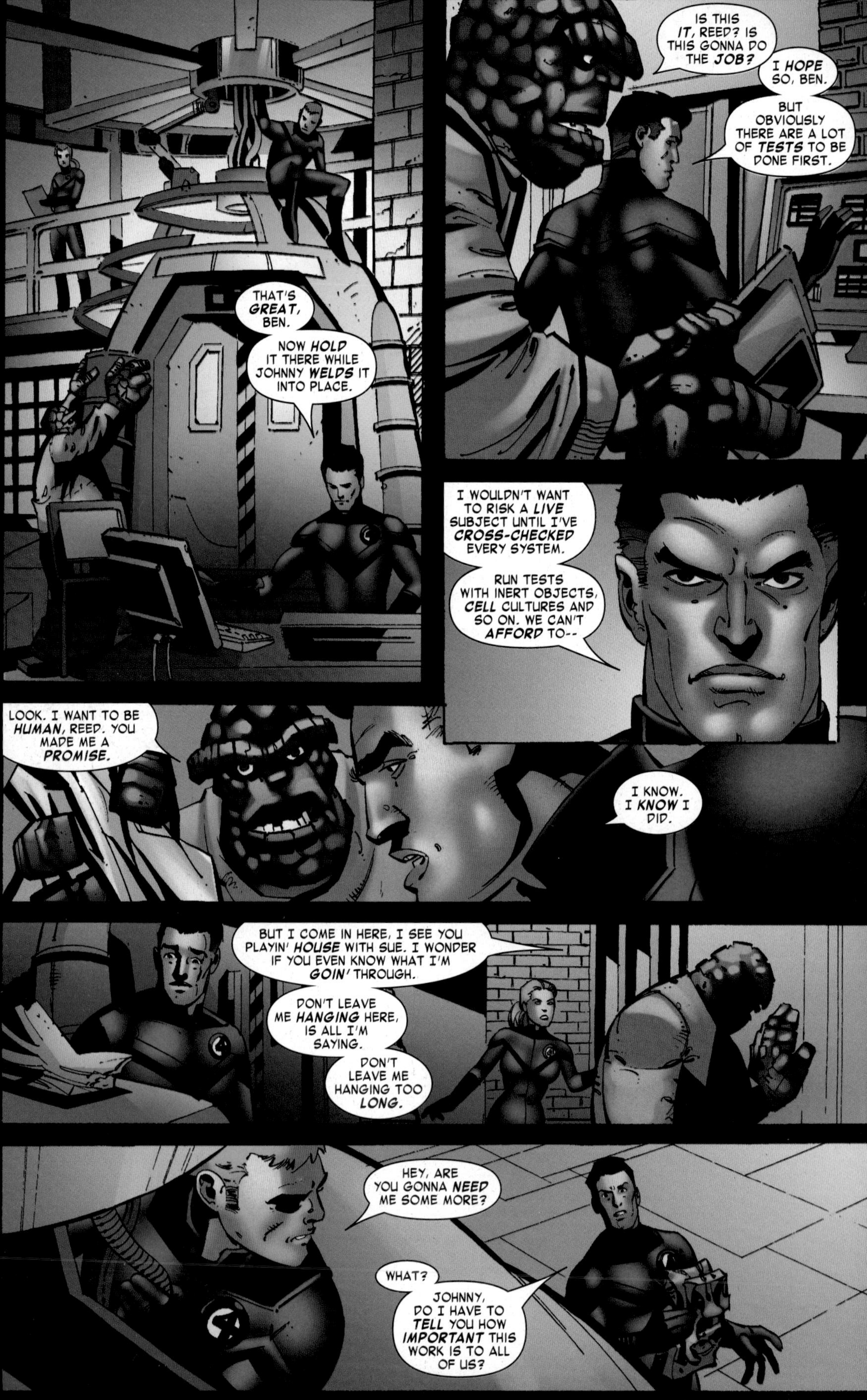
THAT'S GREAT, BEN.
NOW HOLD IT THERE WHILE JOHNNY WELDS IT INTO PLACE.
IS THIS IT, REED? IS THIS GONNA DO THE JOB?
I HOPE SO, BEN.
BUT OBVIOUSLY THERE ARE A LOT OF TESTS TO BE DONE FIRST.
I WOULDN'T WANT TO RISK A LIVE SUBJECT UNTIL I'VE CROSS-CHECKED EVERY SYSTEM.
RUN TESTS WITH INERT OBJECTS, CELL CULTURES AND SO ON. WE CAN'T AFFORD TO--
LOOK. I WANT TO BE HUMAN, REED. YOU MADE ME A PROMISE.
I KNOW. I KNOW I DID.
BUT I COME IN HERE, I SEE YOU PLAYIN' HOUSE WITH SUE. I WONDER IF YOU EVEN KNOW WHAT I'M GOIN' THROUGH.
DON'T LEAVE ME HANGING HERE, IS ALL I'M SAYING.
DON'T LEAVE ME HANGING TOO LONG.
HEY, ARE YOU GONNA NEED ME SOME MORE?
WHAT?
JOHNNY, DO I HAVE TO TELL YOU HOW IMPORTANT THIS WORK IS TO ALL OF US?

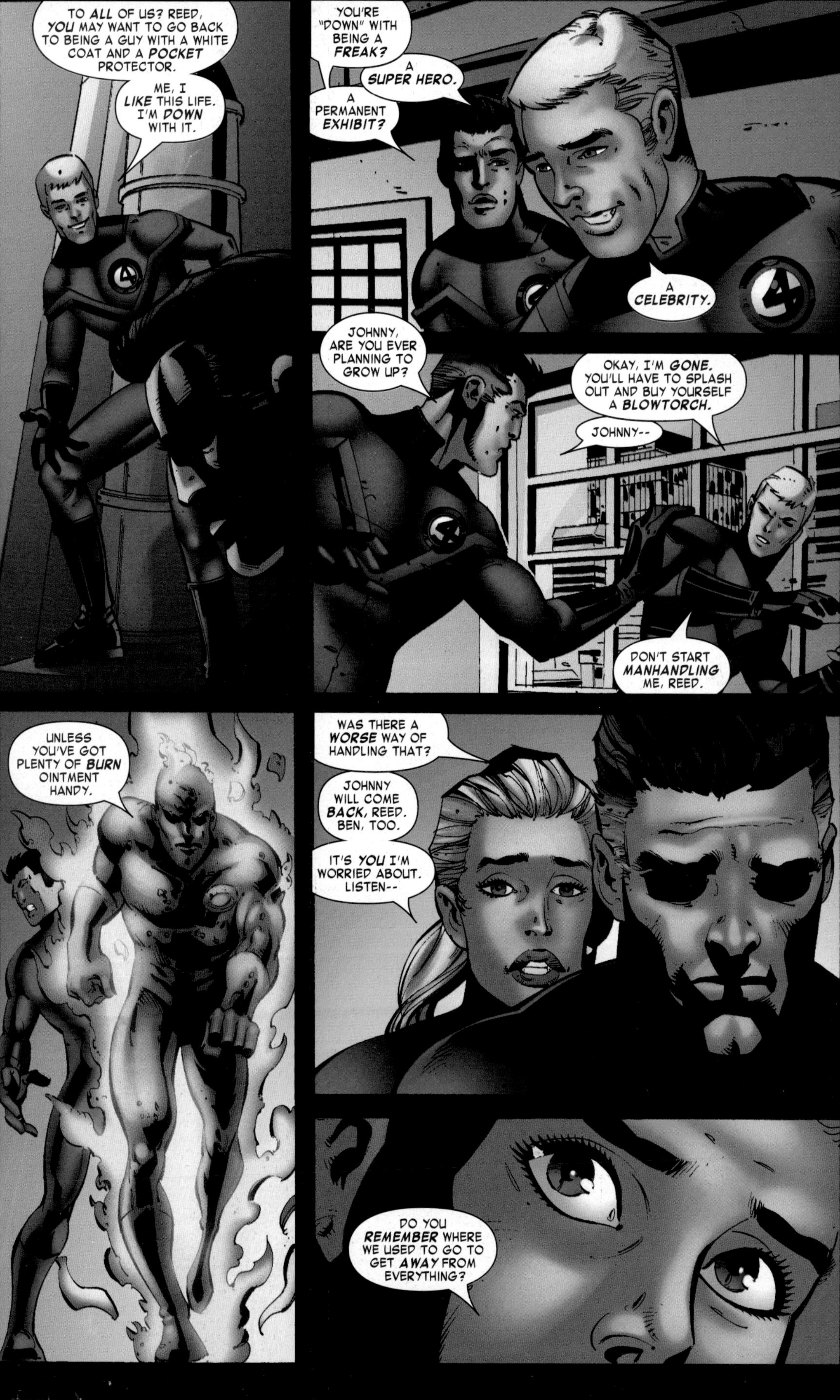
TO ALL OF US? REED, YOU MAY WANT TO GO BACK TO BEING A GUY WITH A WHITE COAT AND A POCKET PROTECTOR.
ME, I LIKE THIS LIFE. I'M DOWN WITH IT.
YOU'RE "DOWN" WITH BEING A FREAK?
A PERMANENT EXHIBIT?
A SUPER HERO.
A CELEBRITY.
JOHNNY, ARE YOU EVER PLANNING TO GROW UP?
OKAY, I'M GONE. YOU'LL HAVE TO SPLASH OUT AND BUY YOURSELF A BLOWTORCH.
JOHNNY--
DON'T START MANHANDLING ME, REED.
UNLESS YOU'VE GOT PLENTY OF BURN OINTMENT HANDY.
WAS THERE A WORSE WAY OF HANDLING THAT?
JOHNNY WILL COME BACK, REED. BEN, TOO.
IT'S YOU I'M WORRIED ABOUT. LISTEN--
DO YOU REMEMBER WHERE WE USED TO GO TO GET AWAY FROM EVERYTHING?

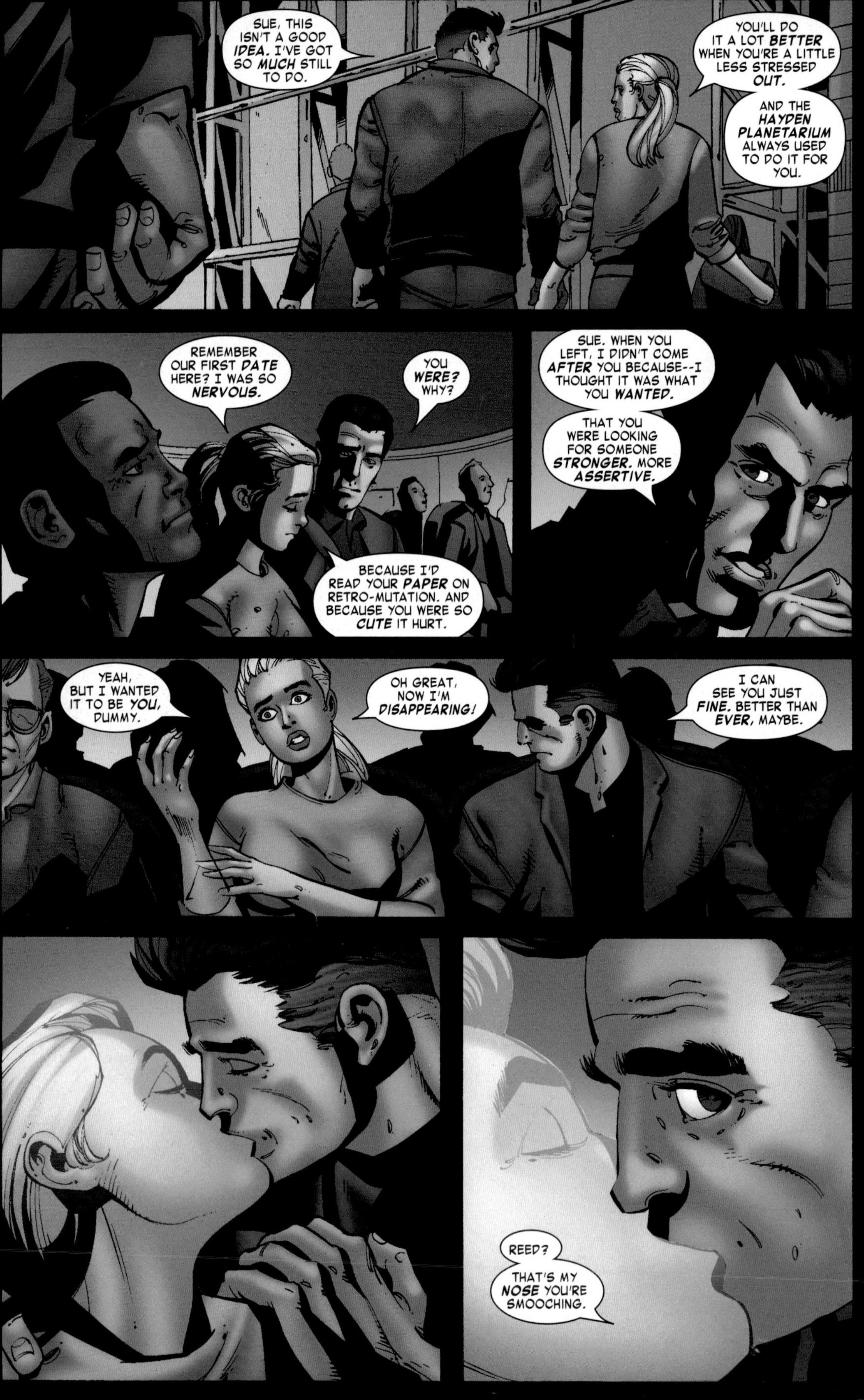
SUE, THIS ISN'T A GOOD IDEA. I'VE GOT SO MUCH STILL TO DO.
YOU'LL DO IT A LOT BETTER WHEN YOU'RE A LITTLE LESS STRESSED OUT.
AND THE HAYDEN PLANETARIUM ALWAYS USED TO DO IT FOR YOU.
REMEMBER OUR FIRST DATE HERE? I WAS SO NERVOUS.
YOU WERE? WHY?
BECAUSE I'D READ YOUR PAPER ON RETRO-MUTATION. AND BECAUSE YOU WERE SO CUTE IT HURT.
SUE. WHEN YOU LEFT, I DIDN'T COME AFTER YOU BECAUSE--I THOUGHT IT WAS WHAT YOU WANTED.
THAT YOU WERE LOOKING FOR SOMEONE STRONGER. MORE ASSERTIVE.
YEAH, BUT I WANTED IT TO BE YOU, DUMMY.
OH GREAT, NOW I'M DISAPPEARING!
I CAN SEE YOU JUST FINE. BETTER THAN EVER, MAYBE.
REED?
THAT'S MY NOSE YOU'RE SMOOCHING.

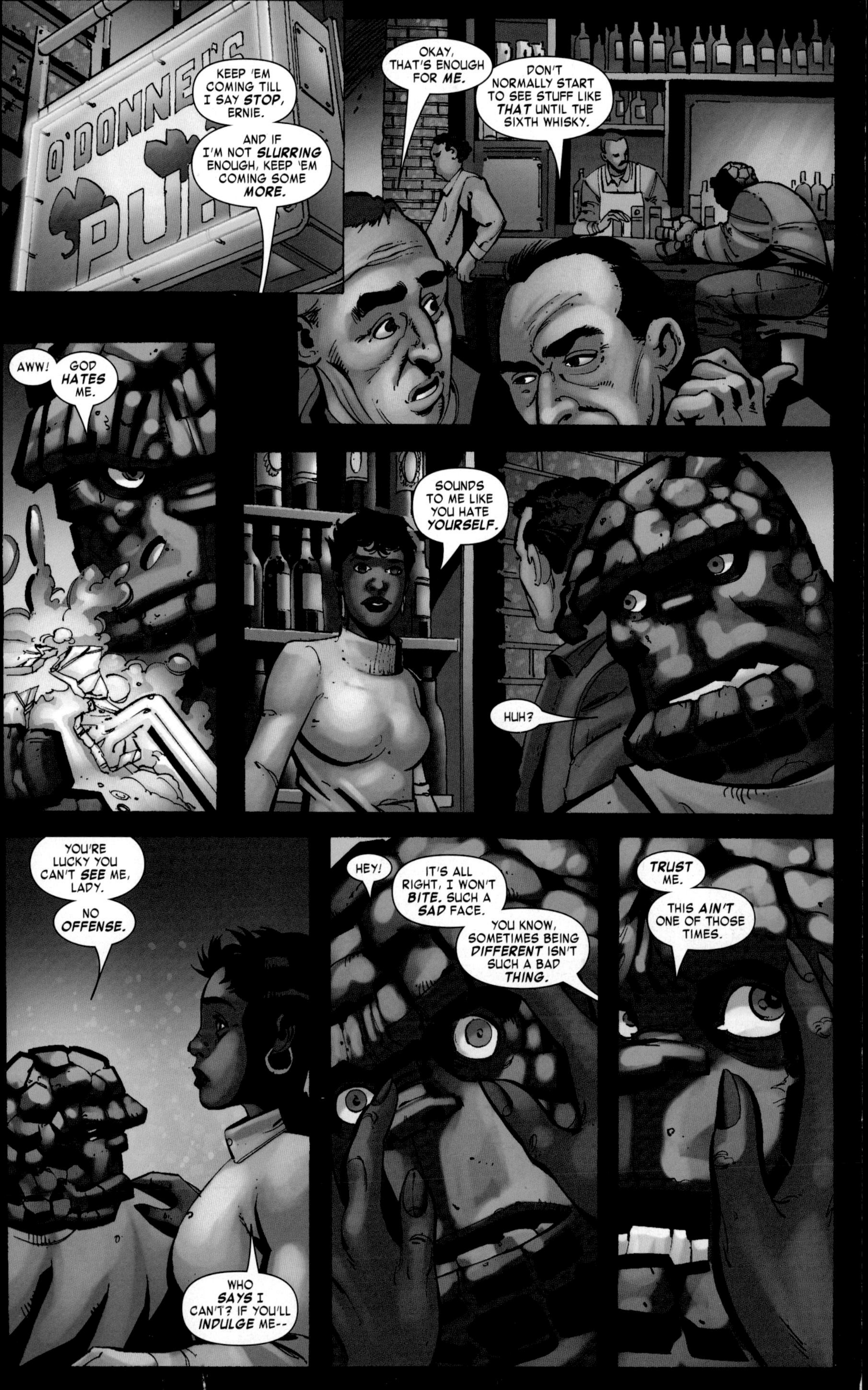
O'DONNELL'S PUB
KEEP 'EM COMING TILL I SAY STOP, ERNIE.
AND IF I'M NOT SLURRING ENOUGH, KEEP 'EM COMING SOME MORE.
OKAY, THAT'S ENOUGH FOR ME.
DON'T NORMALLY START TO SEE STUFF LIKE THAT UNTIL THE SIXTH WHISKY.
AWW!
GOD HATES ME.
SOUNDS TO ME LIKE YOU HATE YOURSELF.
HUH?
YOU'RE LUCKY YOU CAN'T SEE ME, LADY.
NO OFFENSE.
WHO SAYS I CAN'T? IF YOU'LL INDULGE ME--
HEY!
IT'S ALL RIGHT, I WON'T BITE. SUCH A SAD FACE.
YOU KNOW, SOMETIMES BEING DIFFERENT ISN'T SUCH A BAD THING.
TRUST ME.
THIS AIN'T ONE OF THOSE TIMES.

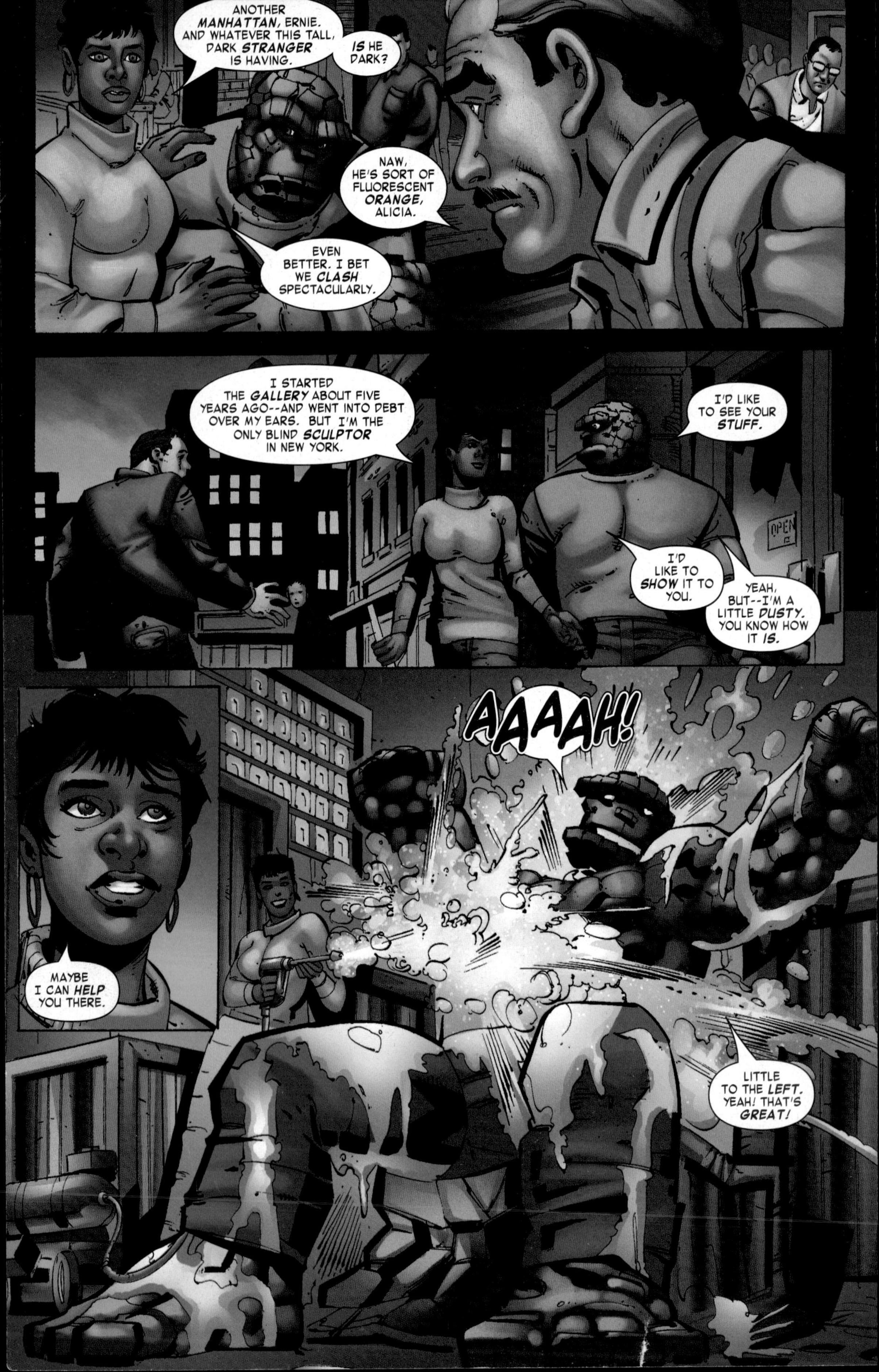
ANOTHER MANHATTAN, ERNIE. AND WHATEVER THIS TALL, DARK STRANGER IS HAVING.
IS HE DARK?
NAW, HE'S SORT OF FLUORESCENT ORANGE, ALICIA.
EVEN BETTER. I BET WE CLASH SPECTACULARLY.
I STARTED THE GALLERY ABOUT FIVE YEARS AGO--AND WENT INTO DEBT OVER MY EARS. BUT I'M THE ONLY BLIND SCULPTOR IN NEW YORK.
I'D LIKE TO SEE YOUR STUFF.
I'D LIKE TO SHOW IT TO YOU.
YEAH, BUT--I'M A LITTLE DUSTY. YOU KNOW HOW IT IS.
OPEN
MAYBE I CAN HELP YOU THERE.
AAAAH!
LITTLE TO THE LEFT. YEAH! THAT'S GREAT!

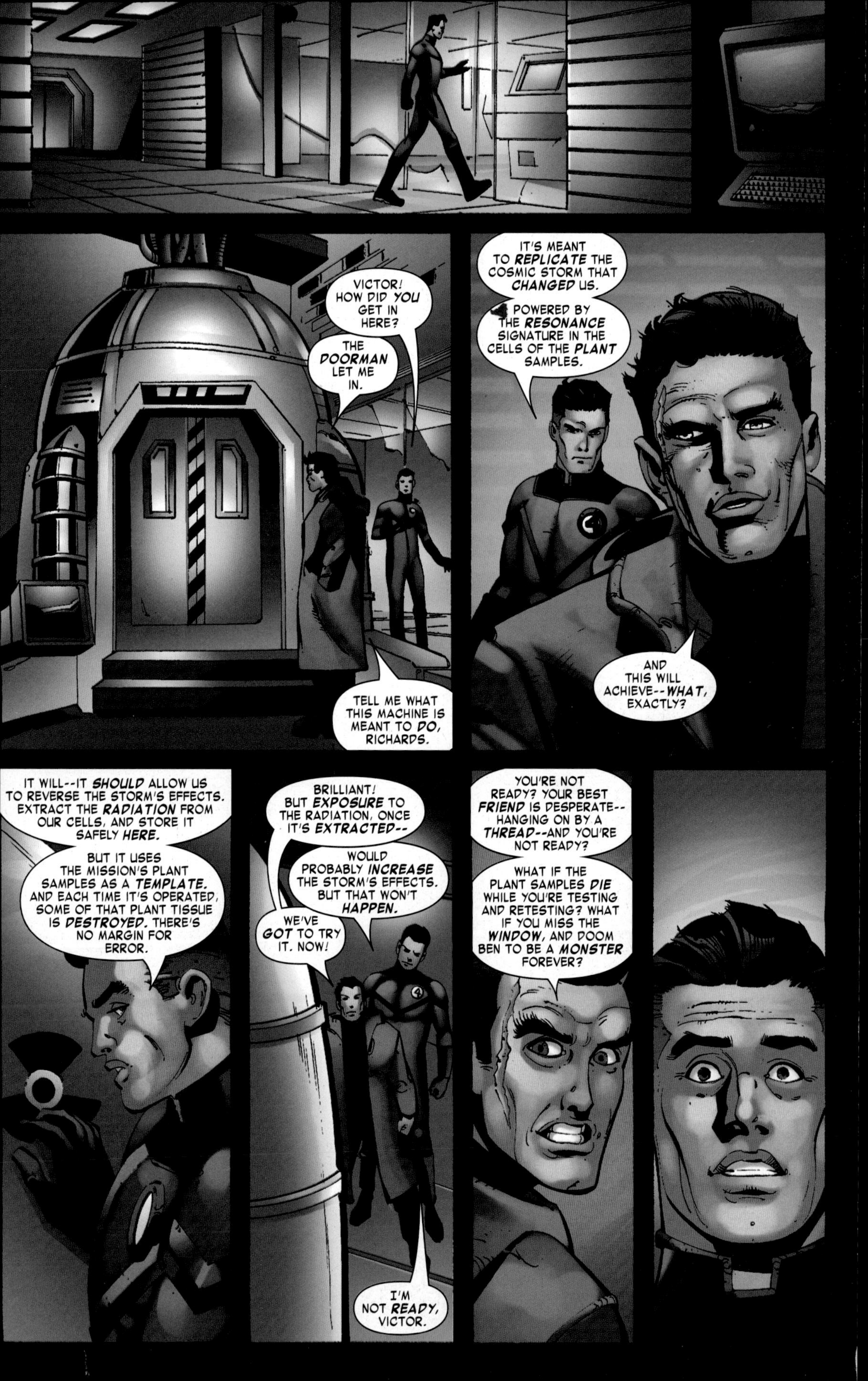
VICTOR! HOW DID YOU GET IN HERE?
THE DOORMAN LET ME IN.
TELL ME WHAT THIS MACHINE IS MEANT TO DO, RICHARDS.
IT'S MEANT TO REPLICATE THE COSMIC STORM THAT CHANGED US.
POWERED BY THE RESONANCE SIGNATURE IN THE CELLS OF THE PLANT SAMPLES.
AND THIS WILL ACHIEVE--WHAT, EXACTLY?
IT WILL--IT SHOULD ALLOW US TO REVERSE THE STORM'S EFFECTS. EXTRACT THE RADIATION FROM OUR CELLS, AND STORE IT SAFELY HERE.
BUT IT USES THE MISSION'S PLANT SAMPLES AS A TEMPLATE. AND EACH TIME IT'S OPERATED, SOME OF THAT PLANT TISSUE IS DESTROYED. THERE'S NO MARGIN FOR ERROR.
BRILLIANT! BUT EXPOSURE TO THE RADIATION, ONCE IT'S EXTRACTED--
WOULD PROBABLY INCREASE THE STORM'S EFFECTS. BUT THAT WON'T HAPPEN.
WE'VE GOT TO TRY IT. NOW!
I'M NOT READY, VICTOR.
YOU'RE NOT READY? YOUR BEST FRIEND IS DESPERATE--HANGING ON BY A THREAD--AND YOU'RE NOT READY?
WHAT IF THE PLANT SAMPLES DIE WHILE YOU'RE TESTING AND RETESTING? WHAT IF YOU MISS THE WINDOW, AND DOOM BEN TO BE A MONSTER FOREVER?

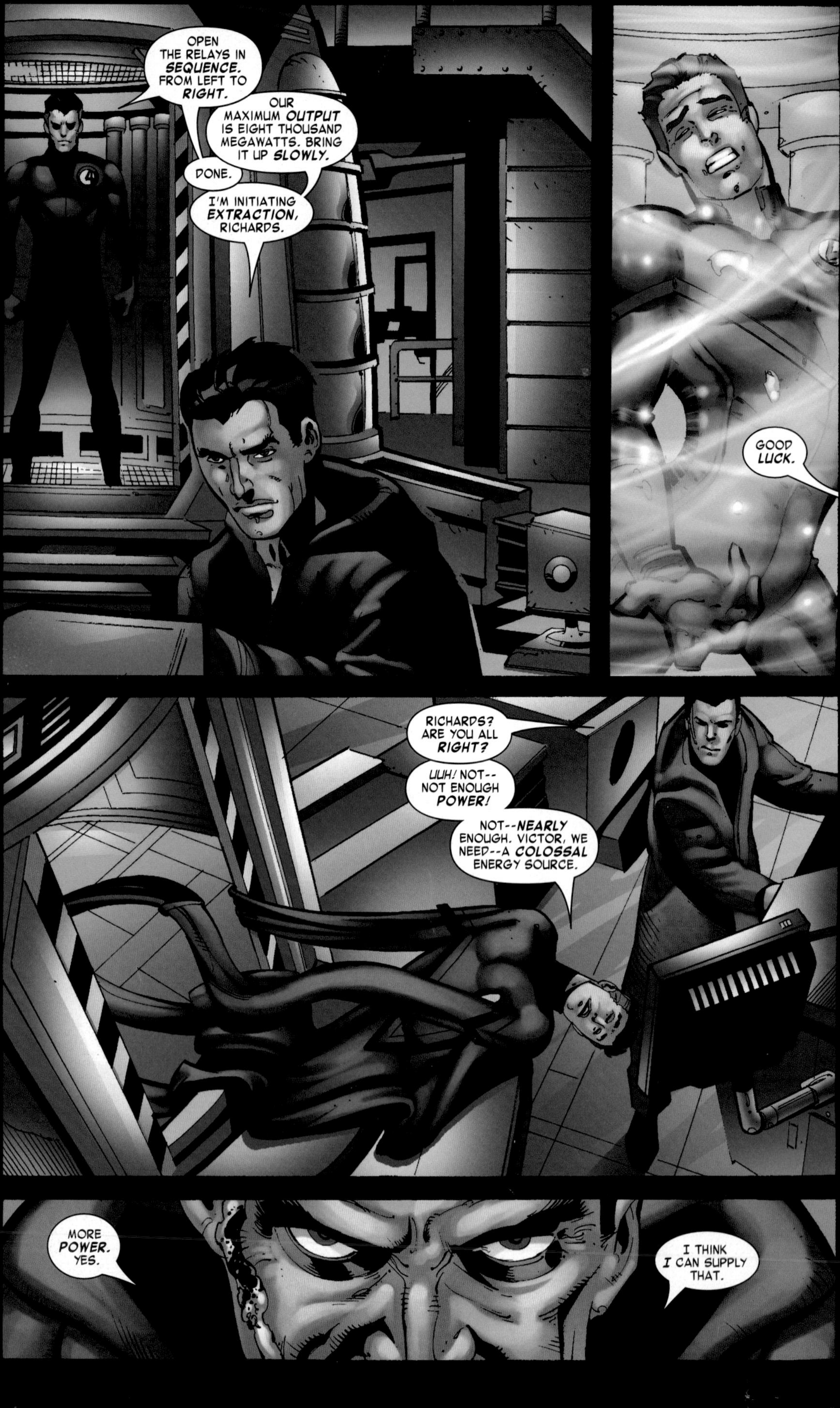
OPEN THE RELAYS IN SEQUENCE. FROM LEFT TO RIGHT.
OUR MAXIMUM OUTPUT IS EIGHT THOUSAND MEGAWATTS. BRING IT UP SLOWLY.
DONE.
I'M INITIATING EXTRACTION, RICHARDS.
GOOD LUCK.
RICHARDS? ARE YOU ALL RIGHT?
UUH! NOT-- NOT ENOUGH POWER!
NOT--NEARLY ENOUGH. VICTOR, WE NEED--A COLOSSAL ENERGY SOURCE.
MORE POWER. YES.
I THINK I CAN SUPPLY THAT.

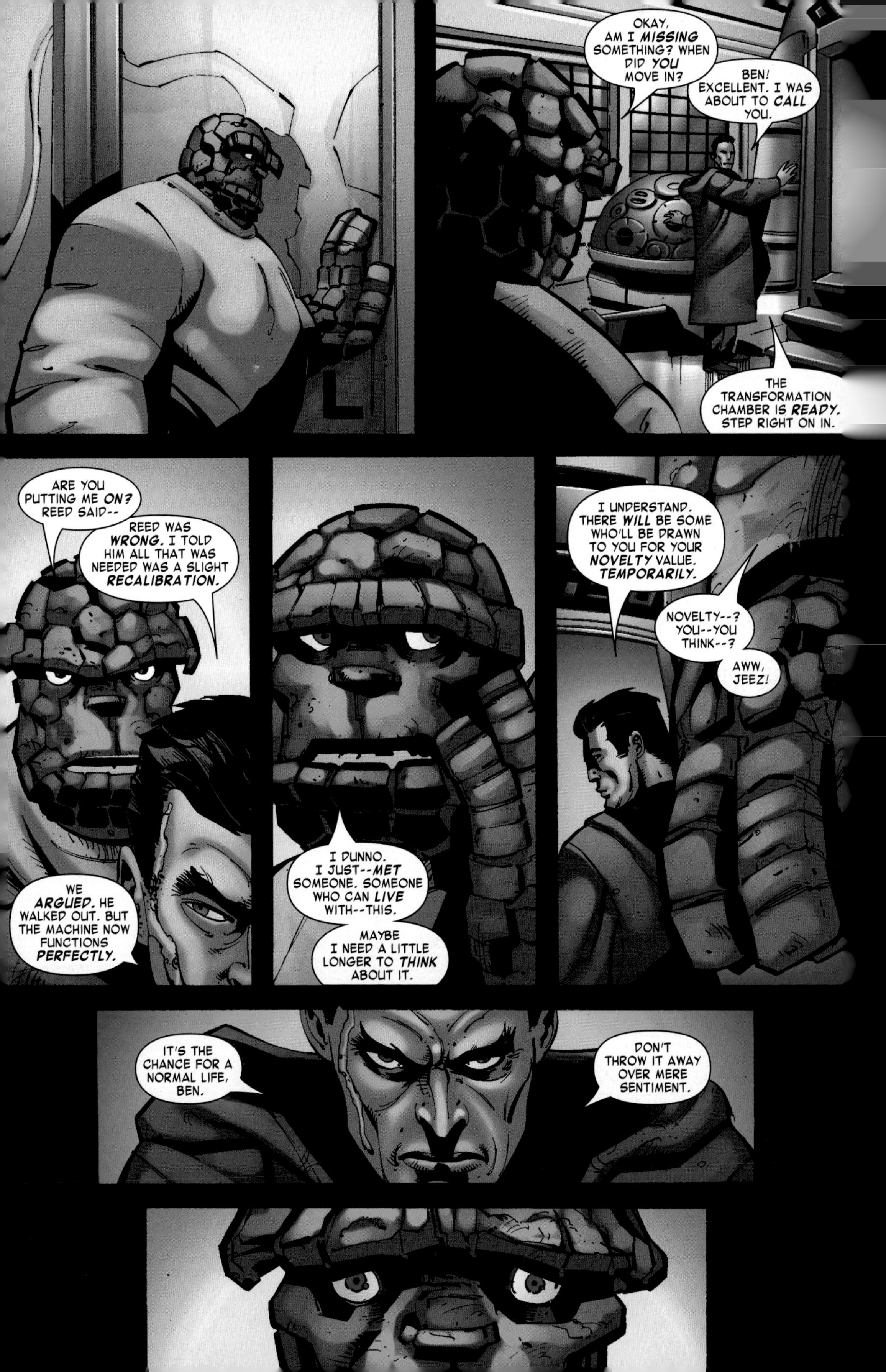
OKAY, AM I MISSING SOMETHING? WHEN DID YOU MOVE IN?
BEN! EXCELLENT. I WAS ABOUT TO CALL YOU.
THE TRANSFORMATION CHAMBER IS READY. STEP RIGHT ON IN.
ARE YOU PUTTING ME ON? REED SAID--
REED WAS WRONG. I TOLD HIM ALL THAT WAS NEEDED WAS A SLIGHT RECALIBRATION.
WE ARGUED. HE WALKED OUT. BUT THE MACHINE NOW FUNCTIONS PERFECTLY.
I DUNNO. I JUST--MET SOMEONE. SOMEONE WHO CAN LIVE WITH--THIS.
MAYBE I NEED A LITTLE LONGER TO THINK ABOUT IT.
I UNDERSTAND. THERE WILL BE SOME WHO'LL BE DRAWN TO YOU FOR YOUR NOVELTY VALUE. TEMPORARILY.
NOVELTY--? YOU--YOU THINK--?
AWW, JEEZ!
IT'S THE CHANCE FOR A NORMAL LIFE, BEN.
DON'T THROW IT AWAY OVER MERE SENTIMENT.

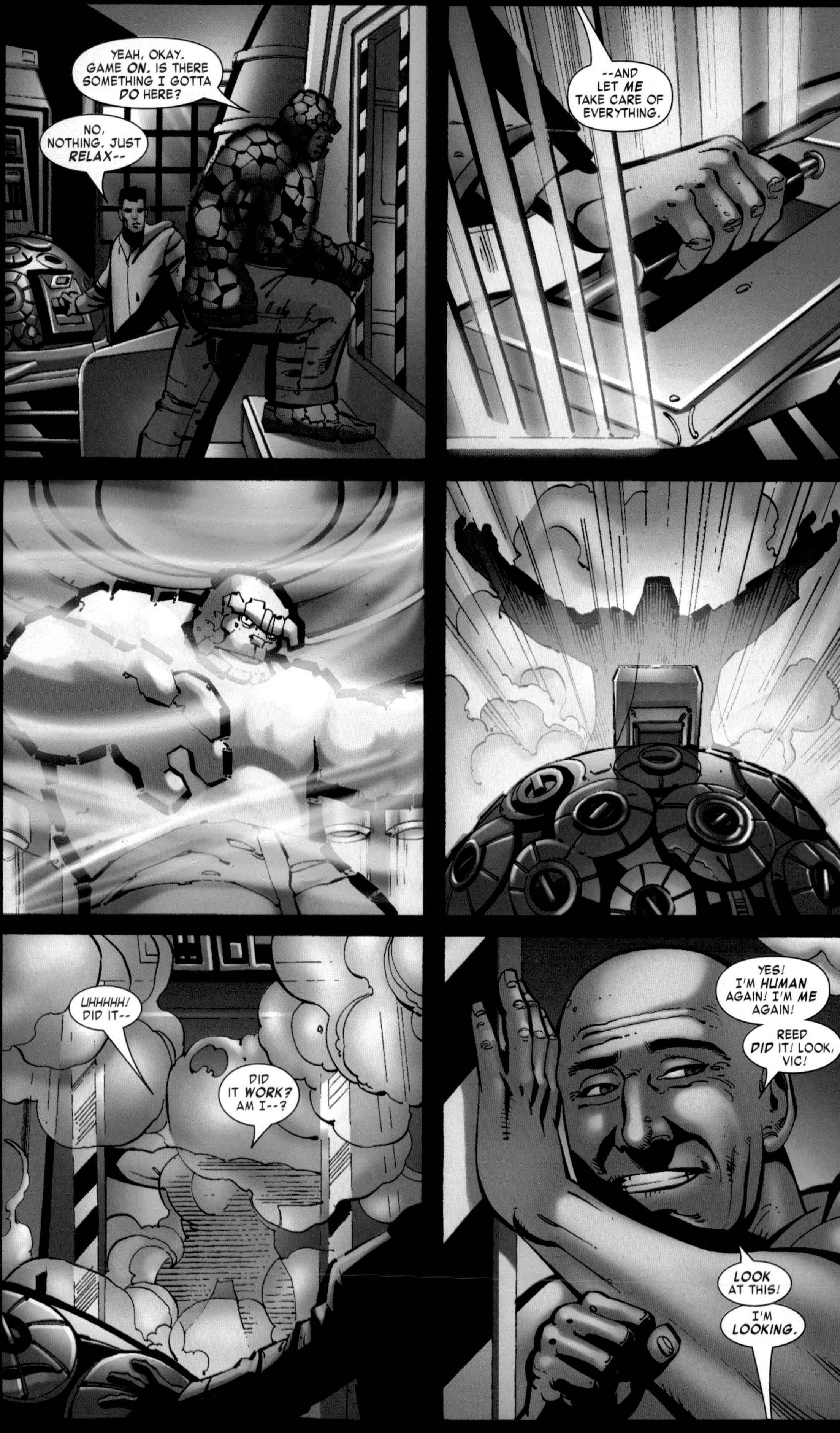

YEAH, OKAY. GAME ON. IS THERE SOMETHING I GOTTA DO HERE?
NO, NOTHING. JUST RELAX--
--AND LET ME TAKE CARE OF EVERYTHING.
UHHHHH! DID IT--
DID IT WORK? AM I--?
YES! I'M HUMAN AGAIN! I'M ME AGAIN!
REED DID IT! LOOK, VIC!
LOOK AT THIS!
I'M LOOKING.

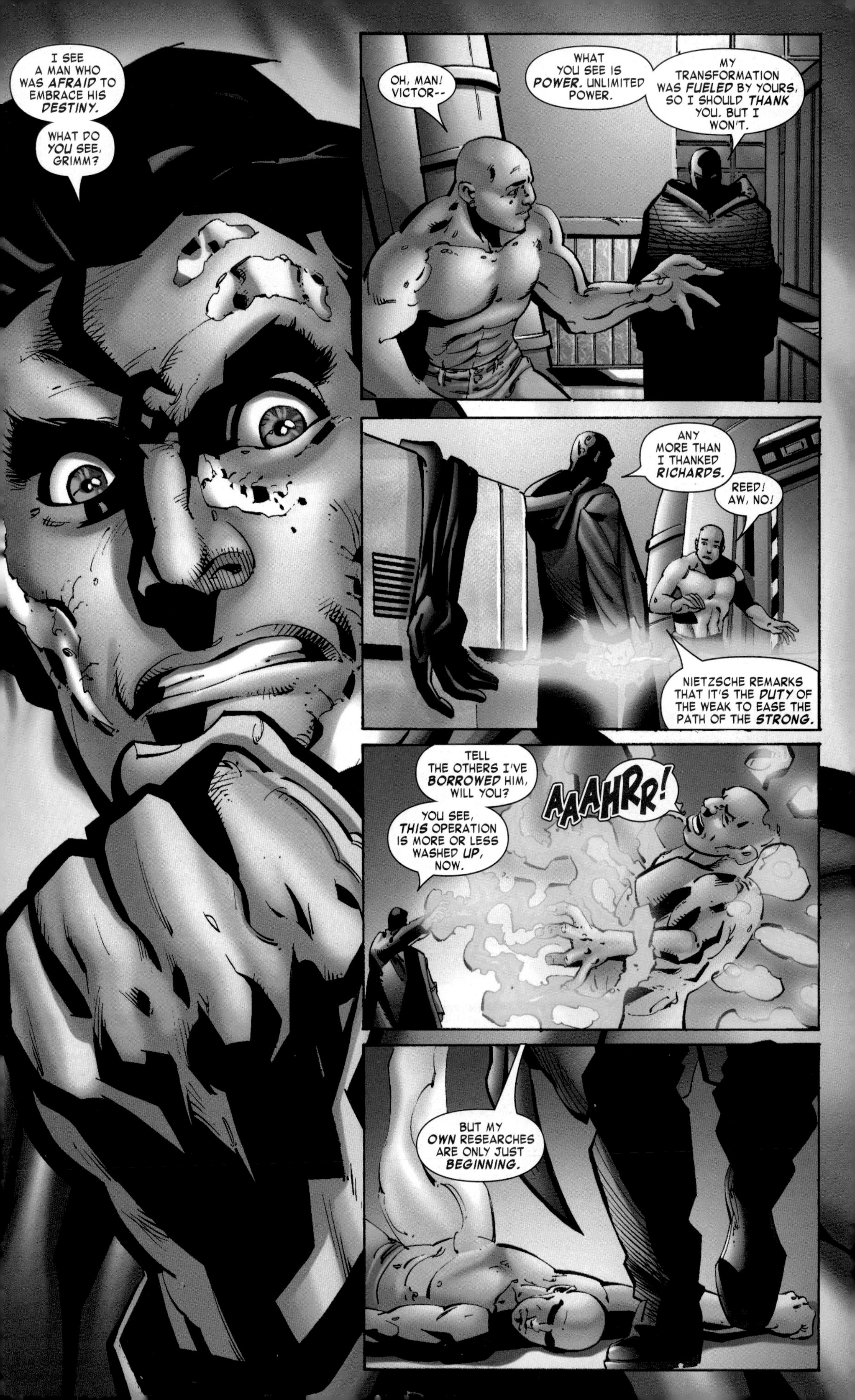

I SEE A MAN WHO WAS AFRAID TO EMBRACE HIS DESTINY.
WHAT DO YOU SEE, GRIMM?
OH, MAN! VICTOR--
WHAT YOU SEE IS POWER. UNLIMITED POWER.
MY TRANSFORMATION WAS FUELED BY YOURS, SO I SHOULD THANK YOU. BUT I WON'T.
ANY MORE THAN I THANKED RICHARDS.
REED! AW, NO!
NIETZSCHE REMARKS THAT IT'S THE DUTY OF THE WEAK TO EASE THE PATH OF THE STRONG.
TELL THE OTHERS I'VE BORROWED HIM, WILL YOU?
YOU SEE, THIS OPERATION IS MORE OR LESS WASHED UP, NOW.
AAAHRR!
BUT MY OWN RESEARCHES ARE ONLY JUST BEGINNING.

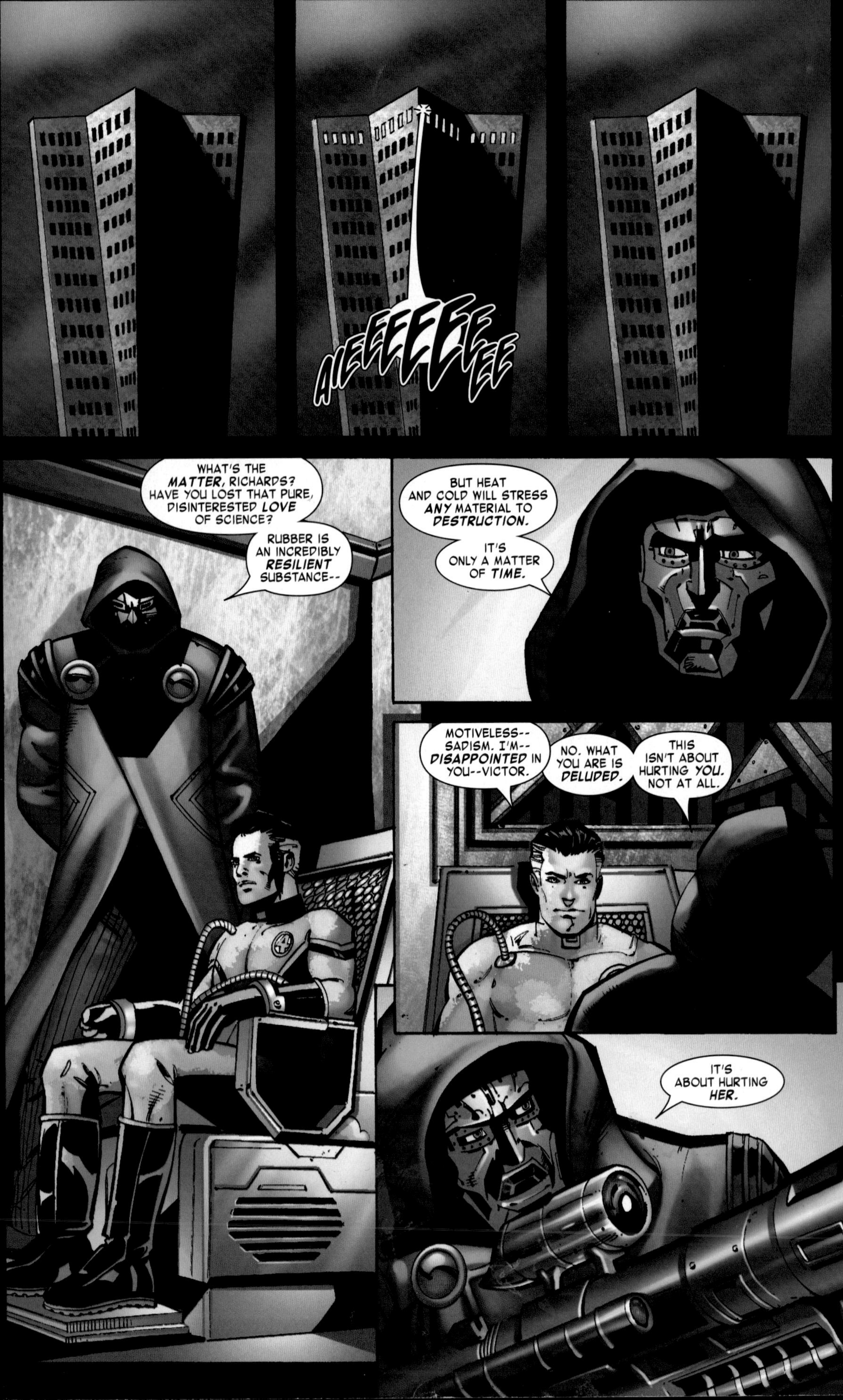

AIEEEEEEEEE
WHAT'S THE MATTER, RICHARDS? HAVE YOU LOST THAT PURE, DISINTERESTED LOVE OF SCIENCE?
RUBBER IS AN INCREDIBLY RESILIENT SUBSTANCE--
BUT HEAT AND COLD WILL STRESS ANY MATERIAL TO DESTRUCTION.
IT'S ONLY A MATTER OF TIME.
MOTIVELESS-- SADISM. I'M-- DISAPPOINTED IN YOU--VICTOR.
NO. WHAT YOU ARE IS DELUDED.
THIS ISN'T ABOUT HURTING YOU. NOT AT ALL.
IT'S ABOUT HURTING HER.

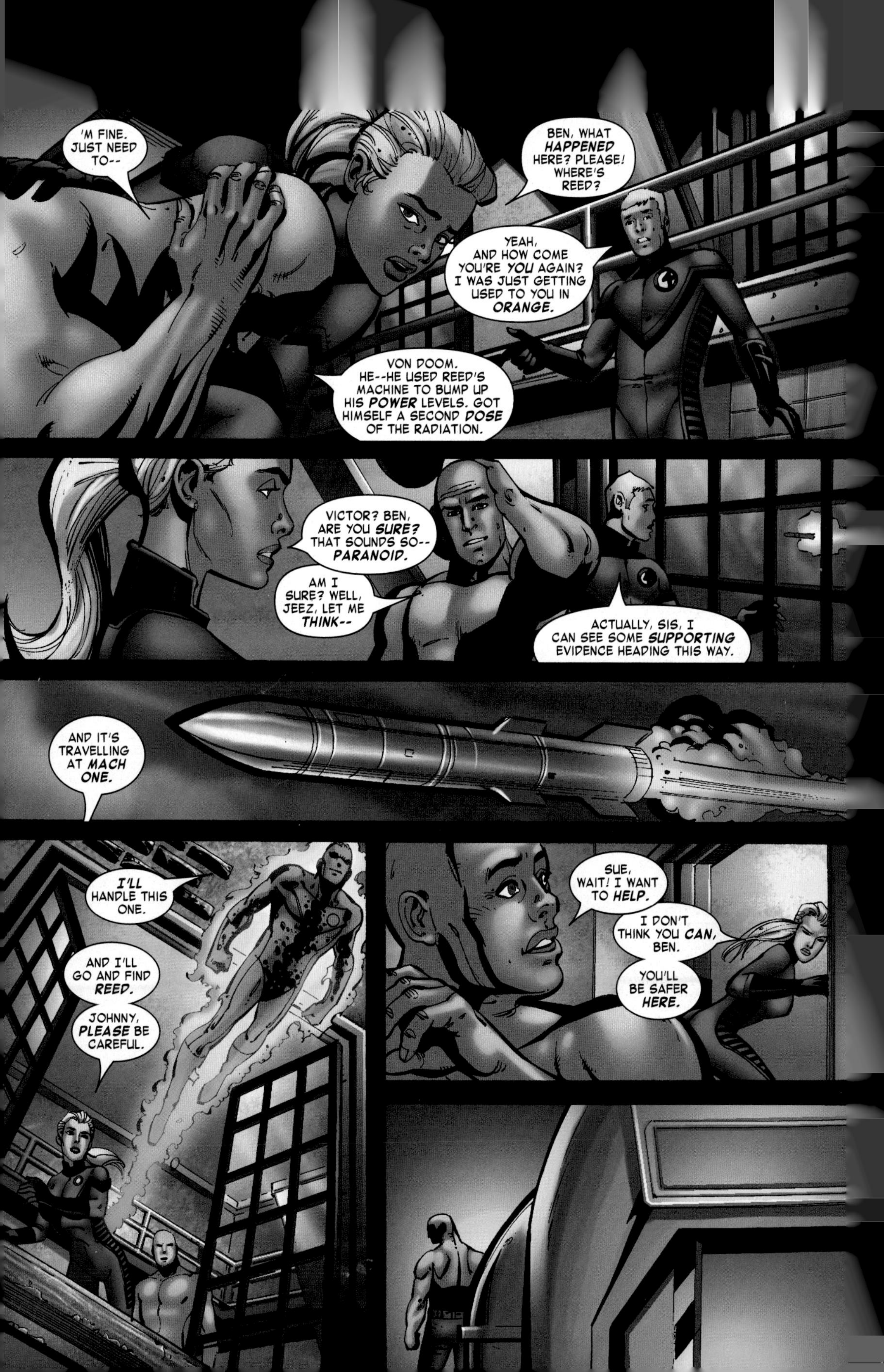
'M FINE. JUST NEED TO--
BEN, WHAT HAPPENED HERE? PLEASE! WHERE'S REED?
YEAH, AND HOW COME YOU'RE YOU AGAIN? I WAS JUST GETTING USED TO YOU IN ORANGE.
VON DOOM. HE--HE USED REED'S MACHINE TO BUMP UP HIS POWER LEVELS. GOT HIMSELF A SECOND DOSE OF THE RADIATION.
VICTOR? BEN, ARE YOU SURE? THAT SOUNDS SO-- PARANOID.
AM I SURE? WELL, JEEZ, LET ME THINK--
ACTUALLY, SIS, I CAN SEE SOME SUPPORTING EVIDENCE HEADING THIS WAY.
AND IT'S TRAVELLING AT MACH ONE.
I'LL HANDLE THIS ONE.
AND I'LL GO AND FIND REED.
JOHNNY, PLEASE BE CAREFUL.
SUE, WAIT! I WANT TO HELP.
I DON'T THINK YOU CAN, BEN.
YOU'LL BE SAFER HERE.

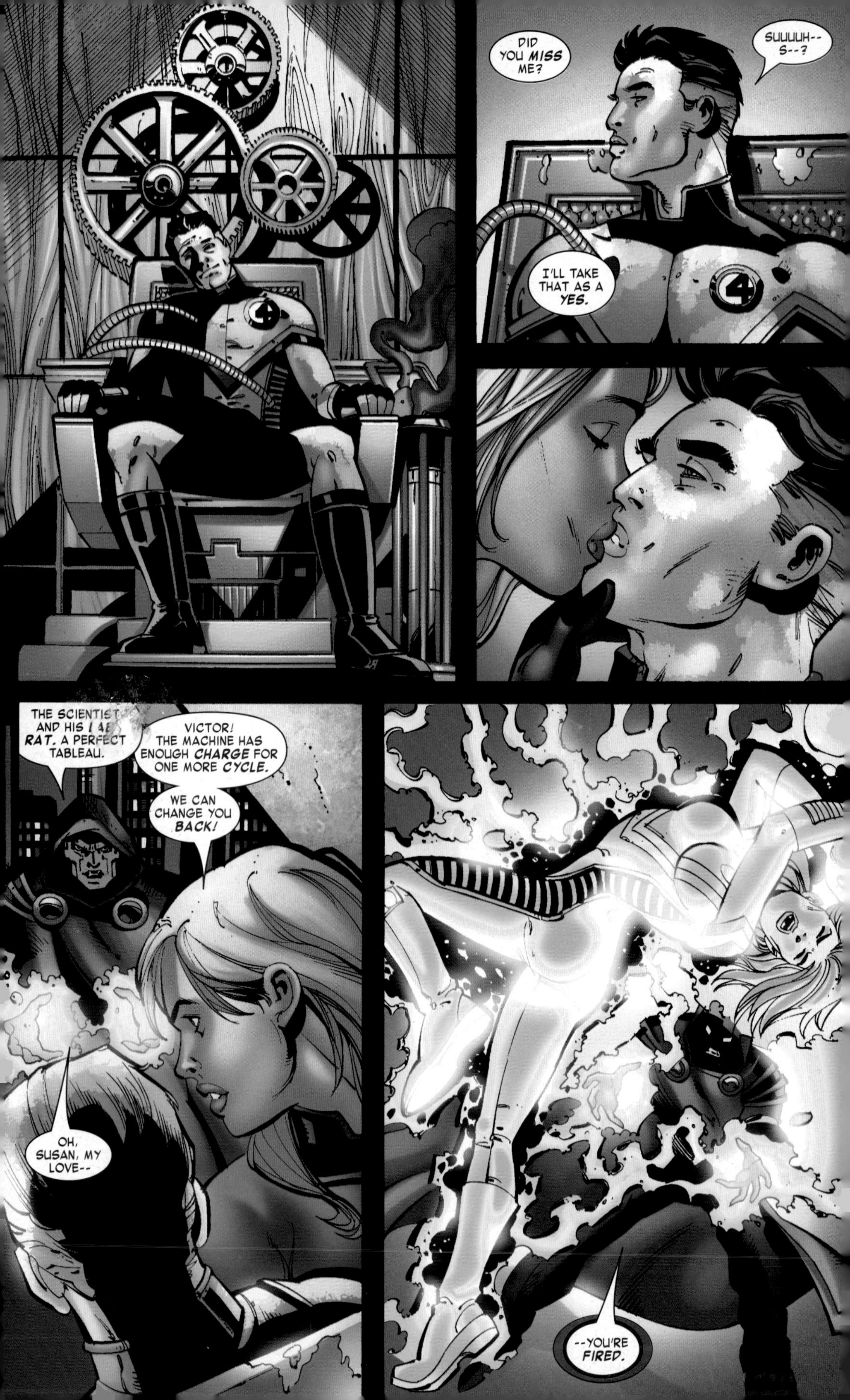

DID YOU MISS ME?
SUUUUH-- S--?
I'LL TAKE THAT AS A YES.
THE SCIENTIST AND HIS LAB RAT. A PERFECT TABLEAU.
VICTOR! THE MACHINE HAS ENOUGH CHARGE FOR ONE MORE CYCLE.
WE CAN CHANGE YOU BACK!
OH, SUSAN, MY LOVE--
--YOU'RE FIRED.

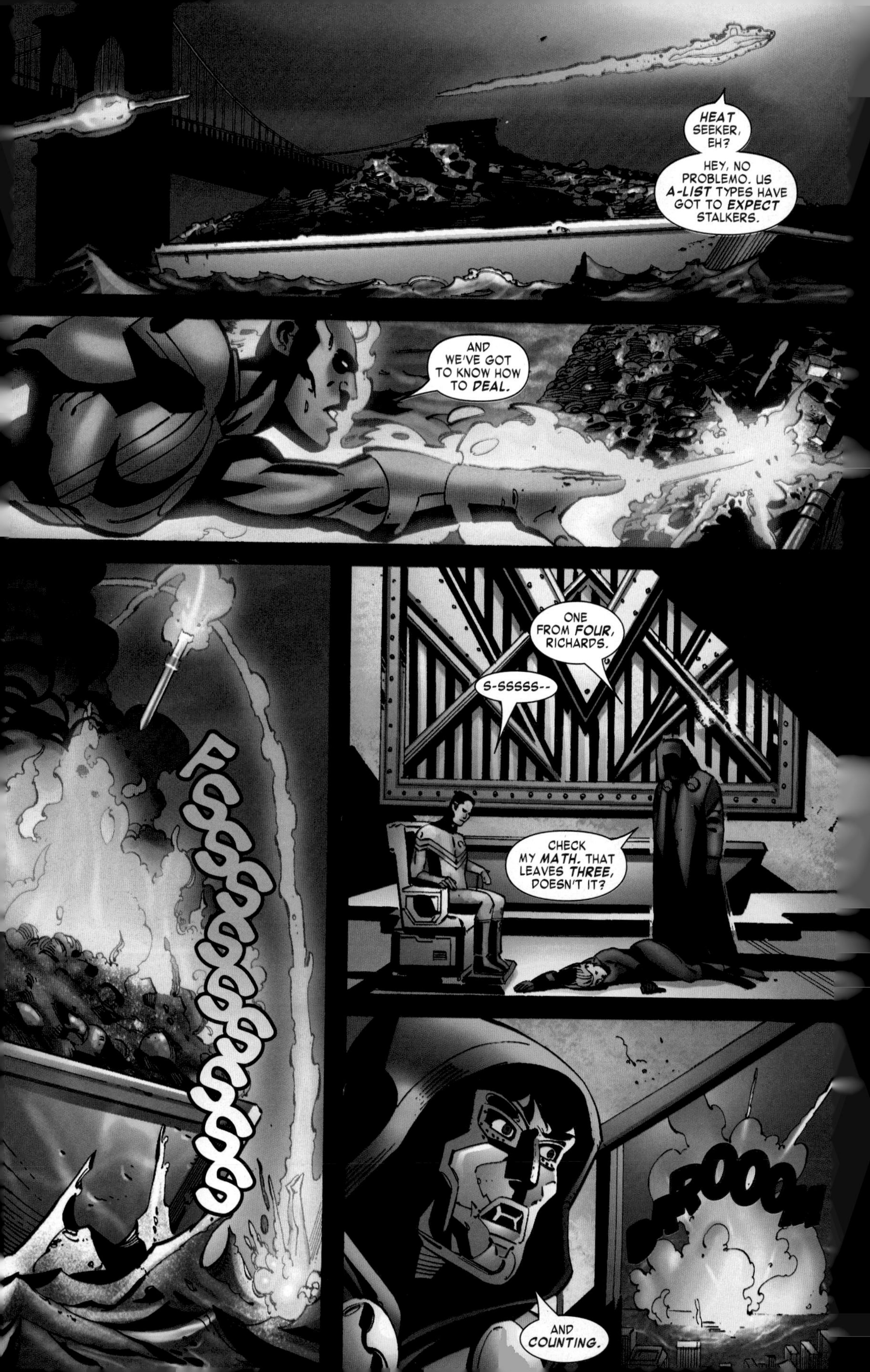
HEAT SEEKER, EH?
HEY, NO PROBLEMO. US A-LIST TYPES HAVE GOT TO EXPECT STALKERS.
AND WE'VE GOT TO KNOW HOW TO DEAL.
FSSSSSSSSSHHHS
ONE FROM FOUR, RICHARDS.
S-SSSSS--
CHECK MY MATH. THAT LEAVES THREE, DOESN'T IT?
AND COUNTING.

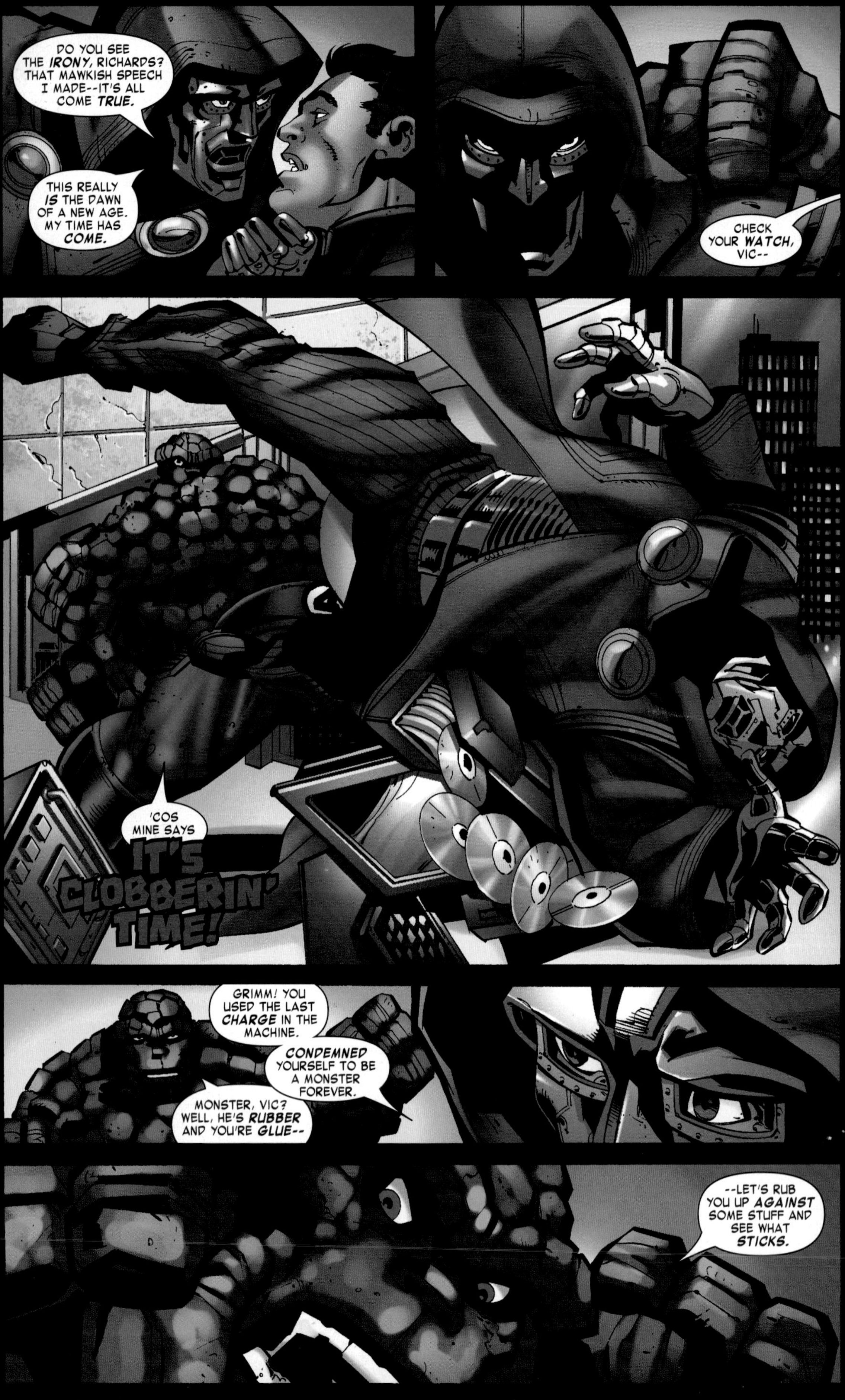

DO YOU SEE THE IRONY, RICHARDS? THAT MAWKISH SPEECH I MADE--IT'S ALL COME TRUE.
THIS REALLY IS THE DAWN OF A NEW AGE. MY TIME HAS COME.
CHECK YOUR WATCH, VIC--
'COS MINE SAYS
IT'S CLOBBERIN' TIME!
GRIMM! YOU USED THE LAST CHARGE IN THE MACHINE.
CONDEMNED YOURSELF TO BE A MONSTER FOREVER.
MONSTER, VIC? WELL, HE'S RUBBER AND YOU'RE GLUE--
--LET'S RUB YOU UP AGAINST SOME STUFF AND SEE WHAT STICKS.

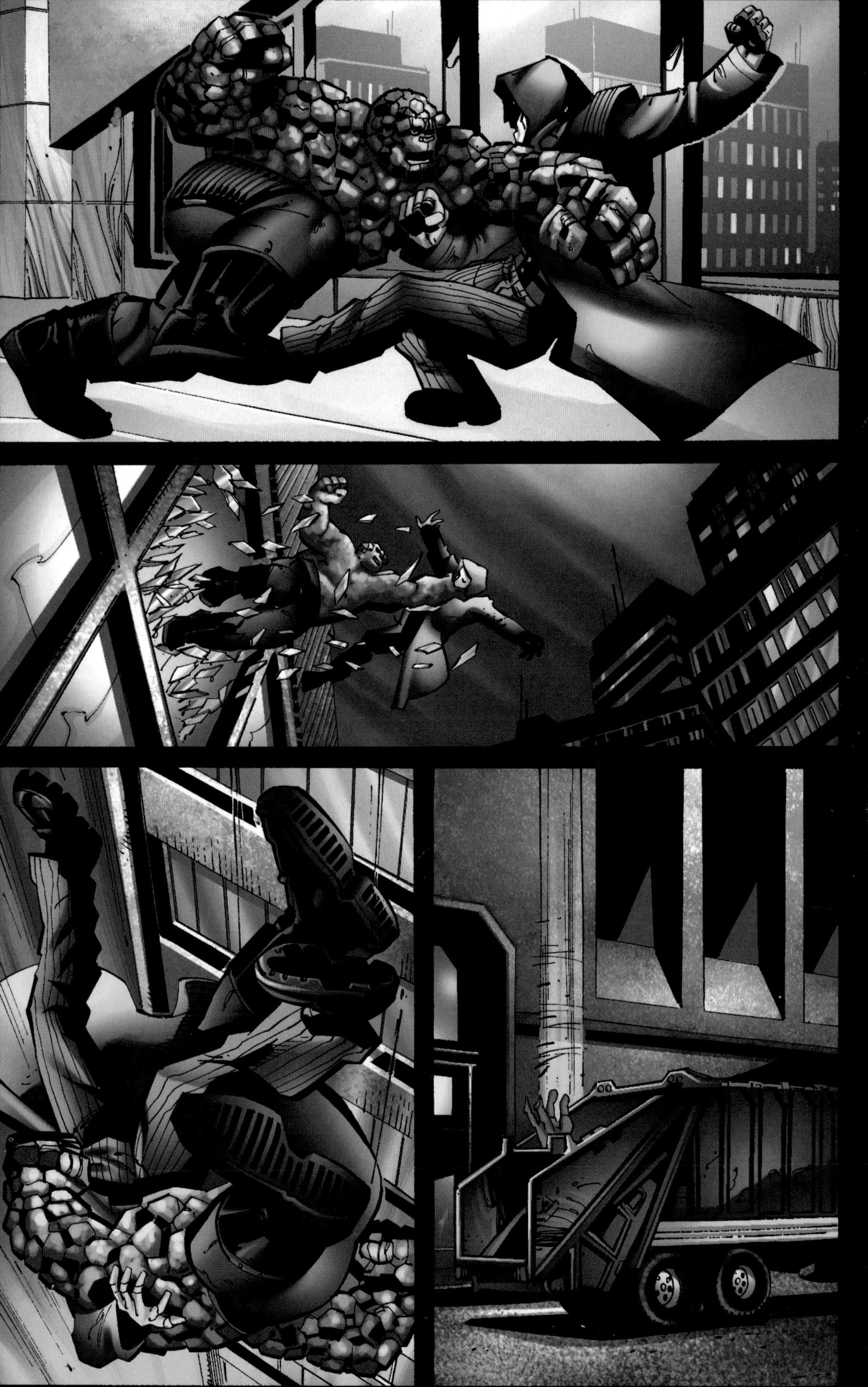

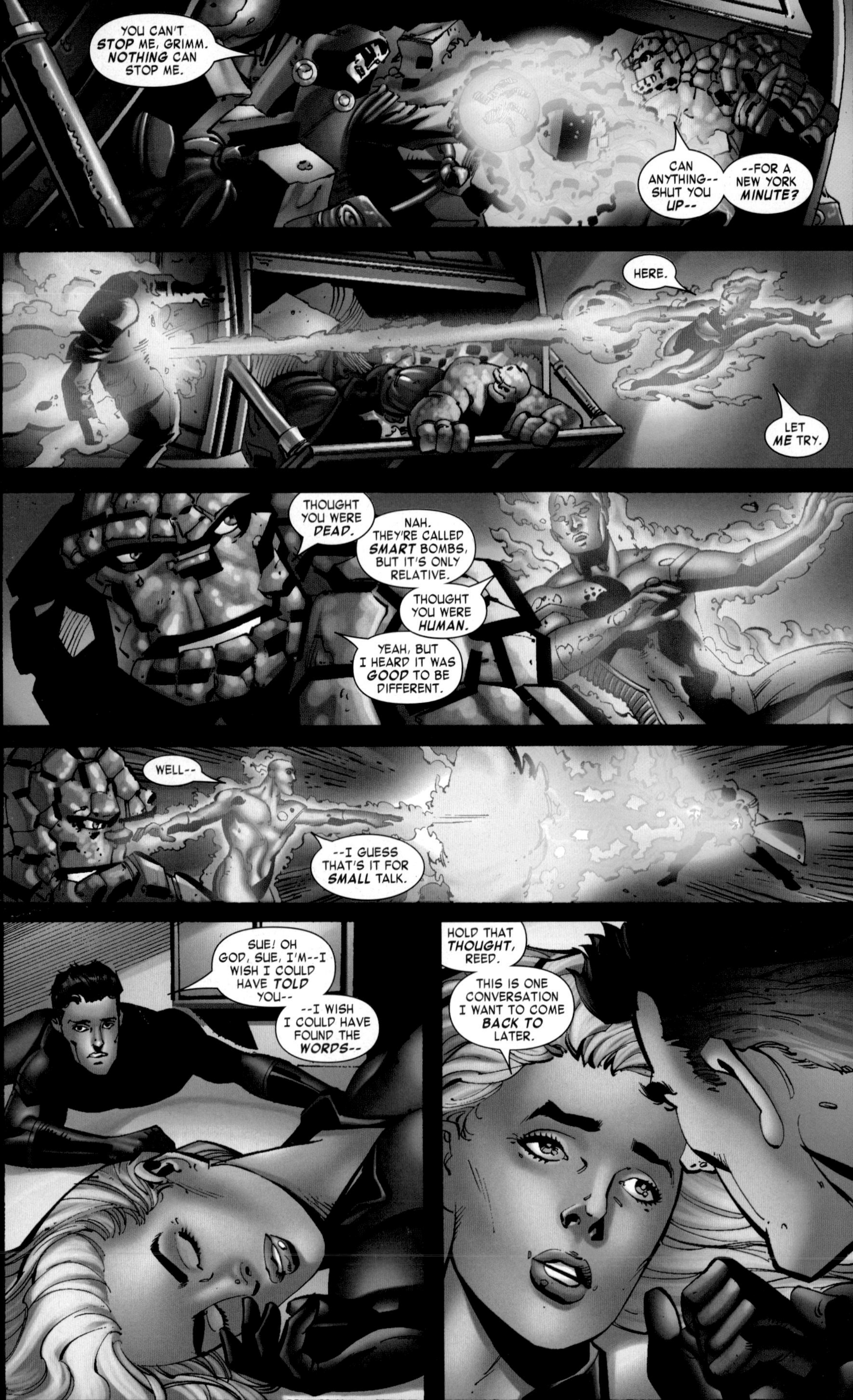
YOU CAN'T STOP ME, GRIMM. NOTHING CAN STOP ME.
CAN ANYTHING-- SHUT YOU UP--
--FOR A NEW YORK MINUTE?
HERE.
LET ME TRY.
THOUGHT YOU WERE DEAD.
NAH. THEY'RE CALLED SMART BOMBS, BUT IT'S ONLY RELATIVE.
THOUGHT YOU WERE HUMAN.
YEAH, BUT I HEARD IT WAS GOOD TO BE DIFFERENT.
WELL--
--I GUESS THAT'S IT FOR SMALL TALK.
SUE! OH GOD, SUE, I'M--I WISH I COULD HAVE TOLD YOU--
--I WISH I COULD HAVE FOUND THE WORDS--
HOLD THAT THOUGHT, REED.
THIS IS ONE CONVERSATION I WANT TO COME BACK TO LATER.

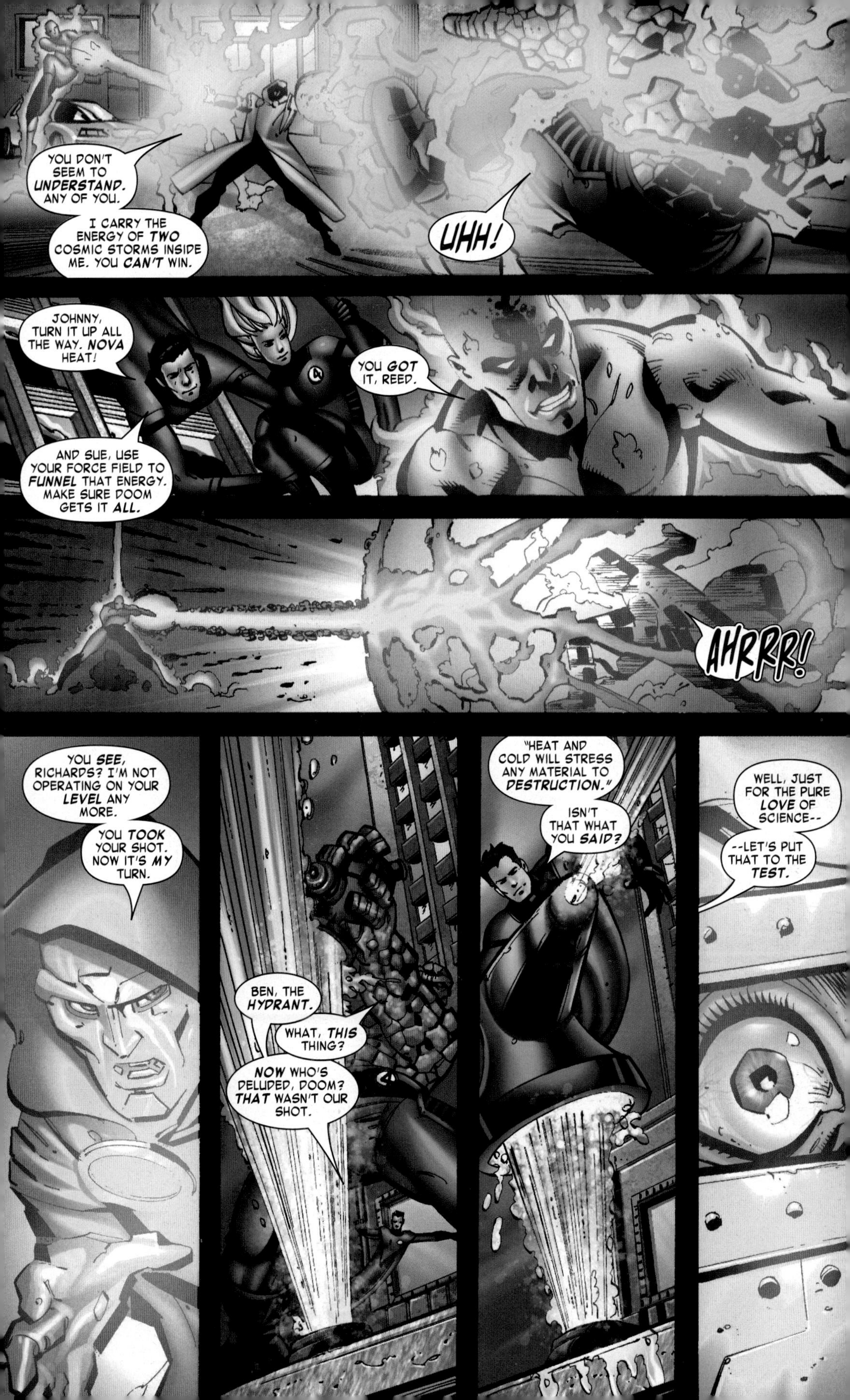
YOU DON'T SEEM TO UNDERSTAND. ANY OF YOU.
I CARRY THE ENERGY OF TWO COSMIC STORMS INSIDE ME. YOU CAN'T WIN.
UHH!
JOHNNY, TURN IT UP ALL THE WAY. NOVA HEAT!
AND SUE, USE YOUR FORCE FIELD TO FUNNEL THAT ENERGY. MAKE SURE DOOM GETS IT ALL.
YOU GOT IT, REED.
AHRRR!
YOU SEE, RICHARDS? I'M NOT OPERATING ON YOUR LEVEL ANY MORE.
YOU TOOK YOUR SHOT. NOW IT'S MY TURN.
BEN, THE HYDRANT.
WHAT, THIS THING?
NOW WHO'S DELUDED, DOOM? THAT WASN'T OUR SHOT.
"HEAT AND COLD WILL STRESS ANY MATERIAL TO DESTRUCTION."
ISN'T THAT WHAT YOU SAID?
WELL, JUST FOR THE PURE LOVE OF SCIENCE--
--LET'S PUT THAT TO THE TEST.

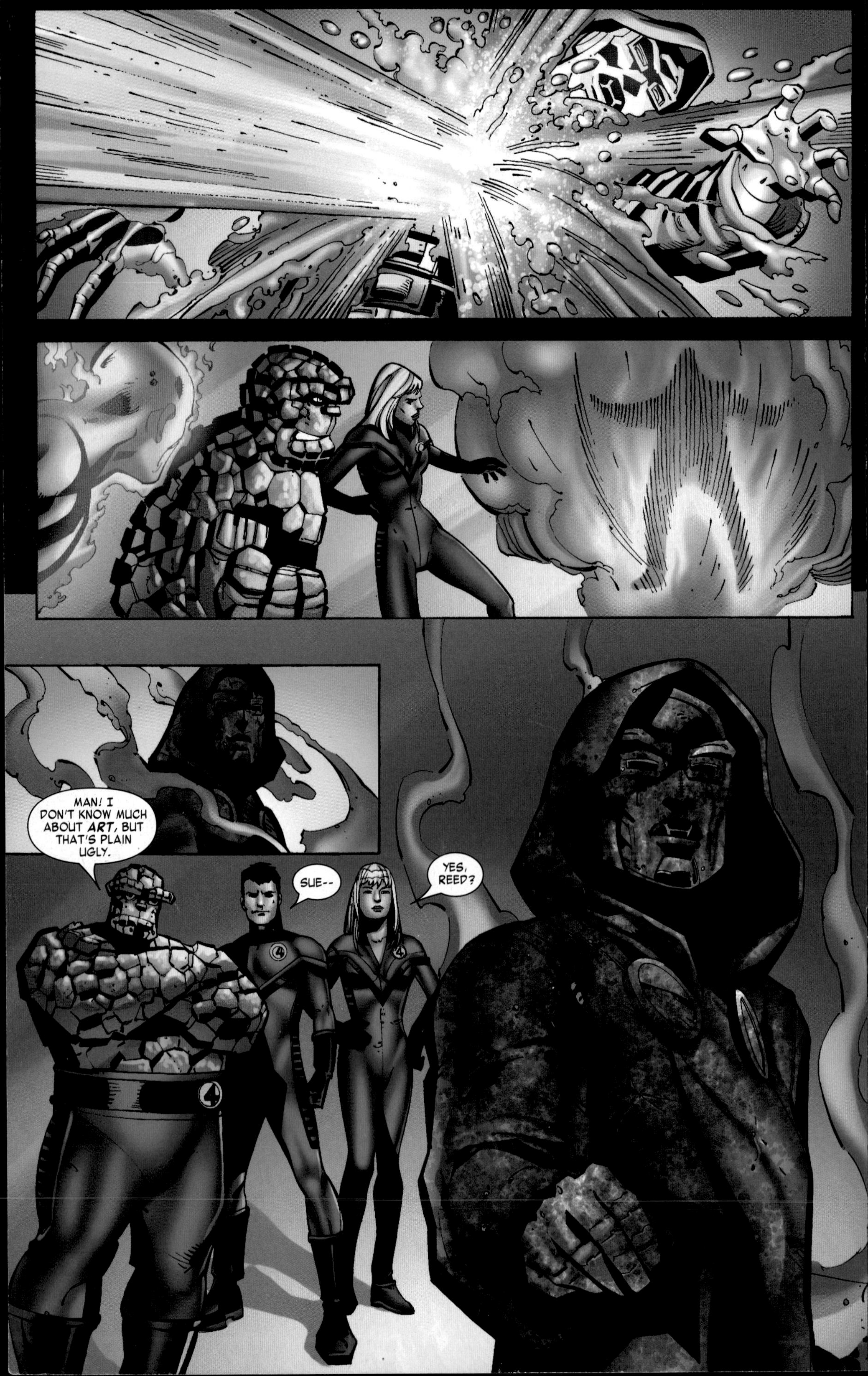
MAN! I DON'T KNOW MUCH ABOUT ART, BUT THAT'S PLAIN UGLY.
SUE--
YES, REED?

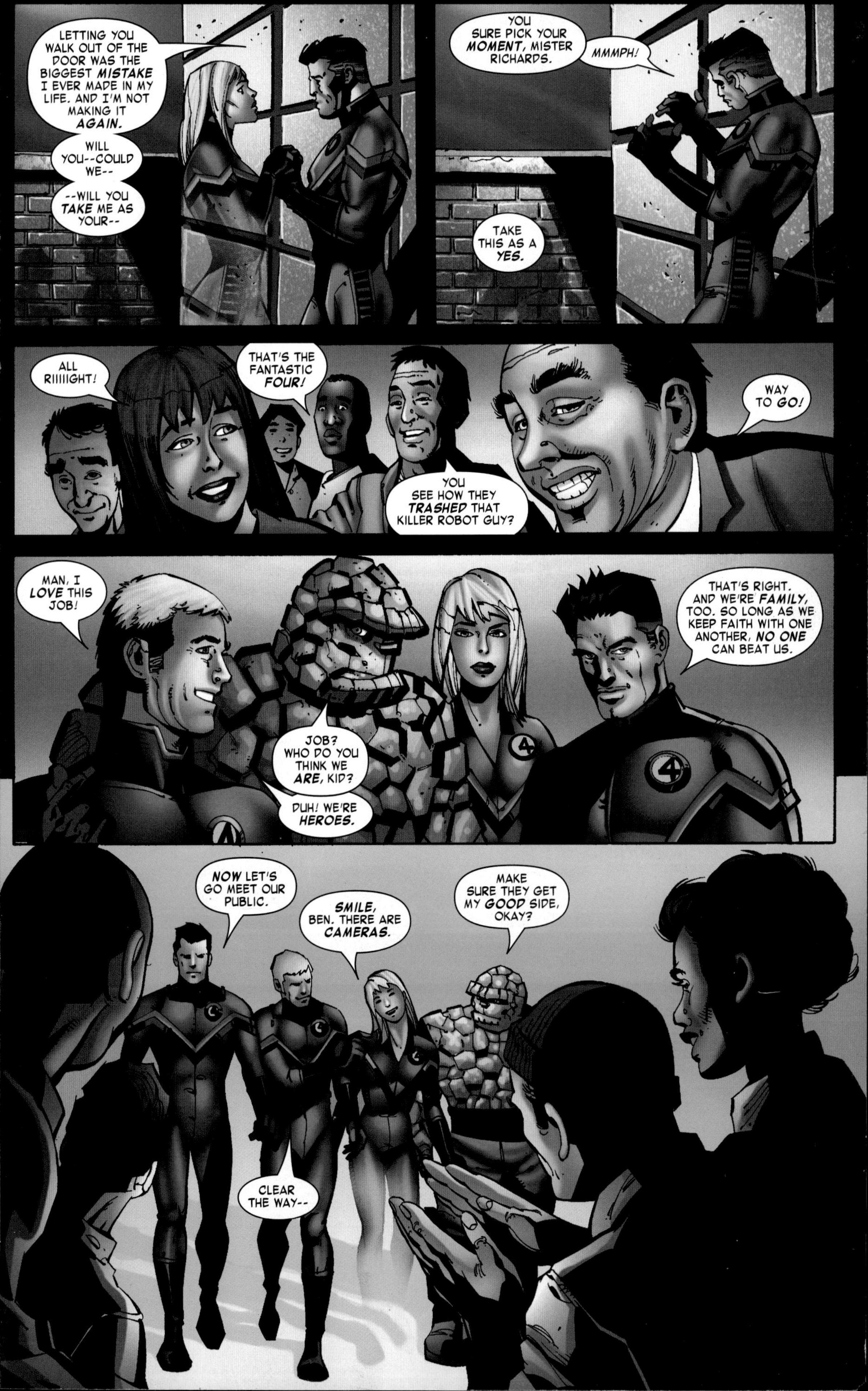
LETTING YOU WALK OUT OF THE DOOR WAS THE BIGGEST MISTAKE I EVER MADE IN MY LIFE. AND I'M NOT MAKING IT AGAIN.
WILL YOU--COULD WE--
--WILL YOU TAKE ME AS YOUR--
YOU SURE PICK YOUR MOMENT, MISTER RICHARDS.
MMMPH!
TAKE THIS AS A YES.
ALL RIIIIIGHT!
THAT'S THE FANTASTIC FOUR!
WAY TO GO!
YOU SEE HOW THEY TRASHED THAT KILLER ROBOT GUY?
MAN, I LOVE THIS JOB!
THAT'S RIGHT. AND WE'RE FAMILY, TOO. SO LONG AS WE KEEP FAITH WITH ONE ANOTHER, NO ONE CAN BEAT US.
JOB? WHO DO YOU THINK WE ARE, KID?
DUH! WE'RE HEROES.
NOW LET'S GO MEET OUR PUBLIC.
SMILE, BEN. THERE ARE CAMERAS.
MAKE SURE THEY GET MY GOOD SIDE, OKAY?
CLEAR THE WAY--

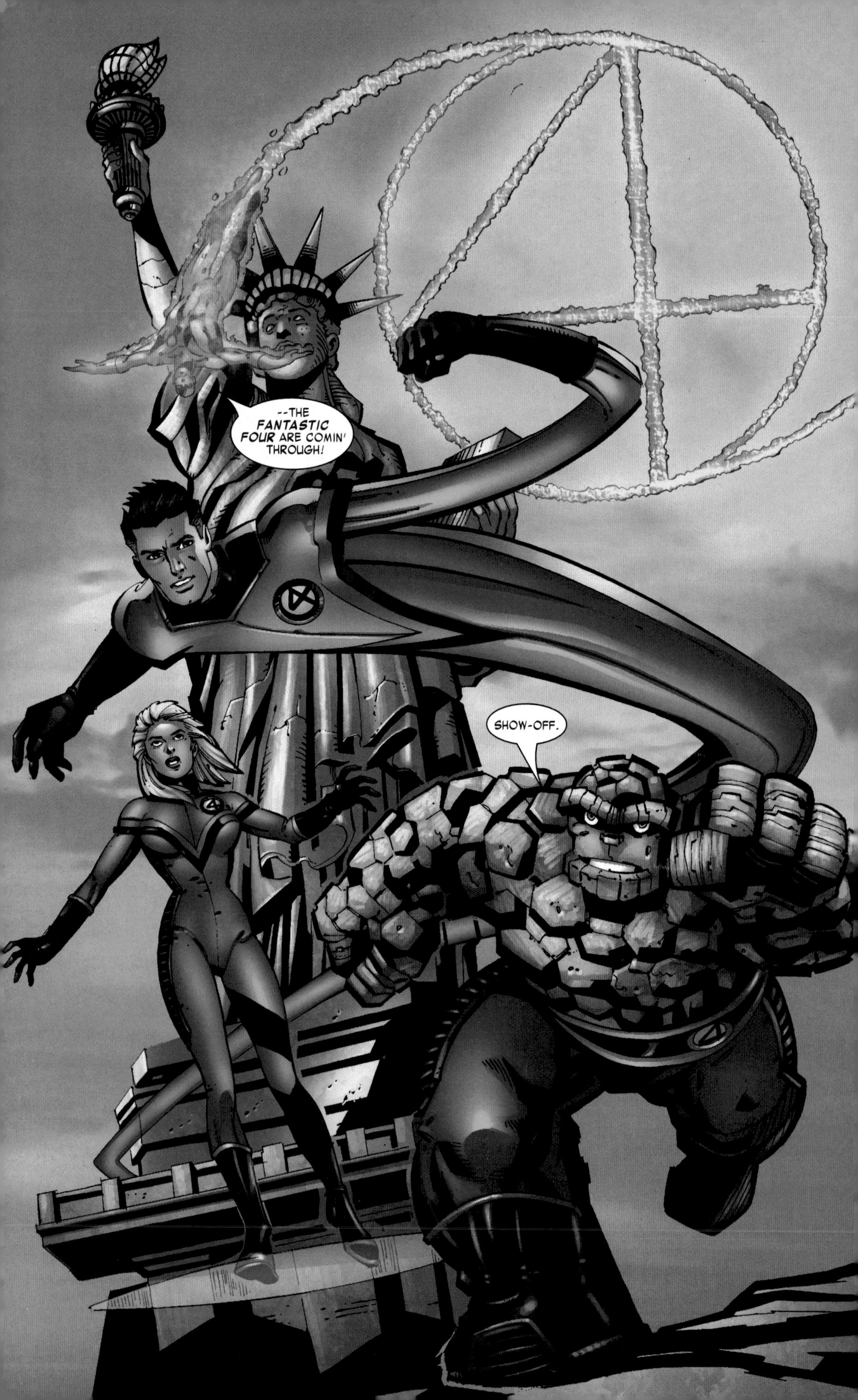
--THE FANTASTIC FOUR ARE COMIN' THROUGH!
SHOW-OFF.

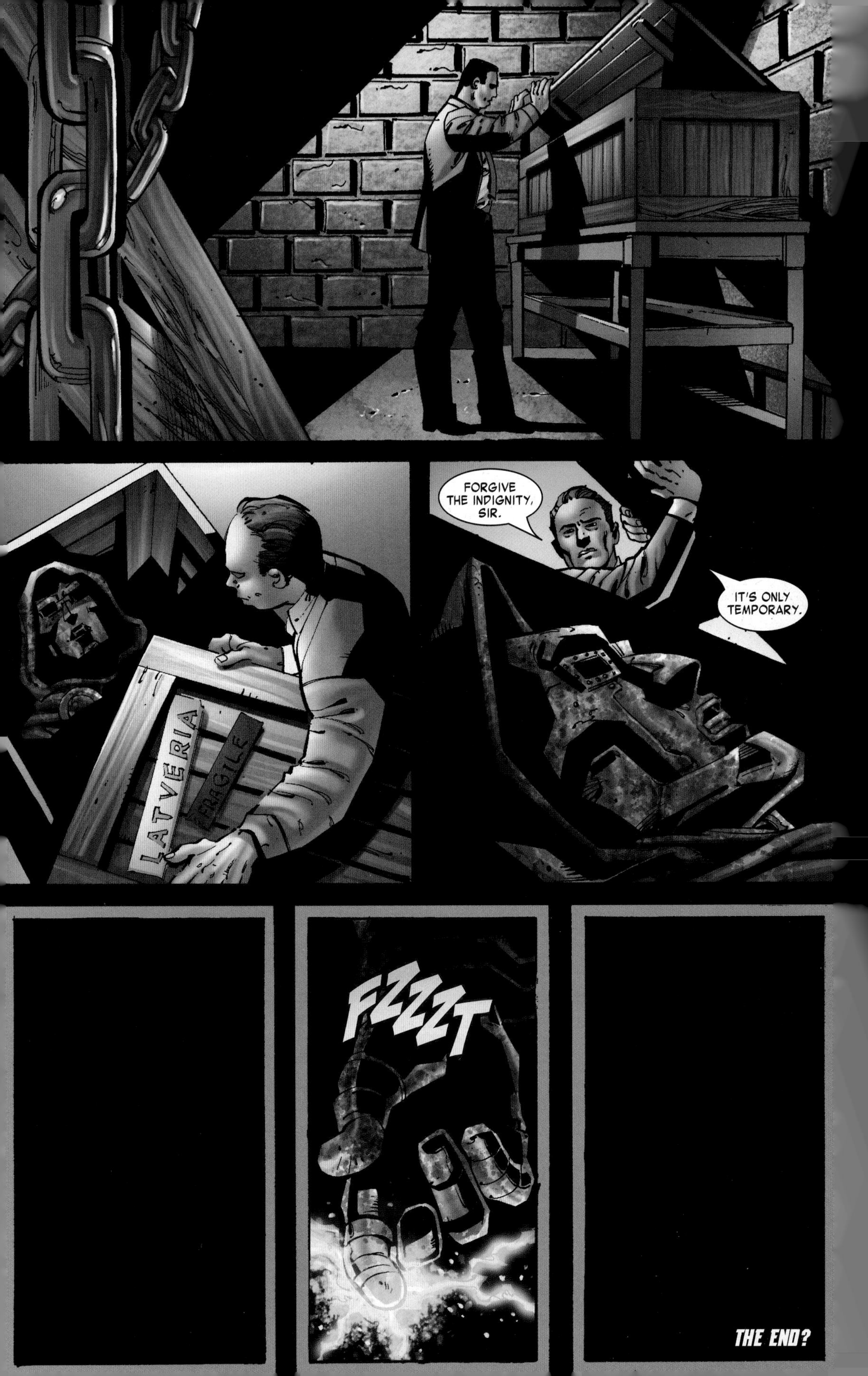
LATVERIA
FRAGILE
FORGIVE THE INDIGNITY, SIR.
IT'S ONLY TEMPORARY.
FZZZT
THE END?

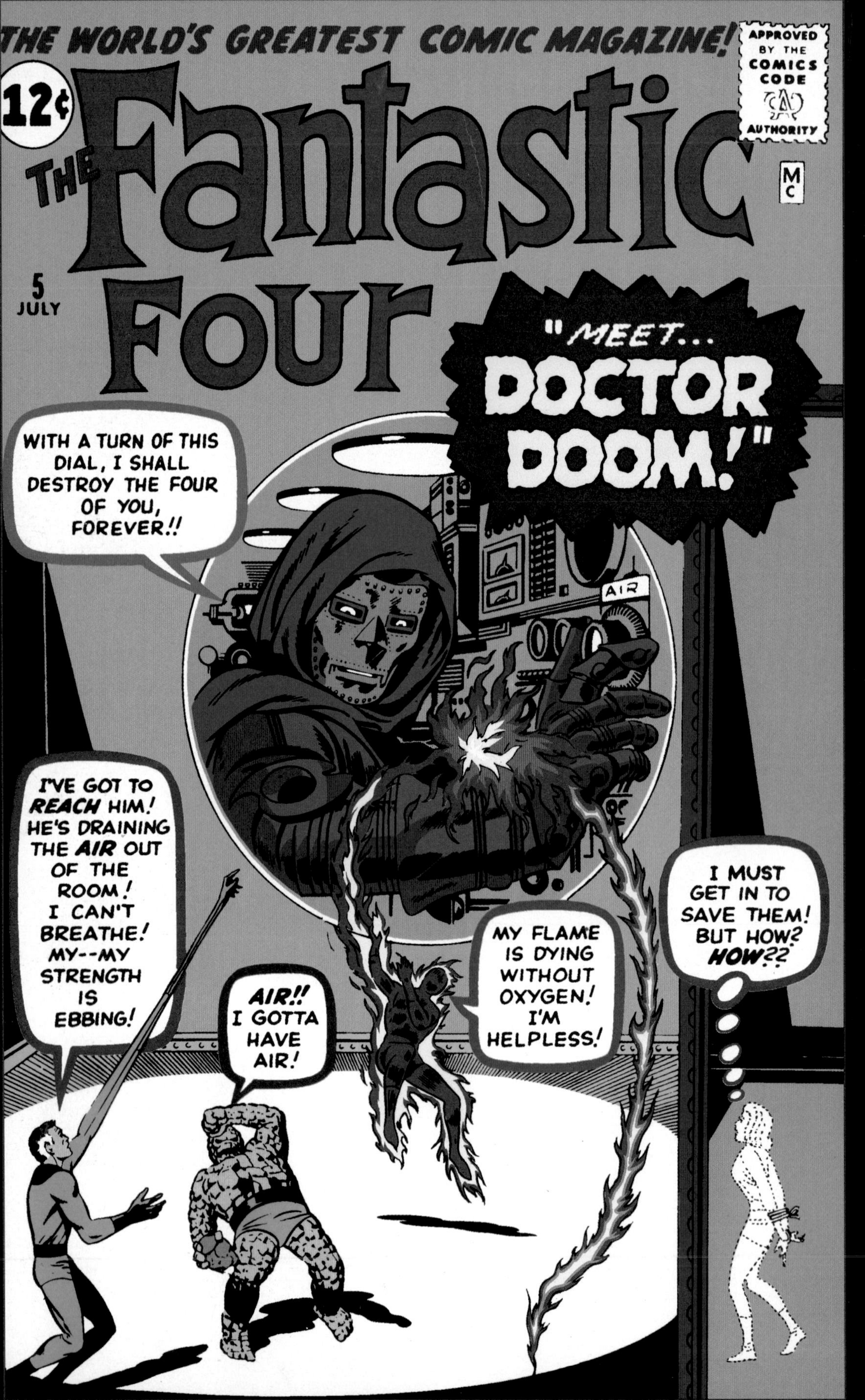
THE WORLD'S GREATEST COMIC MAGAZINE!
APPROVED BY THE COMICS CODE AUTHORITY
12¢
THE Fantastic Four
MC
5 JULY
"MEET... DOCTOR DOOM!"
WITH A TURN OF THIS DIAL, I SHALL DESTROY THE FOUR OF YOU, FOREVER!!
AIR
I'VE GOT TO REACH HIM! HE'S DRAINING THE AIR OUT OF THE ROOM! I CAN'T BREATHE! MY--MY STRENGTH IS EBBING!
AIR!! I GOTTA HAVE AIR!
MY FLAME IS DYING WITHOUT OXYGEN! I'M HELPLESS!
I MUST GET IN TO SAVE THEM! BUT HOW? HOW??

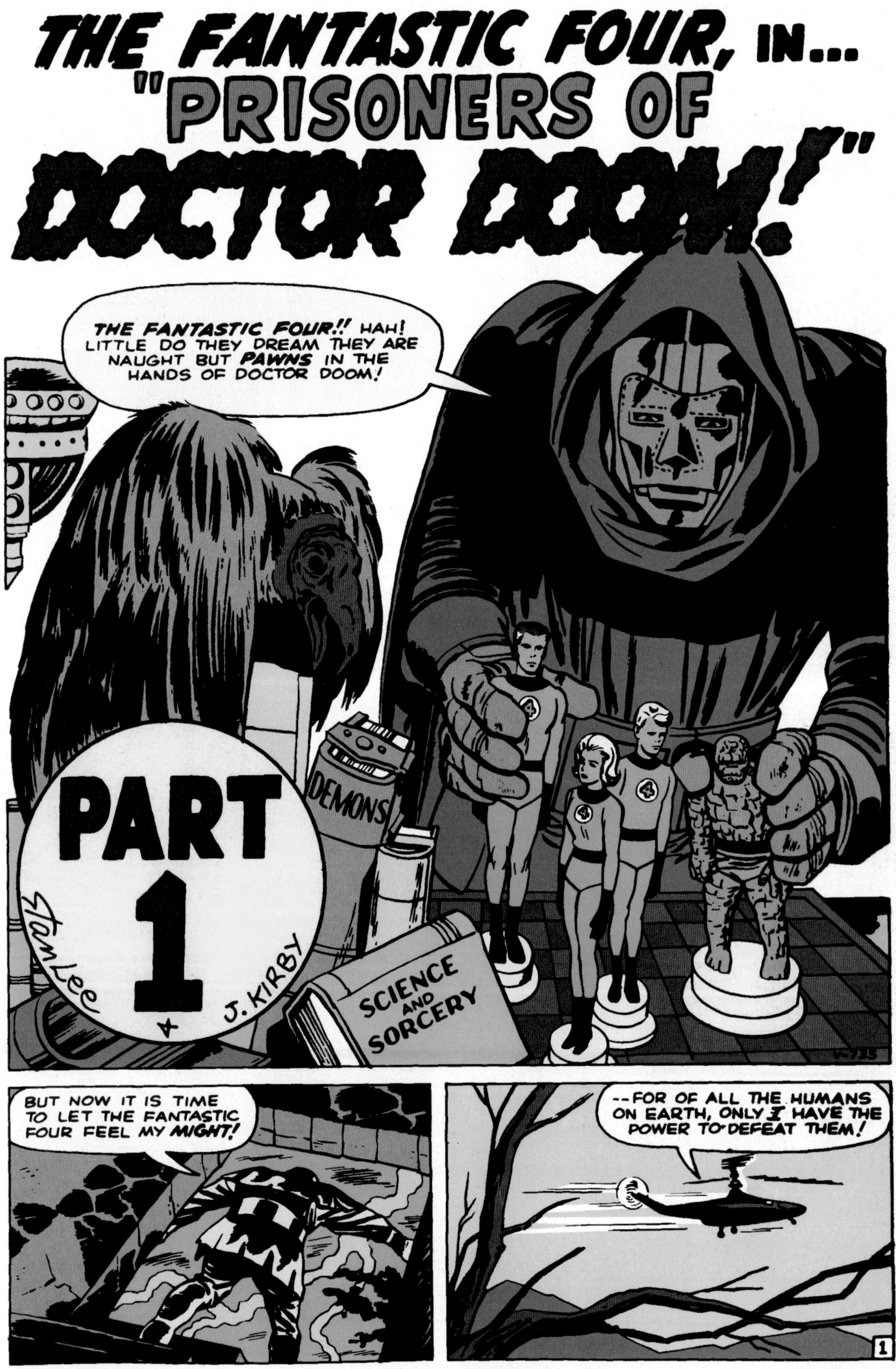
THE FANTASTIC FOUR, IN...
"PRISONERS OF DOCTOR DOOM!"
THE FANTASTIC FOUR!! HAH! LITTLE DO THEY DREAM THEY ARE NAUGHT BUT PAWNS IN THE HANDS OF DOCTOR DOOM!
PART 1
Stan Lee + J. KIRBY
DEMONS
SCIENCE AND SORCERY
BUT NOW IT IS TIME TO LET THE FANTASTIC FOUR FEEL MY MIGHT!
--FOR OF ALL THE HUMANS ON EARTH, ONLY I HAVE THE POWER TO DEFEAT THEM!
1

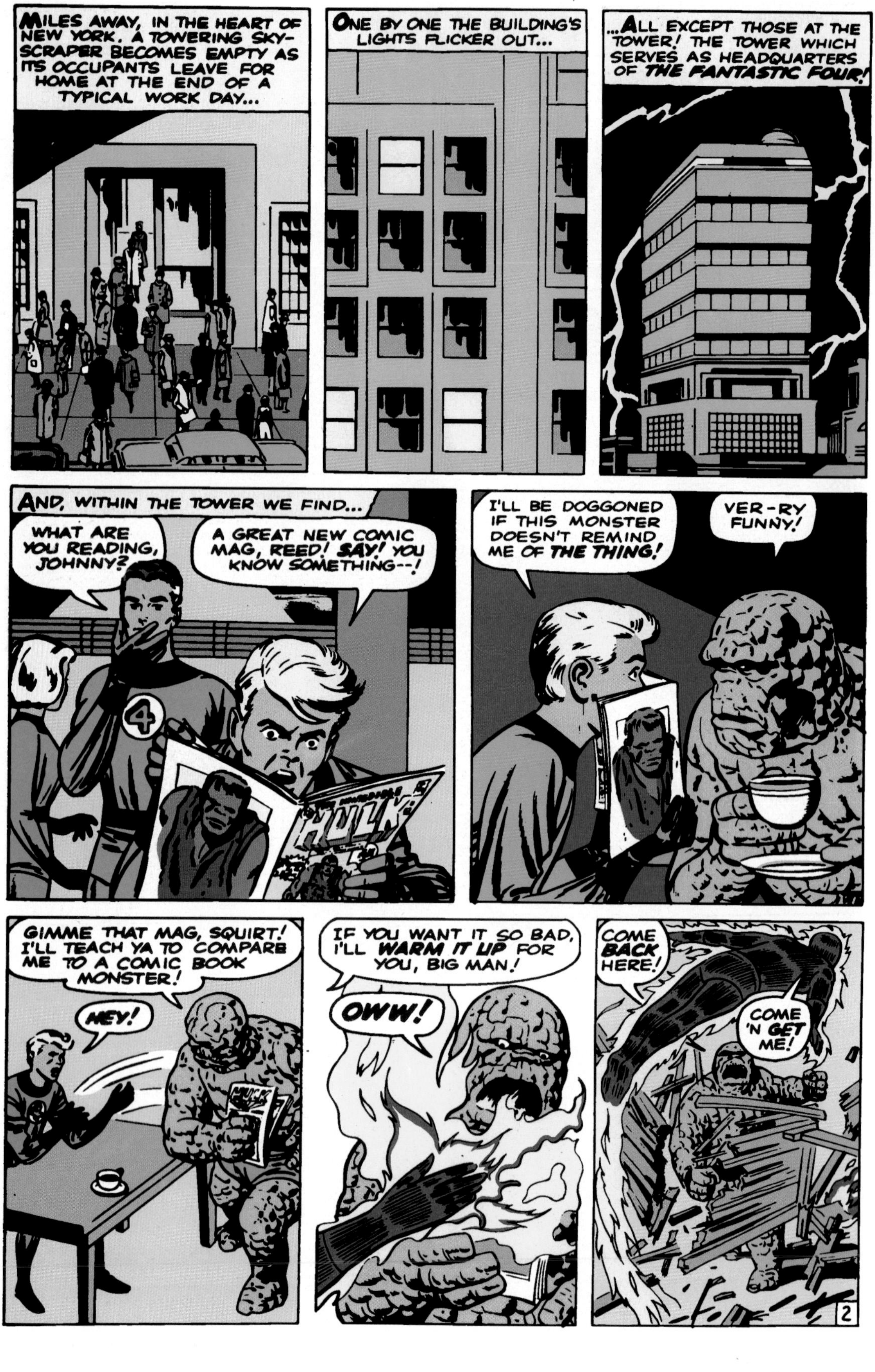
MILES AWAY, IN THE HEART OF NEW YORK, A TOWERING SKY-SCRAPER BECOMES EMPTY AS ITS OCCUPANTS LEAVE FOR HOME AT THE END OF A TYPICAL WORK DAY...
ONE BY ONE THE BUILDING'S LIGHTS FLICKER OUT...
...ALL EXCEPT THOSE AT THE TOWER! THE TOWER WHICH SERVES AS HEADQUARTERS OF THE FANTASTIC FOUR!
AND, WITHIN THE TOWER WE FIND...
WHAT ARE YOU READING, JOHNNY?
A GREAT NEW COMIC MAG, REED! SAY! YOU KNOW SOMETHING--!
HULK
I'LL BE DOGGONED IF THIS MONSTER DOESN'T REMIND ME OF THE THING!
VER-RY FUNNY!
GIMME THAT MAG, SQUIRT! I'LL TEACH YA TO COMPARE ME TO A COMIC BOOK MONSTER!
HEY!
IF YOU WANT IT SO BAD, I'LL WARM IT UP FOR YOU, BIG MAN!
OWW!
COME BACK HERE!
COME 'N GET ME!
2

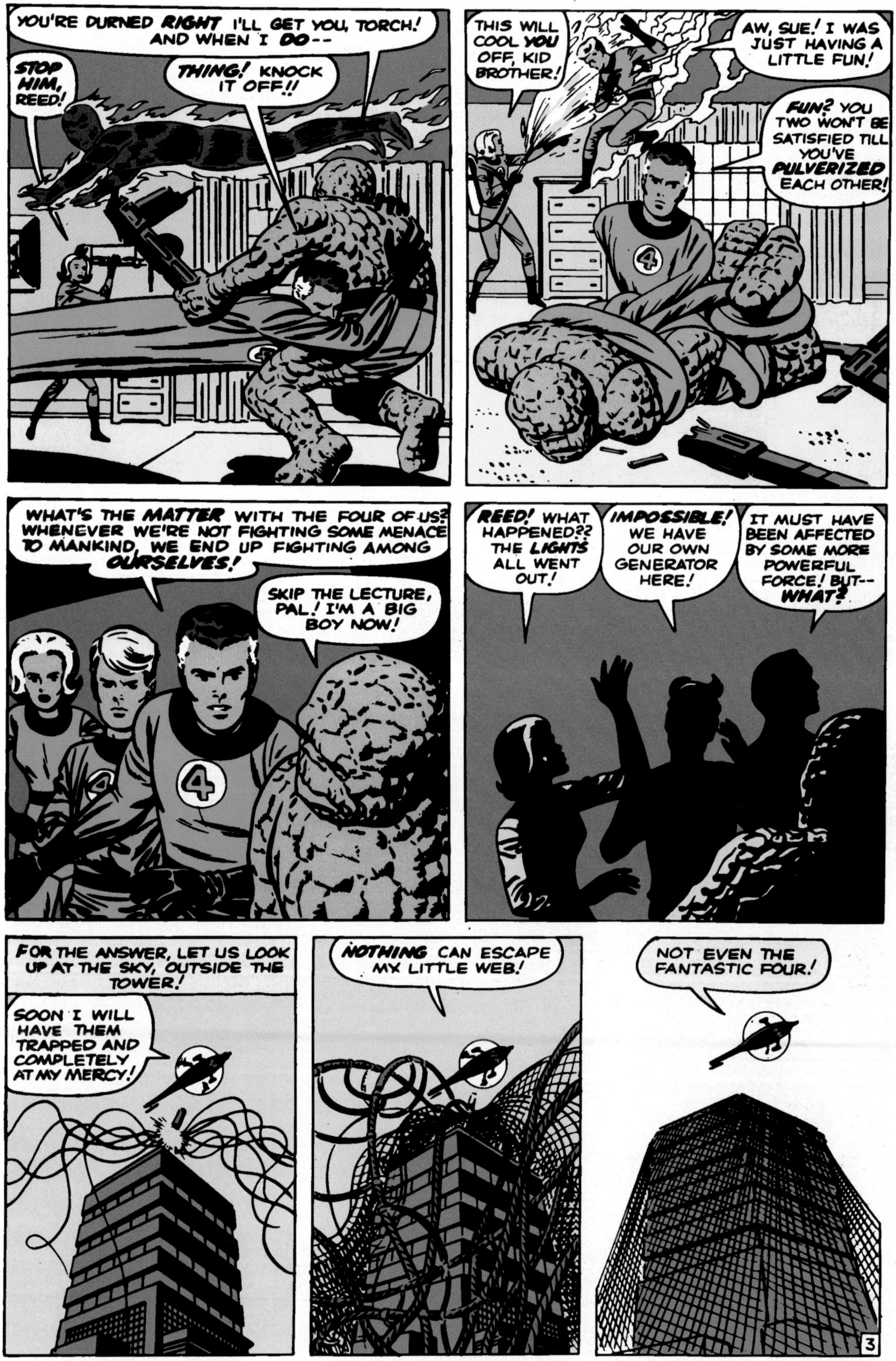
YOU'RE DURNED RIGHT I'LL GET YOU, TORCH! AND WHEN I DO--
STOP HIM, REED!
THING! KNOCK IT OFF!!
THIS WILL COOL YOU OFF, KID BROTHER!
AW, SUE! I WAS JUST HAVING A LITTLE FUN!
FUN? YOU TWO WON'T BE SATISFIED TILL YOU'VE PULVERIZED EACH OTHER!
WHAT'S THE MATTER WITH THE FOUR OF US? WHENEVER WE'RE NOT FIGHTING SOME MENACE TO MANKIND, WE END UP FIGHTING AMONG OURSELVES!
SKIP THE LECTURE, PAL! I'M A BIG BOY NOW!
REED! WHAT HAPPENED?? THE LIGHTS ALL WENT OUT!
IMPOSSIBLE! WE HAVE OUR OWN GENERATOR HERE!
IT MUST HAVE BEEN AFFECTED BY SOME MORE POWERFUL FORCE! BUT-- WHAT?
FOR THE ANSWER, LET US LOOK UP AT THE SKY, OUTSIDE THE TOWER!
SOON I WILL HAVE THEM TRAPPED AND COMPLETELY AT MY MERCY!
NOTHING CAN ESCAPE MY LITTLE WEB!
NOT EVEN THE FANTASTIC FOUR!

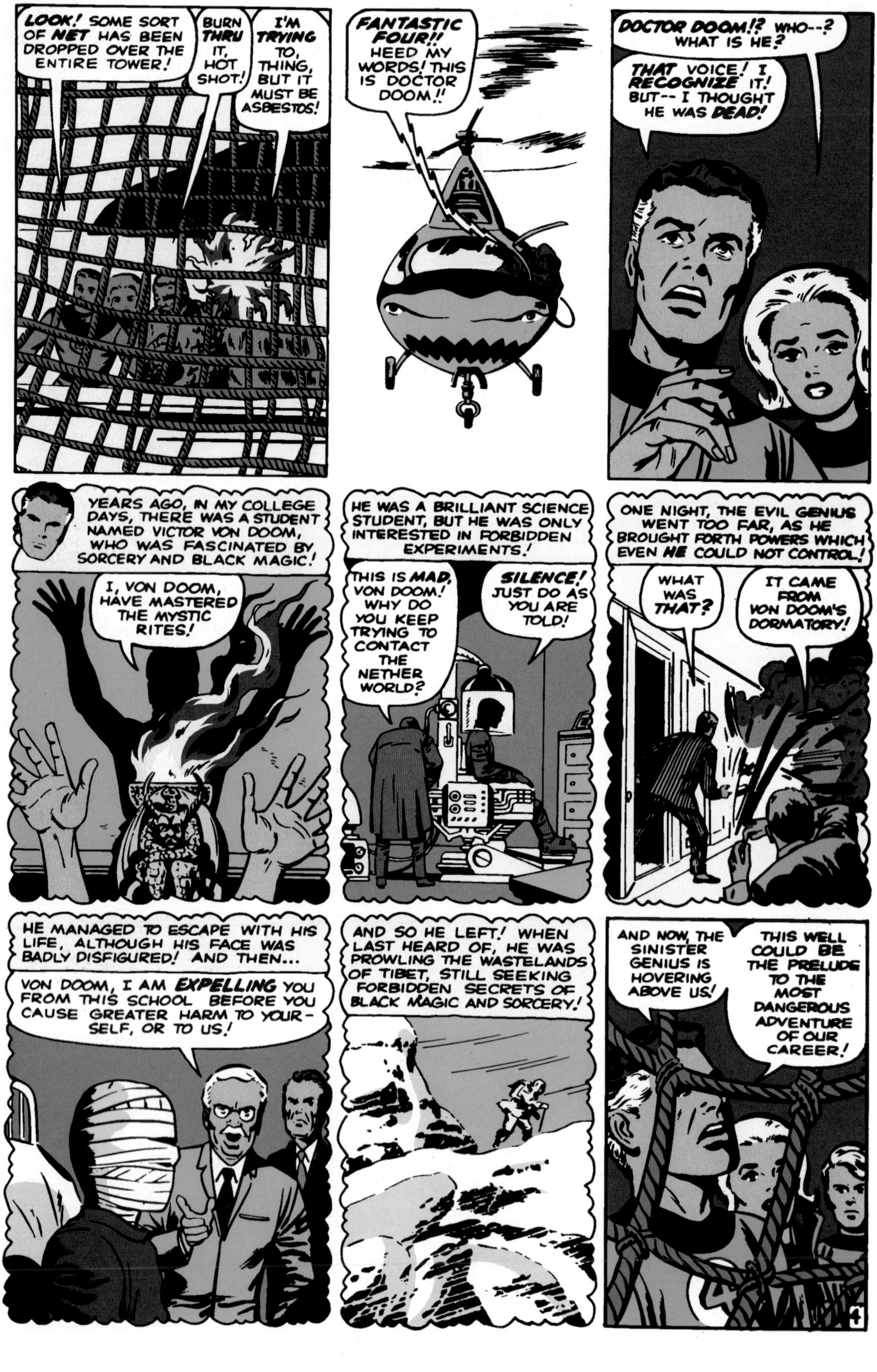
LOOK! SOME SORT OF NET HAS BEEN DROPPED OVER THE ENTIRE TOWER!
BURN THRU IT, HOT SHOT!
I'M TRYING TO, THING, BUT IT MUST BE ASBESTOS!
FANTASTIC FOUR!! HEED MY WORDS! THIS IS DOCTOR DOOM!!
DOCTOR DOOM!? WHO--? WHAT IS HE?
THAT VOICE! I RECOGNIZE IT! BUT-- I THOUGHT HE WAS DEAD!
YEARS AGO, IN MY COLLEGE DAYS, THERE WAS A STUDENT NAMED VICTOR VON DOOM, WHO WAS FASCINATED BY SORCERY AND BLACK MAGIC!
I, VON DOOM, HAVE MASTERED THE MYSTIC RITES!
HE WAS A BRILLIANT SCIENCE STUDENT, BUT HE WAS ONLY INTERESTED IN FORBIDDEN EXPERIMENTS!
THIS IS MAD, VON DOOM! WHY DO YOU KEEP TRYING TO CONTACT THE NETHER WORLD?
SILENCE! JUST DO AS YOU ARE TOLD!
ONE NIGHT, THE EVIL GENIUS WENT TOO FAR, AS HE BROUGHT FORTH POWERS WHICH EVEN HE COULD NOT CONTROL!
WHAT WAS THAT?
IT CAME FROM VON DOOM'S DORMATORY!
HE MANAGED TO ESCAPE WITH HIS LIFE, ALTHOUGH HIS FACE WAS BADLY DISFIGURED! AND THEN...
VON DOOM, I AM EXPELLING YOU FROM THIS SCHOOL BEFORE YOU CAUSE GREATER HARM TO YOURSELF, OR TO US!
AND SO HE LEFT! WHEN LAST HEARD OF, HE WAS PROWLING THE WASTELANDS OF TIBET, STILL SEEKING FORBIDDEN SECRETS OF BLACK MAGIC AND SORCERY!
AND NOW, THE SINISTER GENIUS IS HOVERING ABOVE US!
THIS WELL COULD BE THE PRELUDE TO THE MOST DANGEROUS ADVENTURE OF OUR CAREER!
4

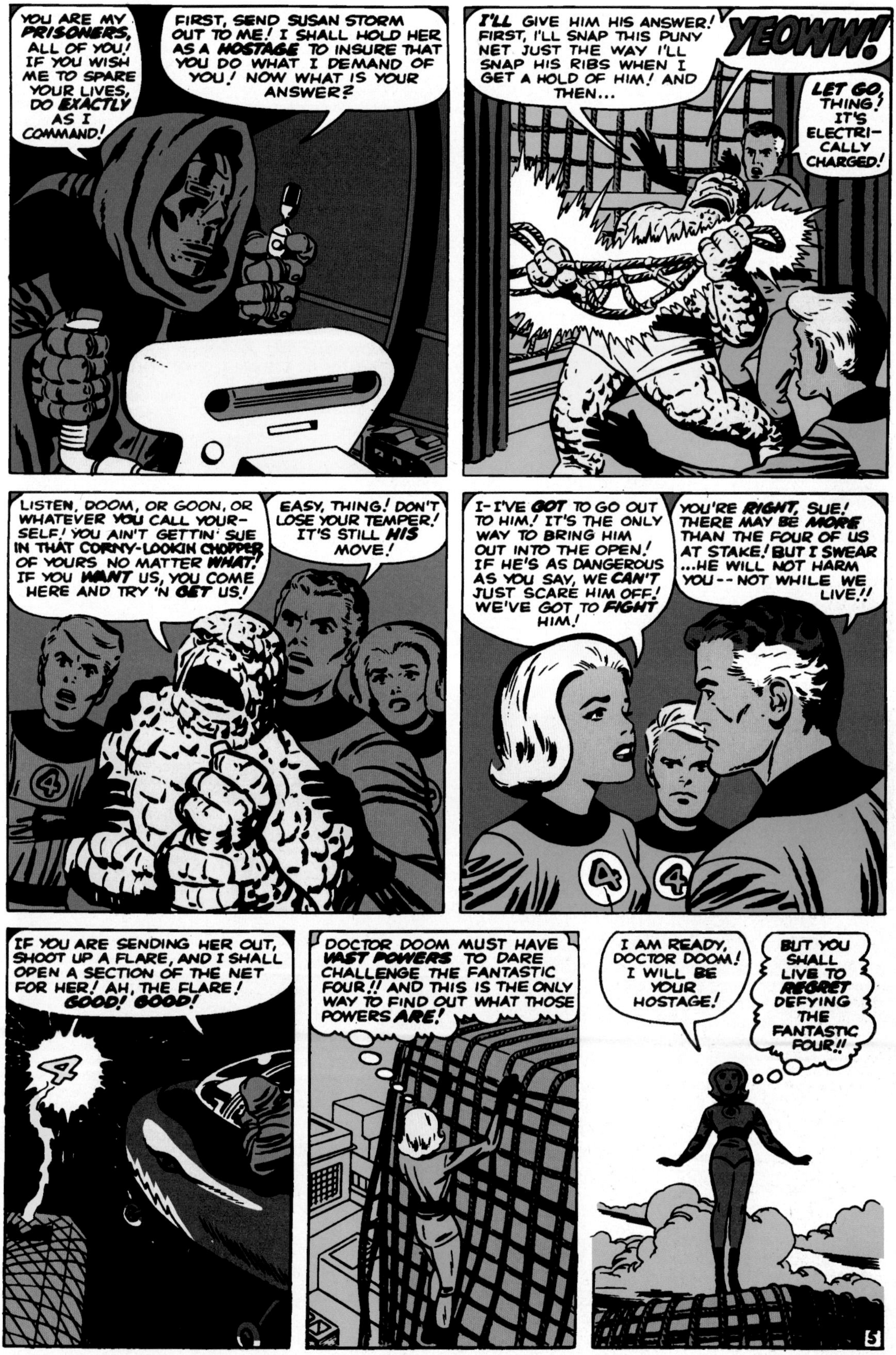
YOU ARE MY PRISONERS, ALL OF YOU! IF YOU WISH ME TO SPARE YOUR LIVES, DO EXACTLY AS I COMMAND!
FIRST, SEND SUSAN STORM OUT TO ME! I SHALL HOLD HER AS A HOSTAGE TO INSURE THAT YOU DO WHAT I DEMAND OF YOU! NOW WHAT IS YOUR ANSWER?
I'LL GIVE HIM HIS ANSWER! FIRST, I'LL SNAP THIS PUNY NET JUST THE WAY I'LL SNAP HIS RIBS WHEN I GET A HOLD OF HIM! AND THEN...
YEOWW!
LET GO, THING! IT'S ELECTRICALLY CHARGED!
LISTEN, DOOM, OR GOON, OR WHATEVER YOU CALL YOURSELF! YOU AIN'T GETTIN' SUE IN THAT CORNY-LOOKIN CHOPPER OF YOURS NO MATTER WHAT! IF YOU WANT US, YOU COME HERE AND TRY 'N GET US!
EASY, THING! DON'T LOSE YOUR TEMPER! IT'S STILL HIS MOVE!
I-I'VE GOT TO GO OUT TO HIM! IT'S THE ONLY WAY TO BRING HIM OUT INTO THE OPEN! IF HE'S AS DANGEROUS AS YOU SAY, WE CAN'T JUST SCARE HIM OFF! WE'VE GOT TO FIGHT HIM!
YOU'RE RIGHT, SUE! THERE MAY BE MORE THAN THE FOUR OF US AT STAKE! BUT I SWEAR ...HE WILL NOT HARM YOU-- NOT WHILE WE LIVE!!
IF YOU ARE SENDING HER OUT, SHOOT UP A FLARE, AND I SHALL OPEN A SECTION OF THE NET FOR HER! AH, THE FLARE! GOOD! GOOD!
DOCTOR DOOM MUST HAVE VAST POWERS TO DARE CHALLENGE THE FANTASTIC FOUR!! AND THIS IS THE ONLY WAY TO FIND OUT WHAT THOSE POWERS ARE!
I AM READY, DOCTOR DOOM! I WILL BE YOUR HOSTAGE!
BUT YOU SHALL LIVE TO REGRET DEFYING THE FANTASTIC FOUR!!
5

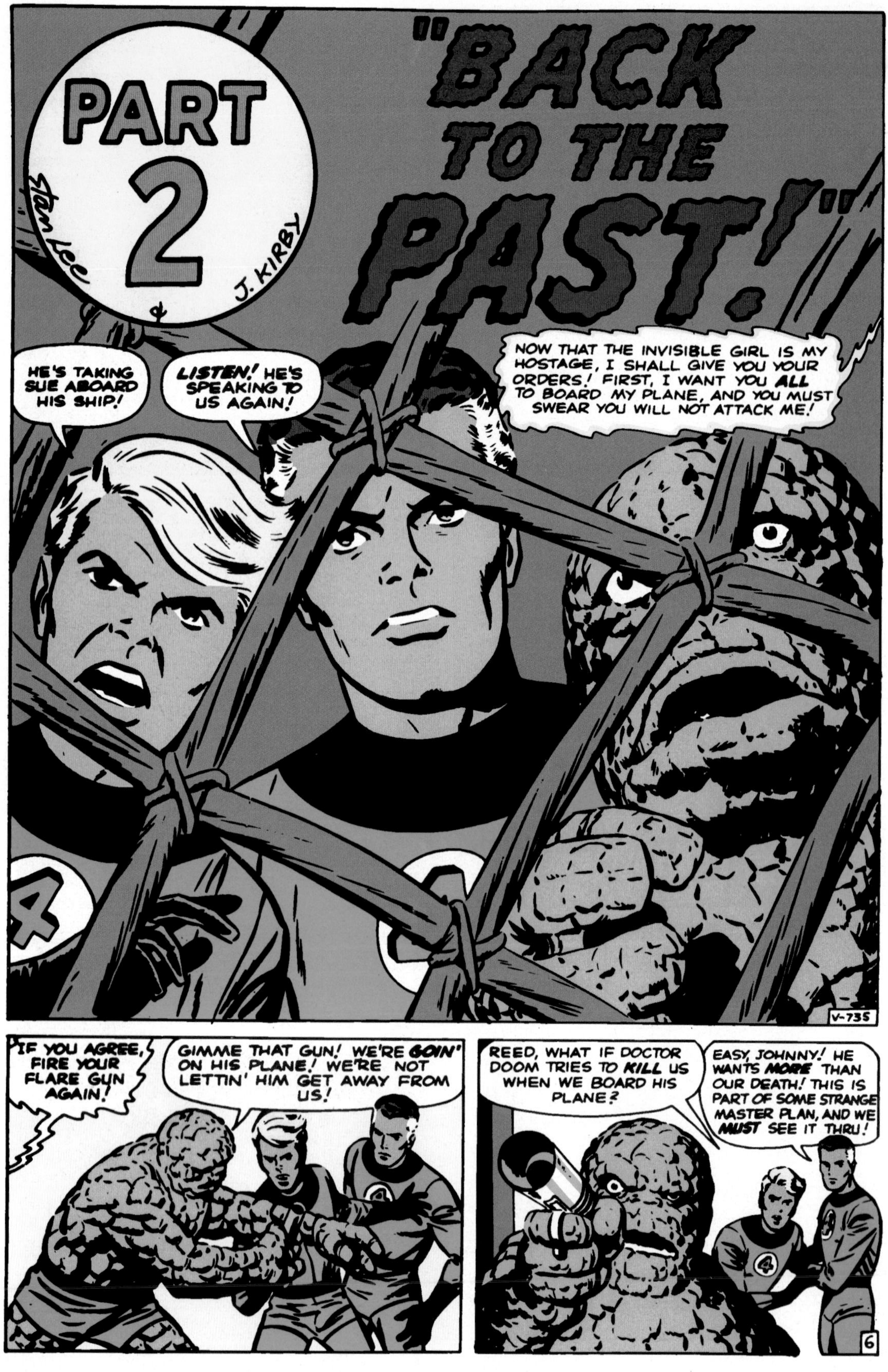

PART 2
"BACK TO THE PAST!"
Stan Lee & J. Kirby
HE'S TAKING SUE ABOARD HIS SHIP!
LISTEN! HE'S SPEAKING TO US AGAIN!
NOW THAT THE INVISIBLE GIRL IS MY HOSTAGE, I SHALL GIVE YOU YOUR ORDERS! FIRST, I WANT YOU ALL TO BOARD MY PLANE, AND YOU MUST SWEAR YOU WILL NOT ATTACK ME!
V-735
IF YOU AGREE, FIRE YOUR FLARE GUN AGAIN!
GIMME THAT GUN! WE'RE GOIN' ON HIS PLANE! WE'RE NOT LETTIN' HIM GET AWAY FROM US!
REED, WHAT IF DOCTOR DOOM TRIES TO KILL US WHEN WE BOARD HIS PLANE?
EASY, JOHNNY! HE WANTS MORE THAN OUR DEATH! THIS IS PART OF SOME STRANGE MASTER PLAN, AND WE MUST SEE IT THRU!
6

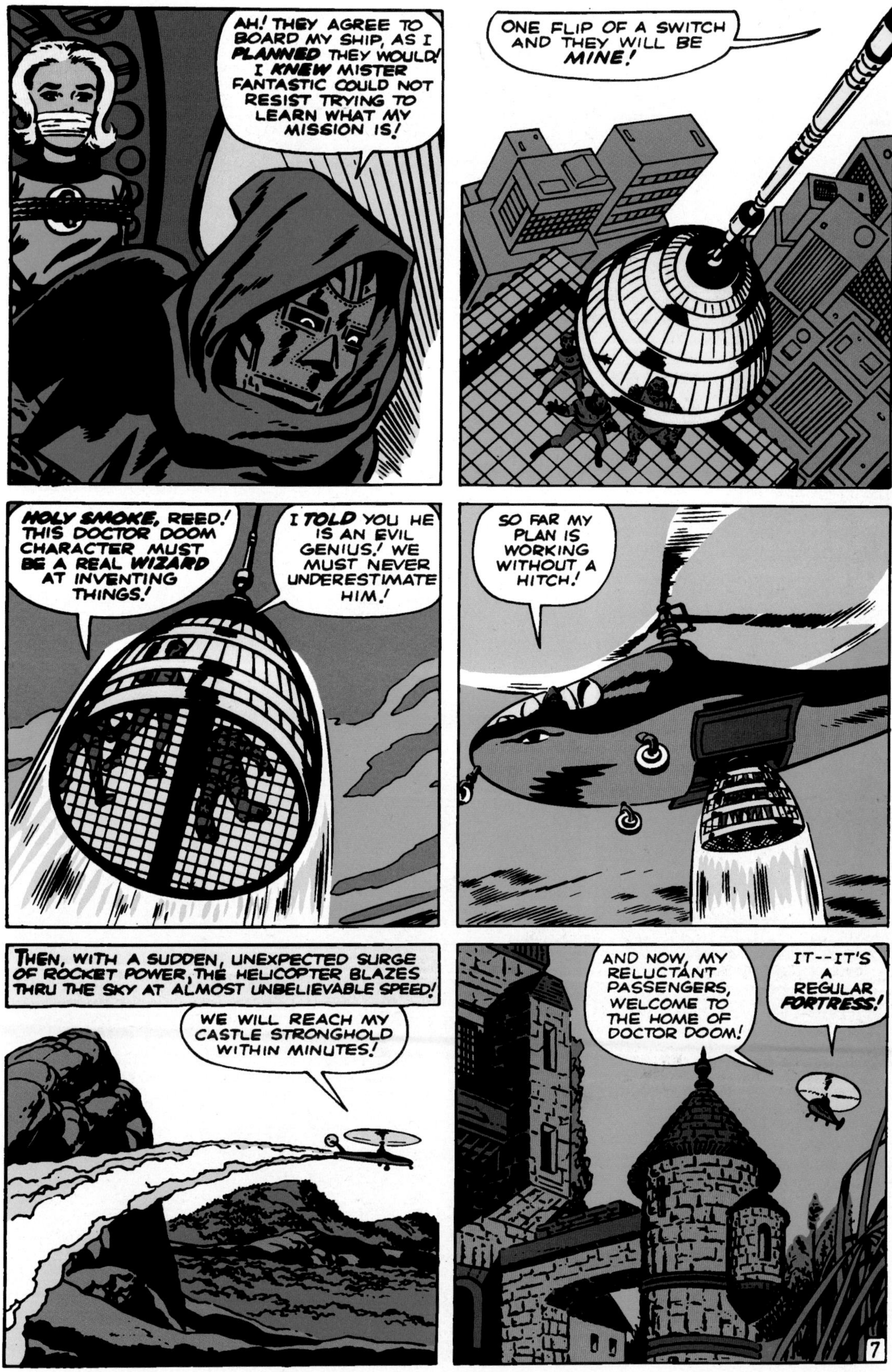
AH! THEY AGREE TO BOARD MY SHIP, AS I PLANNED THEY WOULD! I KNEW MISTER FANTASTIC COULD NOT RESIST TRYING TO LEARN WHAT MY MISSION IS!
ONE FLIP OF A SWITCH AND THEY WILL BE MINE!
HOLY SMOKE, REED! THIS DOCTOR DOOM CHARACTER MUST BE A REAL WIZARD AT INVENTING THINGS!
I TOLD YOU HE IS AN EVIL GENIUS! WE MUST NEVER UNDERESTIMATE HIM!
SO FAR MY PLAN IS WORKING WITHOUT A HITCH!
THEN, WITH A SUDDEN, UNEXPECTED SURGE OF ROCKET POWER, THE HELICOPTER BLAZES THRU THE SKY AT ALMOST UNBELIEVABLE SPEED!
WE WILL REACH MY CASTLE STRONGHOLD WITHIN MINUTES!
AND NOW, MY RELUCTANT PASSENGERS, WELCOME TO THE HOME OF DOCTOR DOOM!
IT--IT'S A REGULAR FORTRESS!

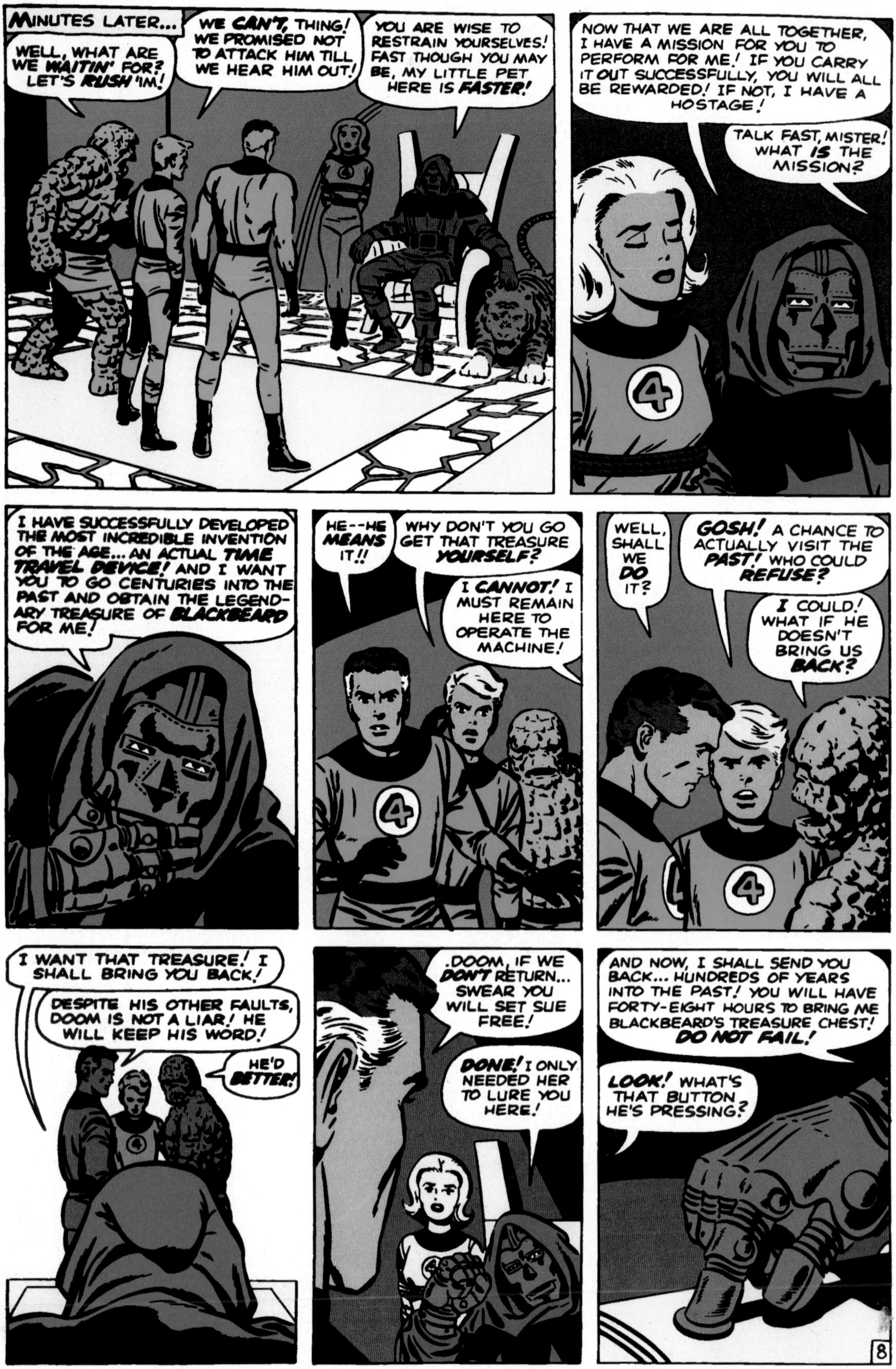
MINUTES LATER...
WELL, WHAT ARE WE WAITIN' FOR? LET'S RUSH 'IM!
WE CAN'T, THING! WE PROMISED NOT TO ATTACK HIM TILL WE HEAR HIM OUT!
YOU ARE WISE TO RESTRAIN YOURSELVES! FAST THOUGH YOU MAY BE, MY LITTLE PET HERE IS FASTER!
NOW THAT WE ARE ALL TOGETHER, I HAVE A MISSION FOR YOU TO PERFORM FOR ME! IF YOU CARRY IT OUT SUCCESSFULLY, YOU WILL ALL BE REWARDED! IF NOT, I HAVE A HOSTAGE!
TALK FAST, MISTER! WHAT IS THE MISSION?
I HAVE SUCCESSFULLY DEVELOPED THE MOST INCREDIBLE INVENTION OF THE AGE... AN ACTUAL TIME TRAVEL DEVICE! AND I WANT YOU TO GO CENTURIES INTO THE PAST AND OBTAIN THE LEGENDARY TREASURE OF BLACKBEARD FOR ME!
HE--HE MEANS IT!!
WHY DON'T YOU GO GET THAT TREASURE YOURSELF?
I CANNOT! I MUST REMAIN HERE TO OPERATE THE MACHINE!
WELL, SHALL WE DO IT?
GOSH! A CHANCE TO ACTUALLY VISIT THE PAST! WHO COULD REFUSE?
I COULD! WHAT IF HE DOESN'T BRING US BACK?
I WANT THAT TREASURE! I SHALL BRING YOU BACK!
DESPITE HIS OTHER FAULTS, DOOM IS NOT A LIAR! HE WILL KEEP HIS WORD!
HE'D BETTER!
.DOOM, IF WE DON'T RETURN... SWEAR YOU WILL SET SUE FREE!
DONE! I ONLY NEEDED HER TO LURE YOU HERE!
AND NOW, I SHALL SEND YOU BACK... HUNDREDS OF YEARS INTO THE PAST! YOU WILL HAVE FORTY-EIGHT HOURS TO BRING ME BLACKBEARD'S TREASURE CHEST! DO NOT FAIL!
LOOK! WHAT'S THAT BUTTON HE'S PRESSING?
8

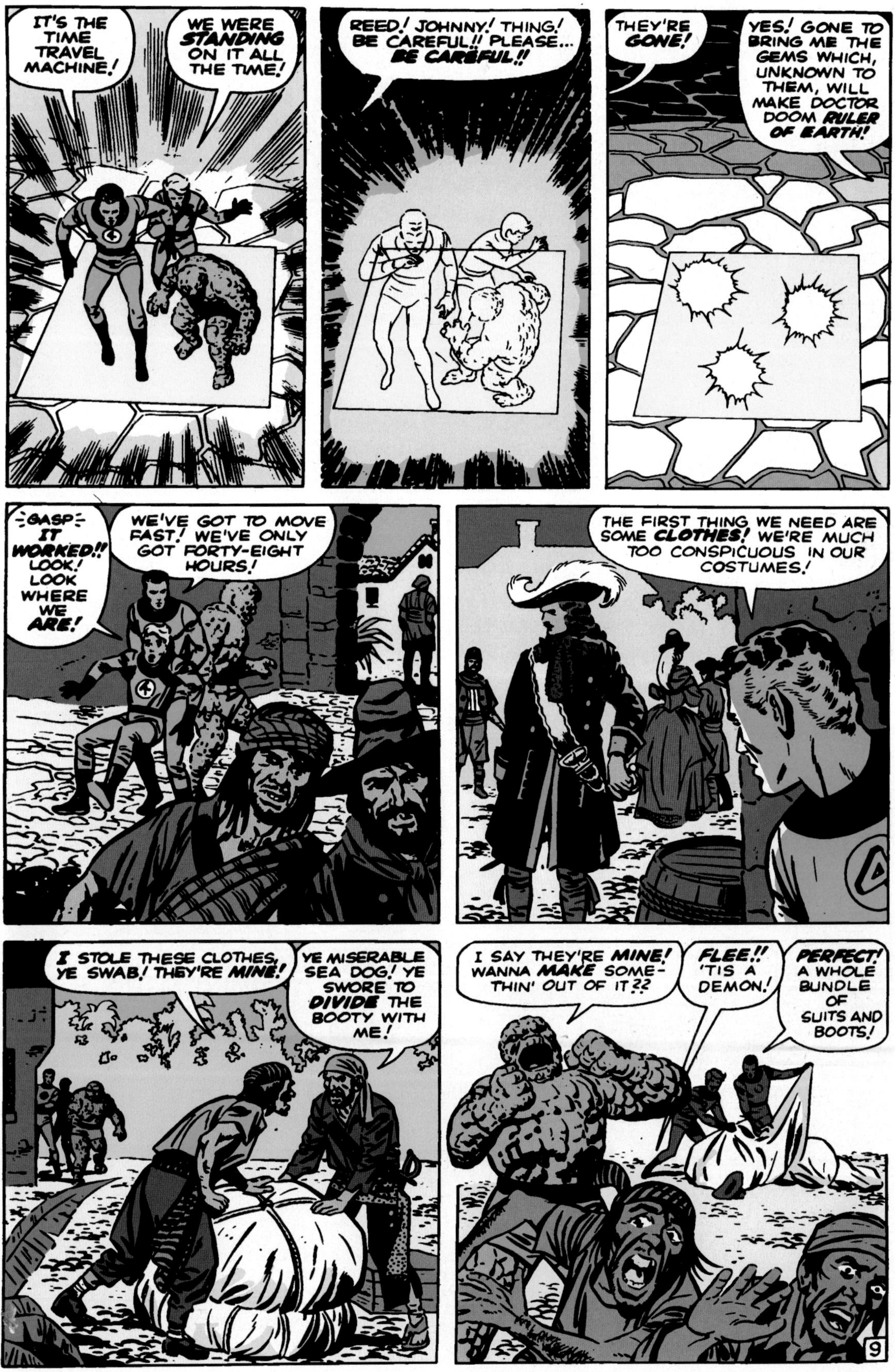
IT'S THE TIME TRAVEL MACHINE!
WE WERE STANDING ON IT ALL THE TIME!
REED! JOHNNY! THING! BE CAREFUL!! PLEASE... BE CAREFUL!!
THEY'RE GONE!
YES! GONE TO BRING ME THE GEMS WHICH, UNKNOWN TO THEM, WILL MAKE DOCTOR DOOM RULER OF EARTH!
-GASP- IT WORKED!! LOOK! LOOK WHERE WE ARE!
WE'VE GOT TO MOVE FAST! WE'VE ONLY GOT FORTY-EIGHT HOURS!
THE FIRST THING WE NEED ARE SOME CLOTHES! WE'RE MUCH TOO CONSPICUOUS IN OUR COSTUMES!
I STOLE THESE CLOTHES, YE SWAB! THEY'RE MINE!
YE MISERABLE SEA DOG! YE SWORE TO DIVIDE THE BOOTY WITH ME!
I SAY THEY'RE MINE! WANNA MAKE SOME-THIN' OUT OF IT??
FLEE!! 'TIS A DEMON!
PERFECT! A WHOLE BUNDLE OF SUITS AND BOOTS!
9

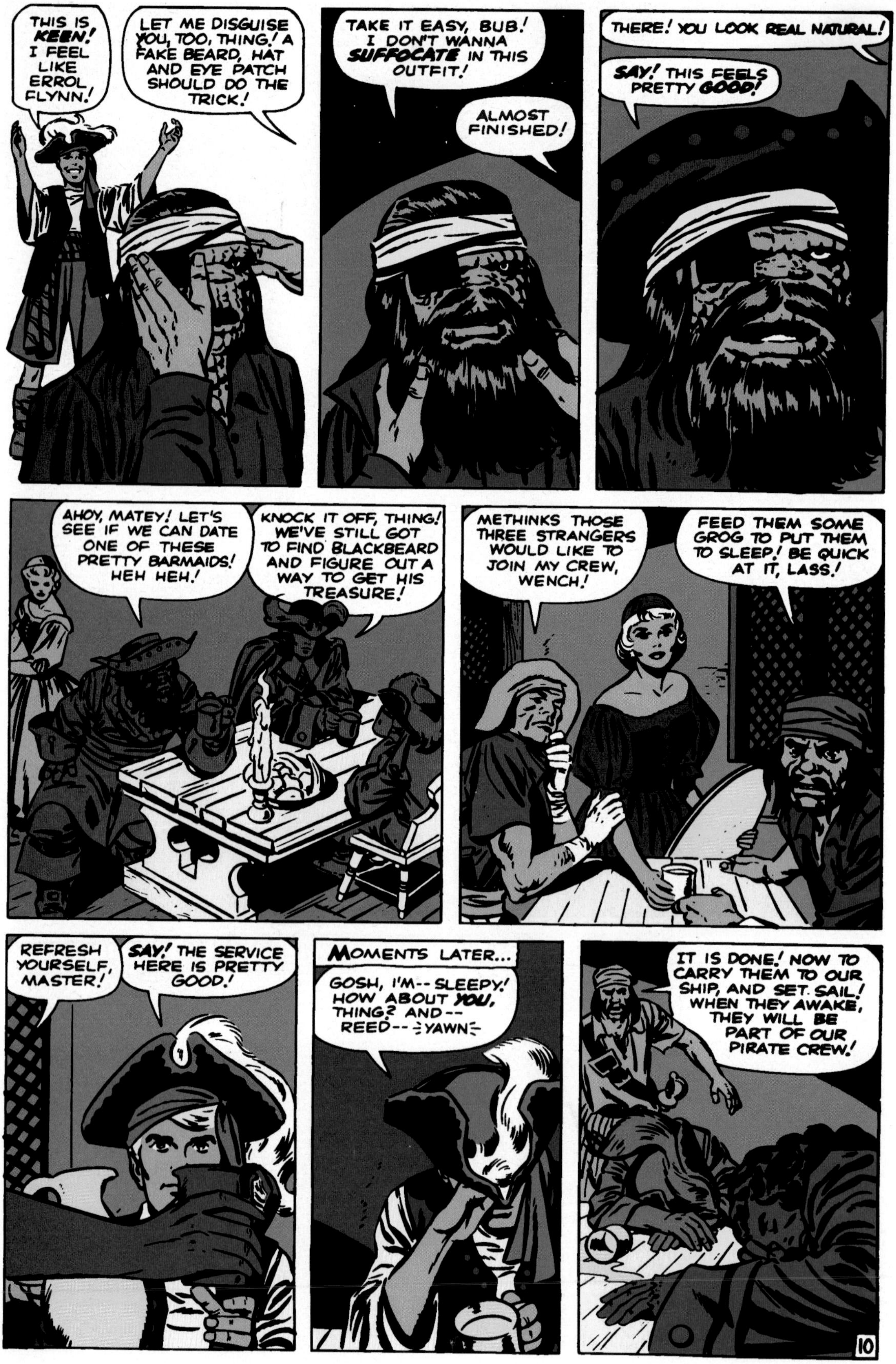
THIS IS KEEN! I FEEL LIKE ERROL FLYNN!
LET ME DISGUISE YOU, TOO, THING! A FAKE BEARD, HAT AND EYE PATCH SHOULD DO THE TRICK!
TAKE IT EASY, BUB! I DON'T WANNA SUFFOCATE IN THIS OUTFIT!
ALMOST FINISHED!
THERE! YOU LOOK REAL NATURAL!
SAY! THIS FEELS PRETTY GOOD!
AHOY, MATEY! LET'S SEE IF WE CAN DATE ONE OF THESE PRETTY BARMAIDS! HEH HEH!
KNOCK IT OFF, THING! WE'VE STILL GOT TO FIND BLACKBEARD AND FIGURE OUT A WAY TO GET HIS TREASURE!
METHINKS THOSE THREE STRANGERS WOULD LIKE TO JOIN MY CREW, WENCH!
FEED THEM SOME GROG TO PUT THEM TO SLEEP! BE QUICK AT IT, LASS!
REFRESH YOURSELF, MASTER!
SAY! THE SERVICE HERE IS PRETTY GOOD!
MOMENTS LATER...
GOSH, I'M-- SLEEPY! HOW ABOUT YOU, THING? AND-- REED-- YAWN
IT IS DONE! NOW TO CARRY THEM TO OUR SHIP, AND SET SAIL! WHEN THEY AWAKE, THEY WILL BE PART OF OUR PIRATE CREW!
10

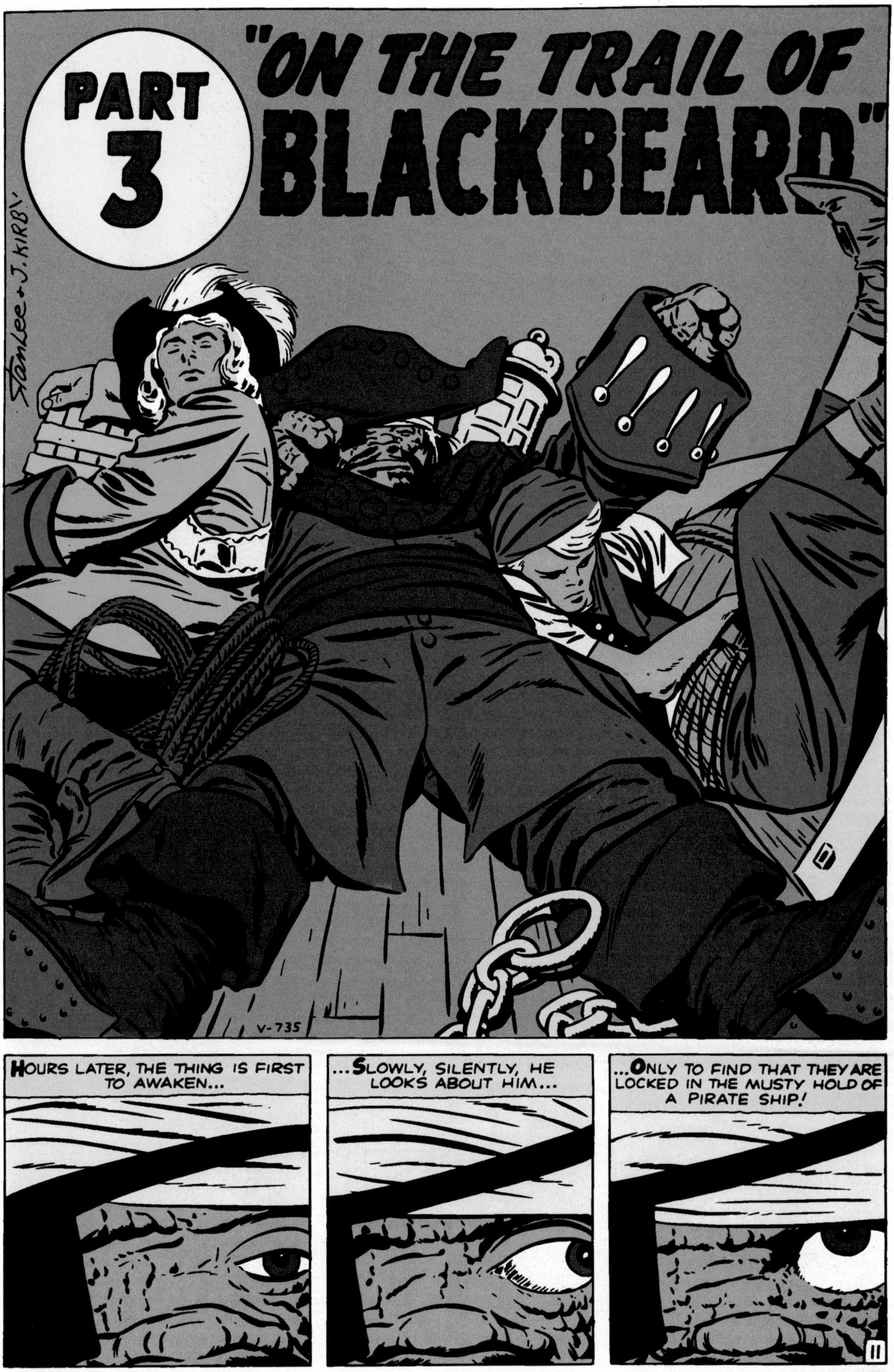
PART 3
"ON THE TRAIL OF BLACKBEARD"
STAN LEE + J. KIRBY
V-735
HOURS LATER, THE THING IS FIRST TO AWAKEN...
...SLOWLY, SILENTLY, HE LOOKS ABOUT HIM...
...ONLY TO FIND THAT THEY ARE LOCKED IN THE MUSTY HOLD OF A PIRATE SHIP!
11

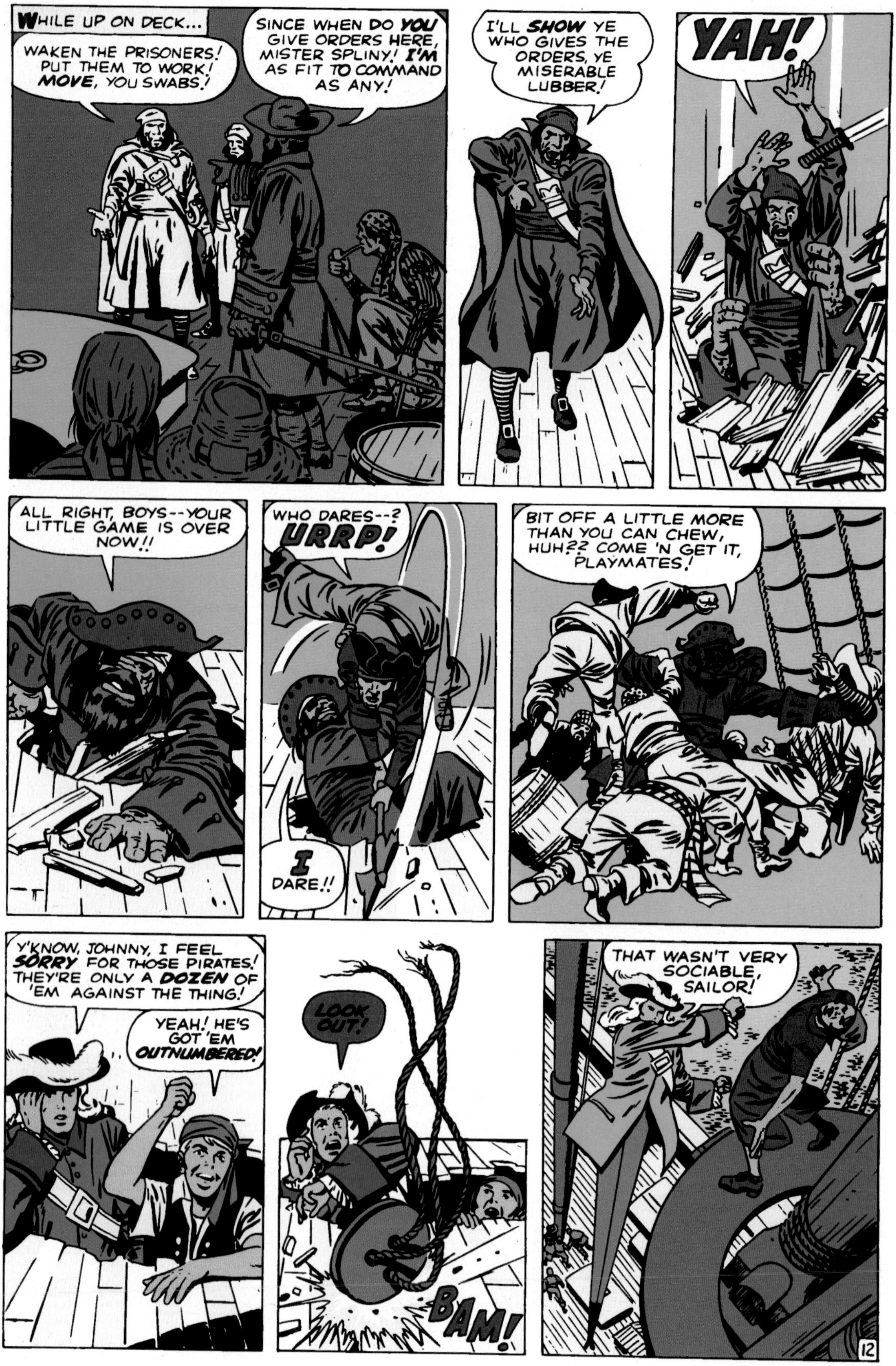
WHILE UP ON DECK...
WAKEN THE PRISONERS! PUT THEM TO WORK! MOVE, YOU SWABS!
SINCE WHEN DO YOU GIVE ORDERS HERE, MISTER SPLINY! I'M AS FIT TO COMMAND AS ANY!
I'LL SHOW YE WHO GIVES THE ORDERS, YE MISERABLE LUBBER!
YAH!
ALL RIGHT, BOYS--YOUR LITTLE GAME IS OVER NOW!!
WHO DARES--? URRP!
I DARE!!
BIT OFF A LITTLE MORE THAN YOU CAN CHEW, HUH?? COME 'N GET IT, PLAYMATES!
Y'KNOW, JOHNNY, I FEEL SORRY FOR THOSE PIRATES! THEY'RE ONLY A DOZEN OF 'EM AGAINST THE THING!
YEAH! HE'S GOT 'EM OUTNUMBERED!
LOOK OUT!
BAM!
THAT WASN'T VERY SOCIABLE, SAILOR!
12

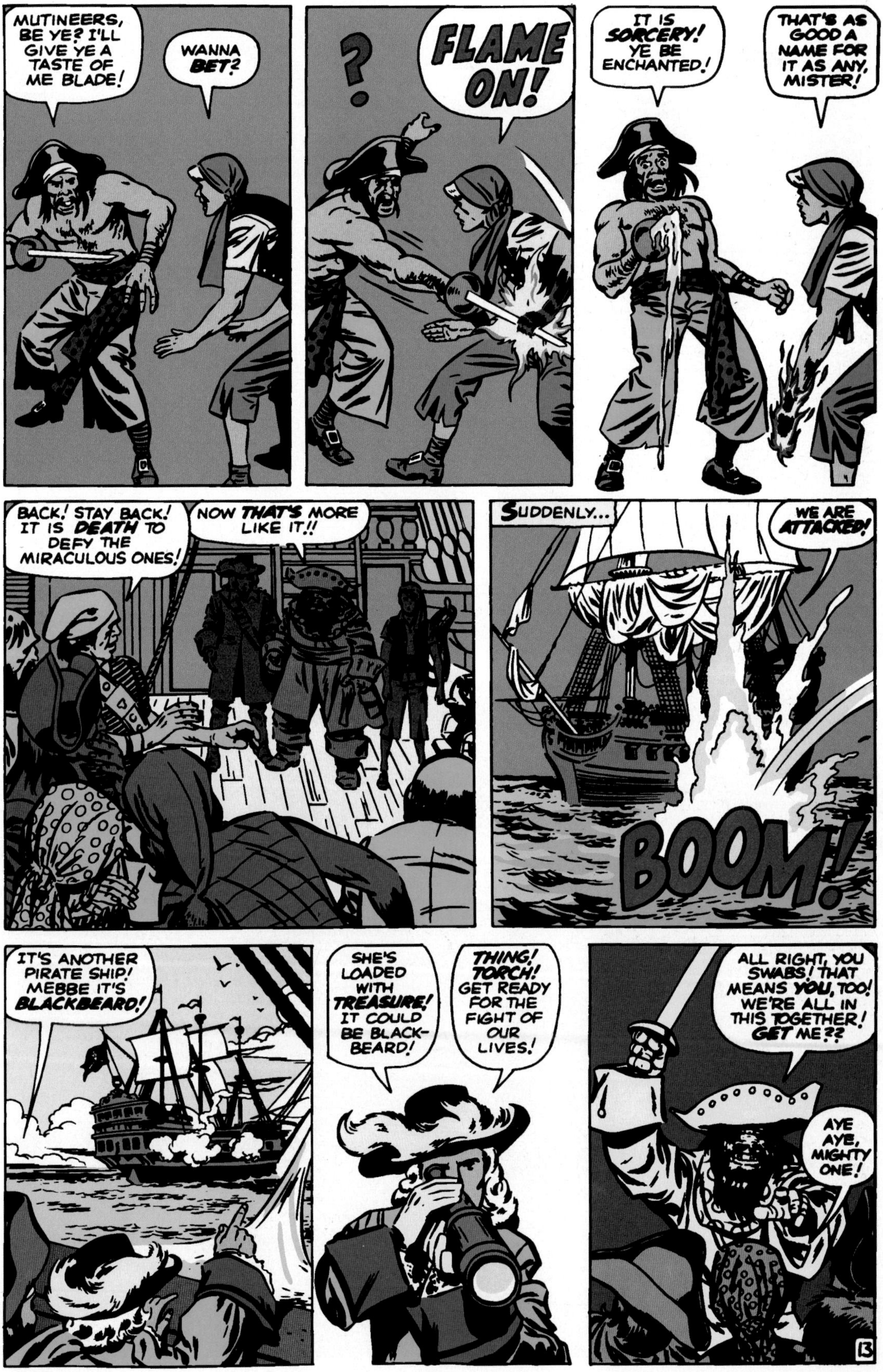
MUTINEERS, BE YE? I'LL GIVE YE A TASTE OF ME BLADE!
WANNA BET?
?
FLAME ON!
IT IS SORCERY! YE BE ENCHANTED!
THAT'S AS GOOD A NAME FOR IT AS ANY, MISTER!
BACK! STAY BACK! IT IS DEATH TO DEFY THE MIRACULOUS ONES!
NOW THAT'S MORE LIKE IT!!
SUDDENLY...
WE ARE ATTACKED!
BOOM!
IT'S ANOTHER PIRATE SHIP! MEBBE IT'S BLACKBEARD!
SHE'S LOADED WITH TREASURE! IT COULD BE BLACK-BEARD!
THING! TORCH! GET READY FOR THE FIGHT OF OUR LIVES!
ALL RIGHT, YOU SWABS! THAT MEANS YOU, TOO! WE'RE ALL IN THIS TOGETHER! GET ME??
AYE AYE, MIGHTY ONE!
13

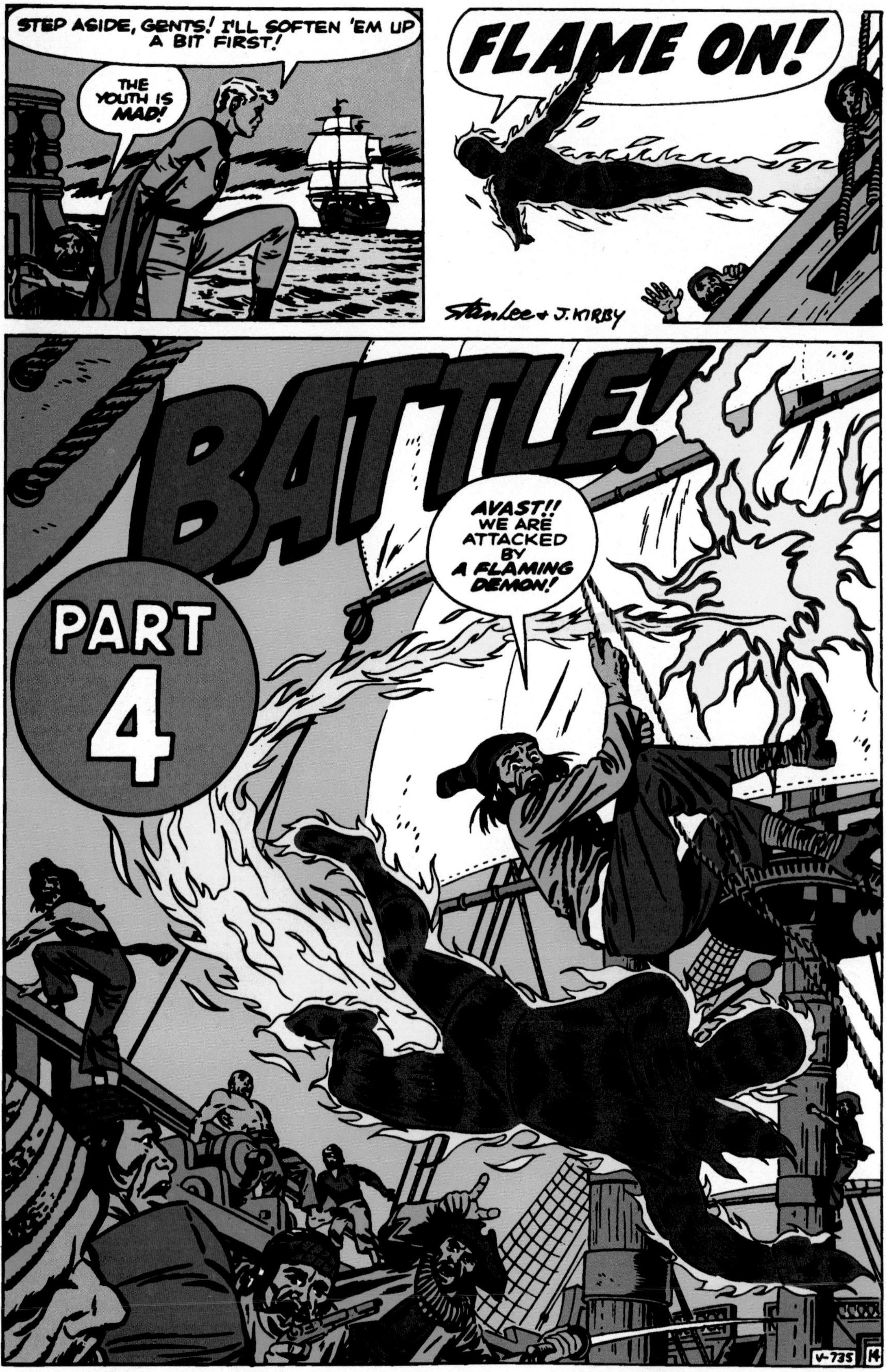

STEP ASIDE, GENTS! I'LL SOFTEN 'EM UP A BIT FIRST!
THE YOUTH IS MAD!
FLAME ON!
StanLee + J. KIRBY
BATTLE!
PART 4
AVAST!! WE ARE ATTACKED BY A FLAMING DEMON!
V-735
14

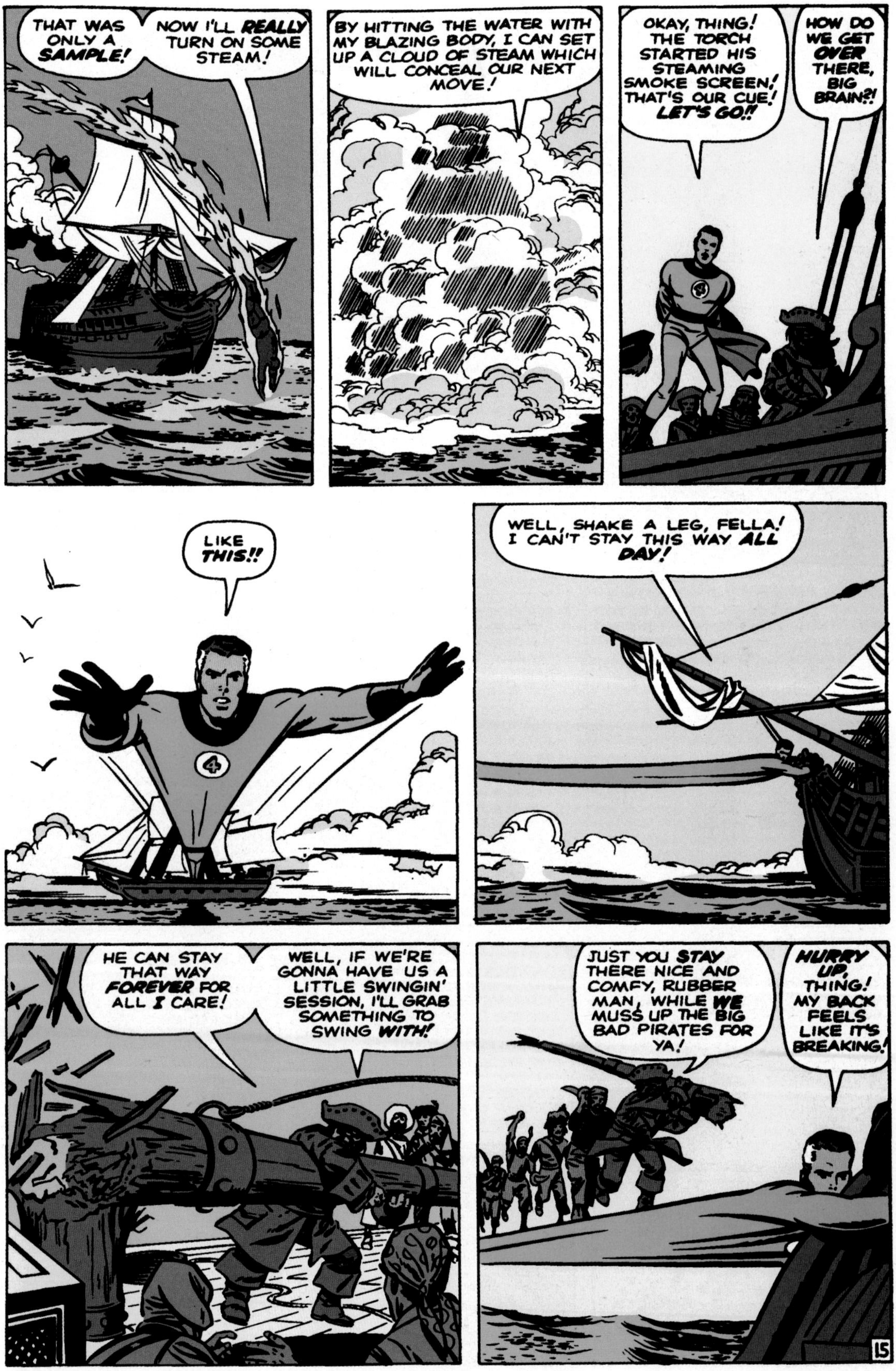
THAT WAS ONLY A SAMPLE!
NOW I'LL REALLY TURN ON SOME STEAM!
BY HITTING THE WATER WITH MY BLAZING BODY, I CAN SET UP A CLOUD OF STEAM WHICH WILL CONCEAL OUR NEXT MOVE!
OKAY, THING! THE TORCH STARTED HIS STEAMING SMOKE SCREEN! THAT'S OUR CUE! LET'S GO!!
HOW DO WE GET OVER THERE, BIG BRAIN?!
LIKE THIS!!
WELL, SHAKE A LEG, FELLA! I CAN'T STAY THIS WAY ALL DAY!
HE CAN STAY THAT WAY FOREVER FOR ALL I CARE!
WELL, IF WE'RE GONNA HAVE US A LITTLE SWINGIN' SESSION, I'LL GRAB SOMETHING TO SWING WITH!
JUST YOU STAY THERE NICE AND COMFY, RUBBER MAN, WHILE WE MUSS UP THE BIG BAD PIRATES FOR YA!
HURRY UP, THING! MY BACK FEELS LIKE IT'S BREAKING!
15

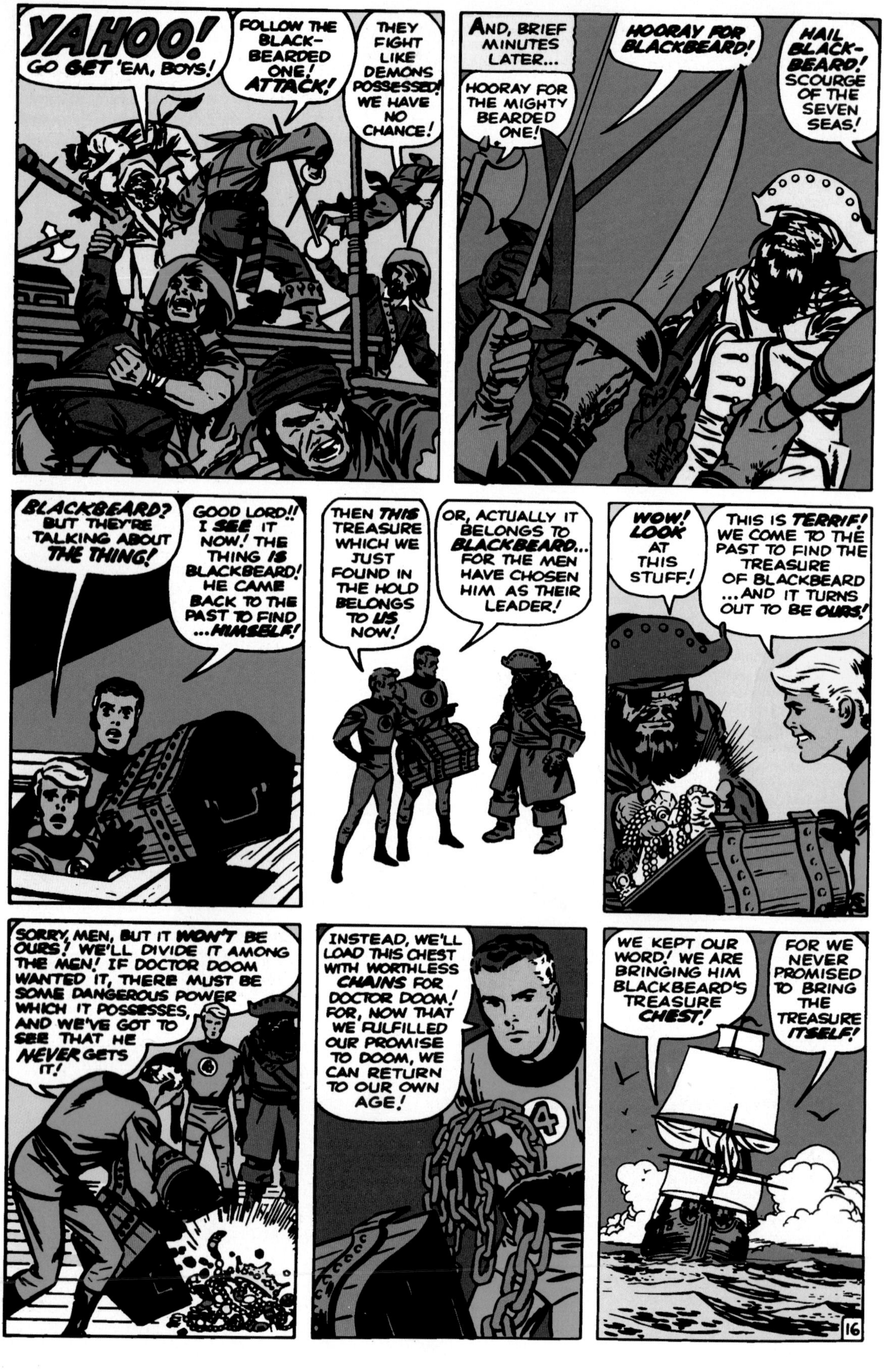

YAHOO! GO GET 'EM, BOYS!
FOLLOW THE BLACK-BEARDED ONE! ATTACK!
THEY FIGHT LIKE DEMONS POSSESSED! WE HAVE NO CHANCE!
AND, BRIEF MINUTES LATER...
HOORAY FOR THE MIGHTY BEARDED ONE!
HOORAY FOR BLACKBEARD!
HAIL BLACK-BEARD! SCOURGE OF THE SEVEN SEAS!
BLACKBEARD? BUT THEY'RE TALKING ABOUT THE THING!
GOOD LORD!! I SEE IT NOW! THE THING IS BLACKBEARD! HE CAME BACK TO THE PAST TO FIND ...HIMSELF!
THEN THIS TREASURE WHICH WE JUST FOUND IN THE HOLD BELONGS TO US NOW!
OR, ACTUALLY IT BELONGS TO BLACKBEARD... FOR THE MEN HAVE CHOSEN HIM AS THEIR LEADER!
WOW! LOOK AT THIS STUFF!
THIS IS TERRIF! WE COME TO THE PAST TO FIND THE TREASURE OF BLACKBEARD ...AND IT TURNS OUT TO BE OURS!
SORRY, MEN, BUT IT WON'T BE OURS! WE'LL DIVIDE IT AMONG THE MEN! IF DOCTOR DOOM WANTED IT, THERE MUST BE SOME DANGEROUS POWER WHICH IT POSSESSES, AND WE'VE GOT TO SEE THAT HE NEVER GETS IT!
INSTEAD, WE'LL LOAD THIS CHEST WITH WORTHLESS CHAINS FOR DOCTOR DOOM! FOR, NOW THAT WE FULFILLED OUR PROMISE TO DOOM, WE CAN RETURN TO OUR OWN AGE!
WE KEPT OUR WORD! WE ARE BRINGING HIM BLACKBEARD'S TREASURE CHEST!
FOR WE NEVER PROMISED TO BRING THE TREASURE ITSELF!
16

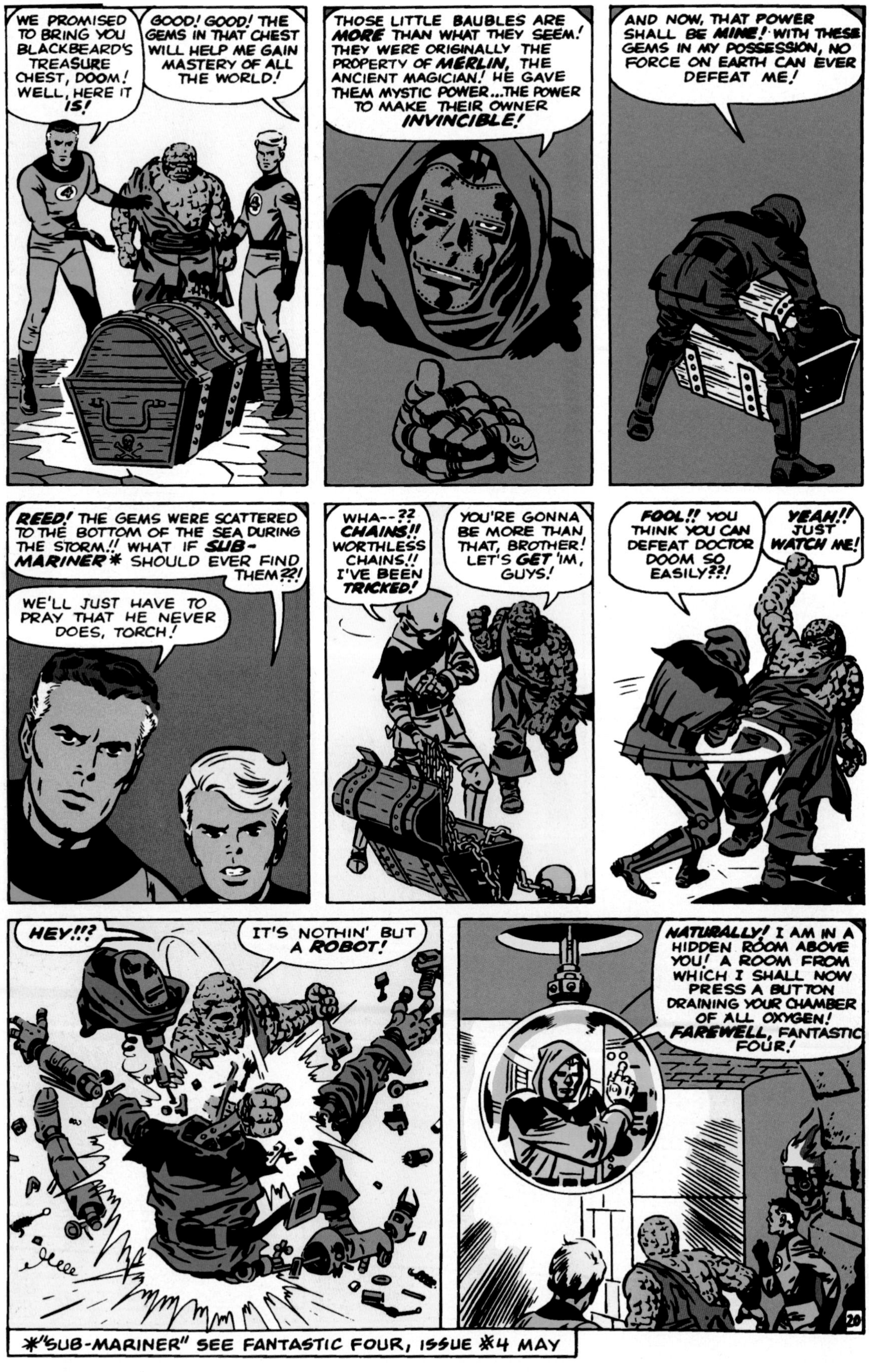
WE PROMISED TO BRING YOU BLACKBEARD'S TREASURE CHEST, DOOM! WELL, HERE IT IS!
GOOD! GOOD! THE GEMS IN THAT CHEST WILL HELP ME GAIN MASTERY OF ALL THE WORLD!
THOSE LITTLE BAUBLES ARE MORE THAN WHAT THEY SEEM! THEY WERE ORIGINALLY THE PROPERTY OF MERLIN, THE ANCIENT MAGICIAN! HE GAVE THEM MYSTIC POWER...THE POWER TO MAKE THEIR OWNER INVINCIBLE!
AND NOW, THAT POWER SHALL BE MINE! WITH THESE GEMS IN MY POSSESSION, NO FORCE ON EARTH CAN EVER DEFEAT ME!
REED! THE GEMS WERE SCATTERED TO THE BOTTOM OF THE SEA DURING THE STORM!! WHAT IF SUB-MARINER* SHOULD EVER FIND THEM??!
WE'LL JUST HAVE TO PRAY THAT HE NEVER DOES, TORCH!
WHA--?? CHAINS!! WORTHLESS CHAINS!! I'VE BEEN TRICKED!
YOU'RE GONNA BE MORE THAN THAT, BROTHER! LET'S GET 'IM, GUYS!
FOOL!! YOU THINK YOU CAN DEFEAT DOCTOR DOOM SO EASILY??!
YEAH!! JUST WATCH ME!
HEY!!?
IT'S NOTHIN' BUT A ROBOT!
NATURALLY! I AM IN A HIDDEN ROOM ABOVE YOU! A ROOM FROM WHICH I SHALL NOW PRESS A BUTTON DRAINING YOUR CHAMBER OF ALL OXYGEN! FAREWELL, FANTASTIC FOUR!

*"SUB-MARINER" SEE FANTASTIC FOUR, ISSUE #4 MAY

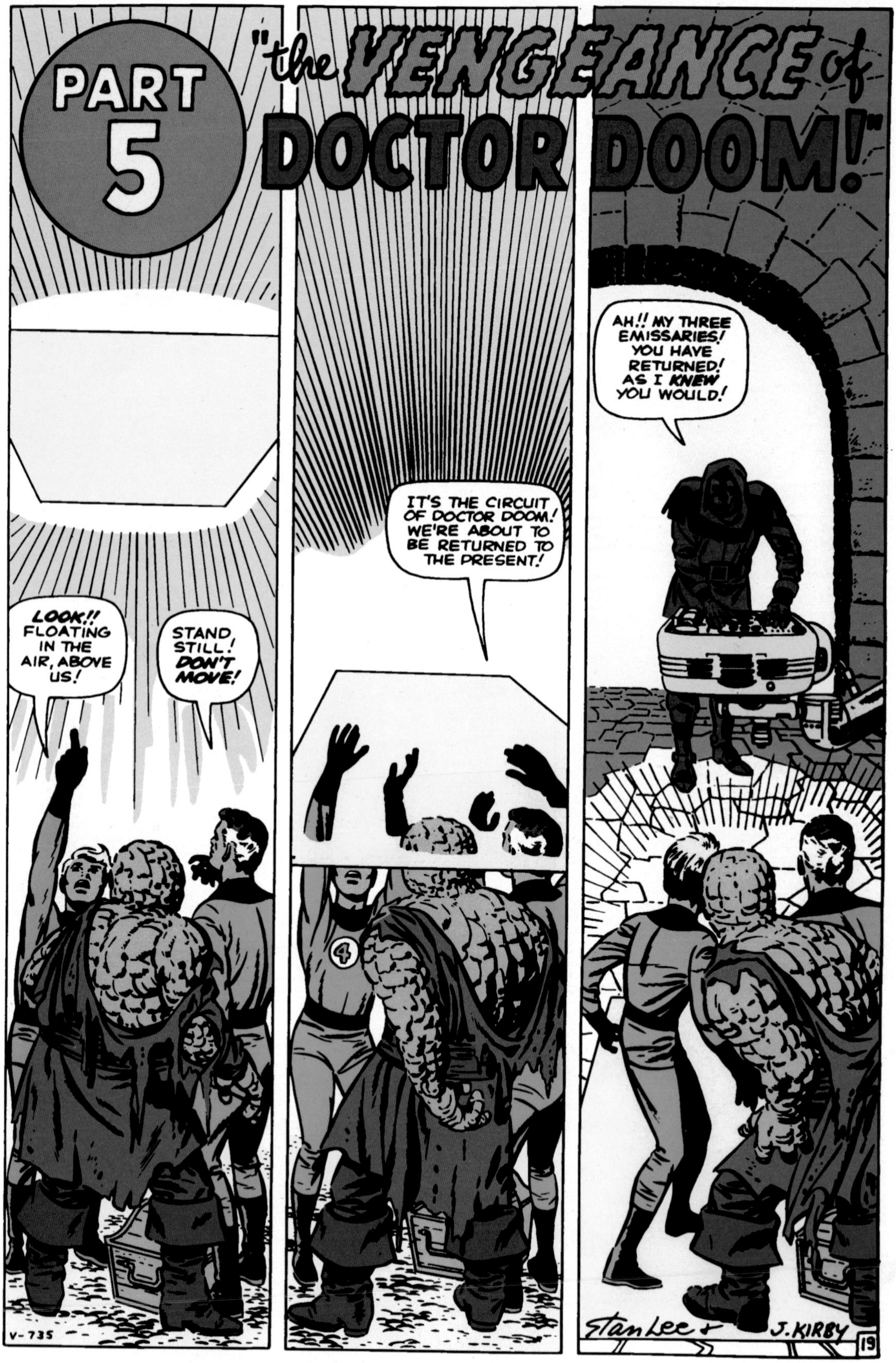
PART 5
"the VENGEANCE of DOCTOR DOOM!"
LOOK!! FLOATING IN THE AIR, ABOVE US!
STAND STILL! DON'T MOVE!
IT'S THE CIRCUIT OF DOCTOR DOOM! WE'RE ABOUT TO BE RETURNED TO THE PRESENT!
AH!! MY THREE EMISSARIES! YOU HAVE RETURNED! AS I KNEW YOU WOULD!
V-735
Stan Lee + J. KIRBY
19

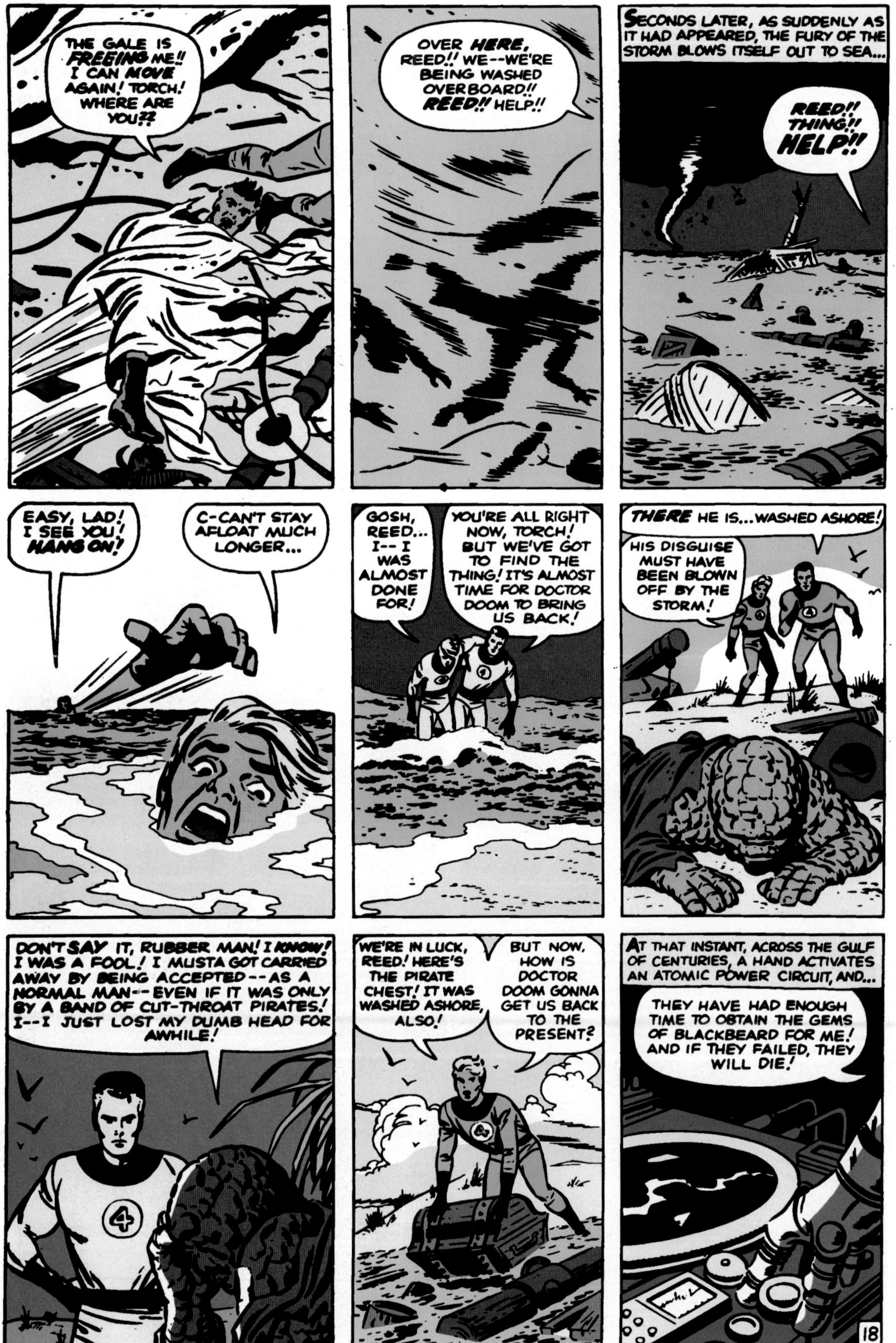
THE GALE IS FREEING ME!! I CAN MOVE AGAIN! TORCH! WHERE ARE YOU??
OVER HERE, REED!! WE--WE'RE BEING WASHED OVERBOARD!! REED!! HELP!!
SECONDS LATER, AS SUDDENLY AS IT HAD APPEARED, THE FURY OF THE STORM BLOWS ITSELF OUT TO SEA...
REED!! THING!! HELP!!
EASY, LAD! I SEE YOU! HANG ON!
C-CAN'T STAY AFLOAT MUCH LONGER...
GOSH, REED... I-- I WAS ALMOST DONE FOR!
YOU'RE ALL RIGHT NOW, TORCH! BUT WE'VE GOT TO FIND THE THING! IT'S ALMOST TIME FOR DOCTOR DOOM TO BRING US BACK!
THERE HE IS...WASHED ASHORE!
HIS DISGUISE MUST HAVE BEEN BLOWN OFF BY THE STORM!
DON'T SAY IT, RUBBER MAN! I KNOW! I WAS A FOOL! I MUSTA GOT CARRIED AWAY BY BEING ACCEPTED--AS A NORMAL MAN--EVEN IF IT WAS ONLY BY A BAND OF CUT-THROAT PIRATES! I--I JUST LOST MY DUMB HEAD FOR AWHILE!
WE'RE IN LUCK, REED! HERE'S THE PIRATE CHEST! IT WAS WASHED ASHORE, ALSO!
BUT NOW, HOW IS DOCTOR DOOM GONNA GET US BACK TO THE PRESENT?
AT THAT INSTANT, ACROSS THE GULF OF CENTURIES, A HAND ACTIVATES AN ATOMIC POWER CIRCUIT, AND...
THEY HAVE HAD ENOUGH TIME TO OBTAIN THE GEMS OF BLACKBEARD FOR ME! AND IF THEY FAILED, THEY WILL DIE!
18

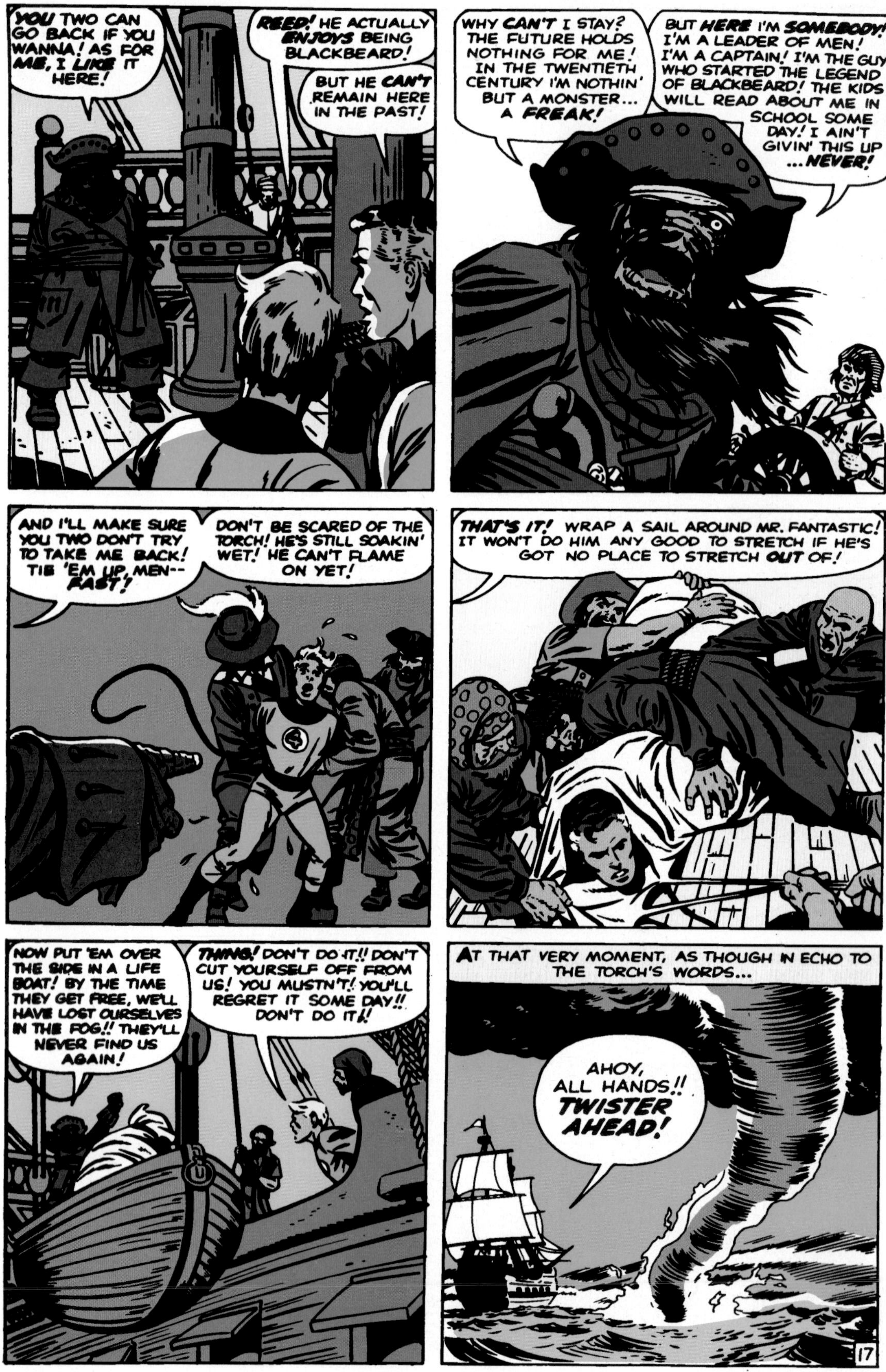
YOU TWO CAN GO BACK IF YOU WANNA! AS FOR ME, I LIKE IT HERE!
REED! HE ACTUALLY ENJOYS BEING BLACKBEARD!
BUT HE CAN'T REMAIN HERE IN THE PAST!
WHY CAN'T I STAY? THE FUTURE HOLDS NOTHING FOR ME! IN THE TWENTIETH CENTURY I'M NOTHIN' BUT A MONSTER... A FREAK!
BUT HERE I'M SOMEBODY! I'M A LEADER OF MEN! I'M A CAPTAIN! I'M THE GUY WHO STARTED THE LEGEND OF BLACKBEARD! THE KIDS WILL READ ABOUT ME IN SCHOOL SOME DAY! I AIN'T GIVIN' THIS UP ...NEVER!
AND I'LL MAKE SURE YOU TWO DON'T TRY TO TAKE ME BACK! TIE 'EM UP, MEN-- FAST!
DON'T BE SCARED OF THE TORCH! HE'S STILL SOAKIN' WET! HE CAN'T FLAME ON YET!
THAT'S IT! WRAP A SAIL AROUND MR. FANTASTIC! IT WON'T DO HIM ANY GOOD TO STRETCH IF HE'S GOT NO PLACE TO STRETCH OUT OF!
NOW PUT 'EM OVER THE SIDE IN A LIFE BOAT! BY THE TIME THEY GET FREE, WE'LL HAVE LOST OURSELVES IN THE FOG!! THEY'LL NEVER FIND US AGAIN!
THING! DON'T DO IT!! DON'T CUT YOURSELF OFF FROM US! YOU MUSTN'T! YOU'LL REGRET IT SOME DAY!! DON'T DO IT!!
AT THAT VERY MOMENT, AS THOUGH IN ECHO TO THE TORCH'S WORDS...
AHOY, ALL HANDS!! TWISTER AHEAD!
17

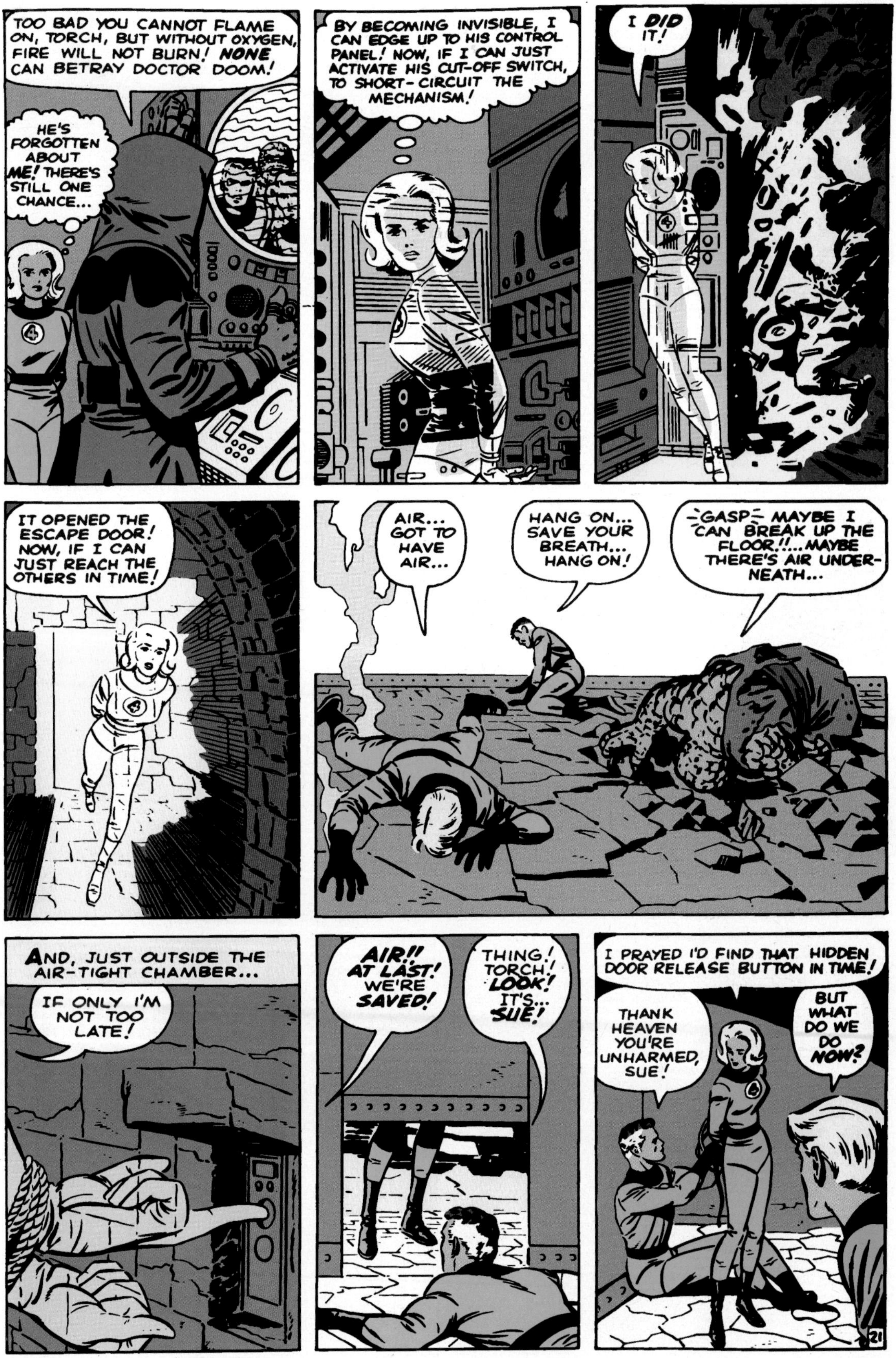
TOO BAD YOU CANNOT FLAME ON, TORCH, BUT WITHOUT OXYGEN, FIRE WILL NOT BURN! NONE CAN BETRAY DOCTOR DOOM!
HE'S FORGOTTEN ABOUT ME! THERE'S STILL ONE CHANCE...
BY BECOMING INVISIBLE, I CAN EDGE UP TO HIS CONTROL PANEL! NOW, IF I CAN JUST ACTIVATE HIS CUT-OFF SWITCH, TO SHORT-CIRCUIT THE MECHANISM!
I DID IT!
IT OPENED THE ESCAPE DOOR! NOW, IF I CAN JUST REACH THE OTHERS IN TIME!
AIR... GOT TO HAVE AIR...
HANG ON... SAVE YOUR BREATH... HANG ON!
-GASP- MAYBE I CAN BREAK UP THE FLOOR!!... MAYBE THERE'S AIR UNDERNEATH...
AND, JUST OUTSIDE THE AIR-TIGHT CHAMBER...
IF ONLY I'M NOT TOO LATE!
AIR!! AT LAST! WE'RE SAVED!
THING! TORCH! LOOK! IT'S... SUE!
I PRAYED I'D FIND THAT HIDDEN DOOR RELEASE BUTTON IN TIME!
THANK HEAVEN YOU'RE UNHARMED, SUE!
BUT WHAT DO WE DO NOW?
21

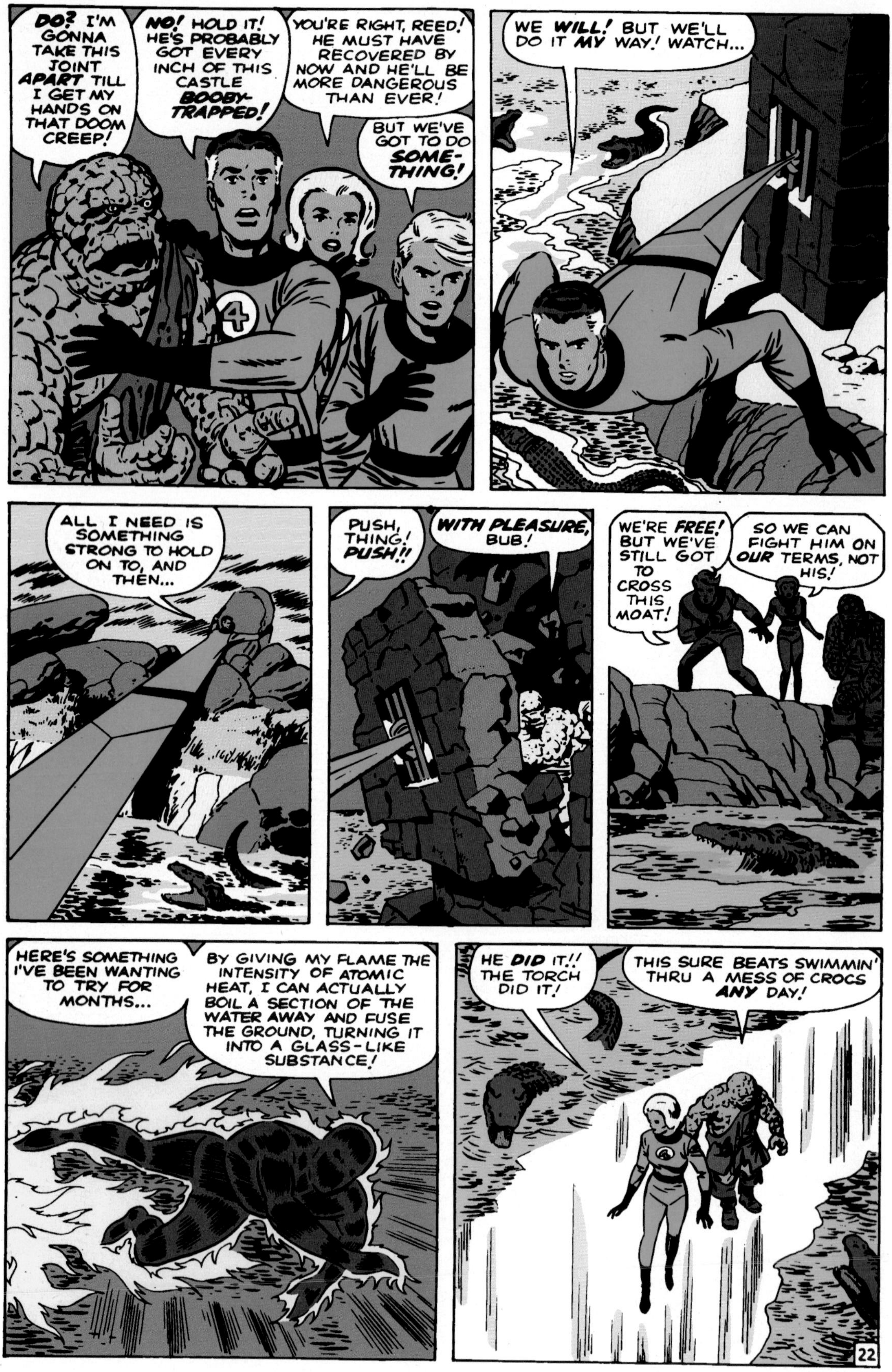
DO? I'M GONNA TAKE THIS JOINT APART TILL I GET MY HANDS ON THAT DOOM CREEP!
NO! HOLD IT! HE'S PROBABLY GOT EVERY INCH OF THIS CASTLE BOOBY-TRAPPED!
YOU'RE RIGHT, REED! HE MUST HAVE RECOVERED BY NOW AND HE'LL BE MORE DANGEROUS THAN EVER!
BUT WE'VE GOT TO DO SOME-THING!
WE WILL! BUT WE'LL DO IT MY WAY! WATCH...
ALL I NEED IS SOMETHING STRONG TO HOLD ON TO, AND THEN...
PUSH, THING! PUSH!!
WITH PLEASURE, BUB!
WE'RE FREE! BUT WE'VE STILL GOT TO CROSS THIS MOAT!
SO WE CAN FIGHT HIM ON OUR TERMS, NOT HIS!
HERE'S SOMETHING I'VE BEEN WANTING TO TRY FOR MONTHS...
BY GIVING MY FLAME THE INTENSITY OF ATOMIC HEAT, I CAN ACTUALLY BOIL A SECTION OF THE WATER AWAY AND FUSE THE GROUND, TURNING IT INTO A GLASS-LIKE SUBSTANCE!
HE DID IT!! THE TORCH DID IT!
THIS SURE BEATS SWIMMIN' THRU A MESS OF CROCS ANY DAY!
22

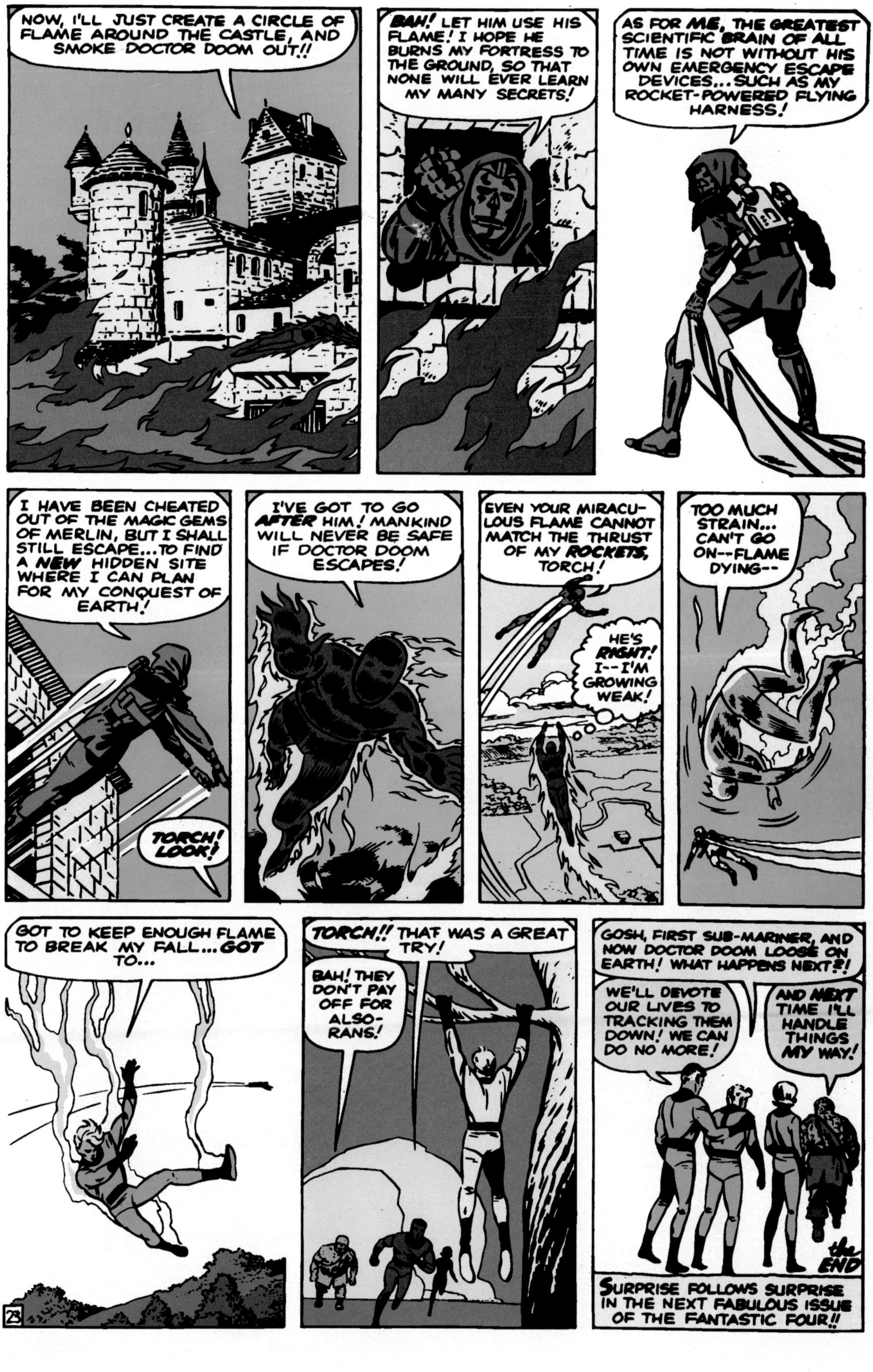

NOW, I'LL JUST CREATE A CIRCLE OF FLAME AROUND THE CASTLE, AND SMOKE DOCTOR DOOM OUT!!
BAH! LET HIM USE HIS FLAME! I HOPE HE BURNS MY FORTRESS TO THE GROUND, SO THAT NONE WILL EVER LEARN MY MANY SECRETS!
AS FOR ME, THE GREATEST SCIENTIFIC BRAIN OF ALL TIME IS NOT WITHOUT HIS OWN EMERGENCY ESCAPE DEVICES...SUCH AS MY ROCKET-POWERED FLYING HARNESS!
I HAVE BEEN CHEATED OUT OF THE MAGIC GEMS OF MERLIN, BUT I SHALL STILL ESCAPE...TO FIND A NEW HIDDEN SITE WHERE I CAN PLAN FOR MY CONQUEST OF EARTH!
TORCH! LOOK!
I'VE GOT TO GO AFTER HIM! MANKIND WILL NEVER BE SAFE IF DOCTOR DOOM ESCAPES!
EVEN YOUR MIRACULOUS FLAME CANNOT MATCH THE THRUST OF MY ROCKETS, TORCH!
HE'S RIGHT! I--I'M GROWING WEAK!
TOO MUCH STRAIN... CAN'T GO ON--FLAME DYING--
GOT TO KEEP ENOUGH FLAME TO BREAK MY FALL...GOT TO...
23
TORCH!! THAT WAS A GREAT TRY!
BAH! THEY DON'T PAY OFF FOR ALSO-RANS!
GOSH, FIRST SUB-MARINER, AND NOW DOCTOR DOOM LOOSE ON EARTH! WHAT HAPPENS NEXT?!
WE'LL DEVOTE OUR LIVES TO TRACKING THEM DOWN! WE CAN DO NO MORE!
AND NEXT TIME I'LL HANDLE THINGS MY WAY!
the END
SURPRISE FOLLOWS SURPRISE IN THE NEXT FABULOUS ISSUE OF THE FANTASTIC FOUR!!

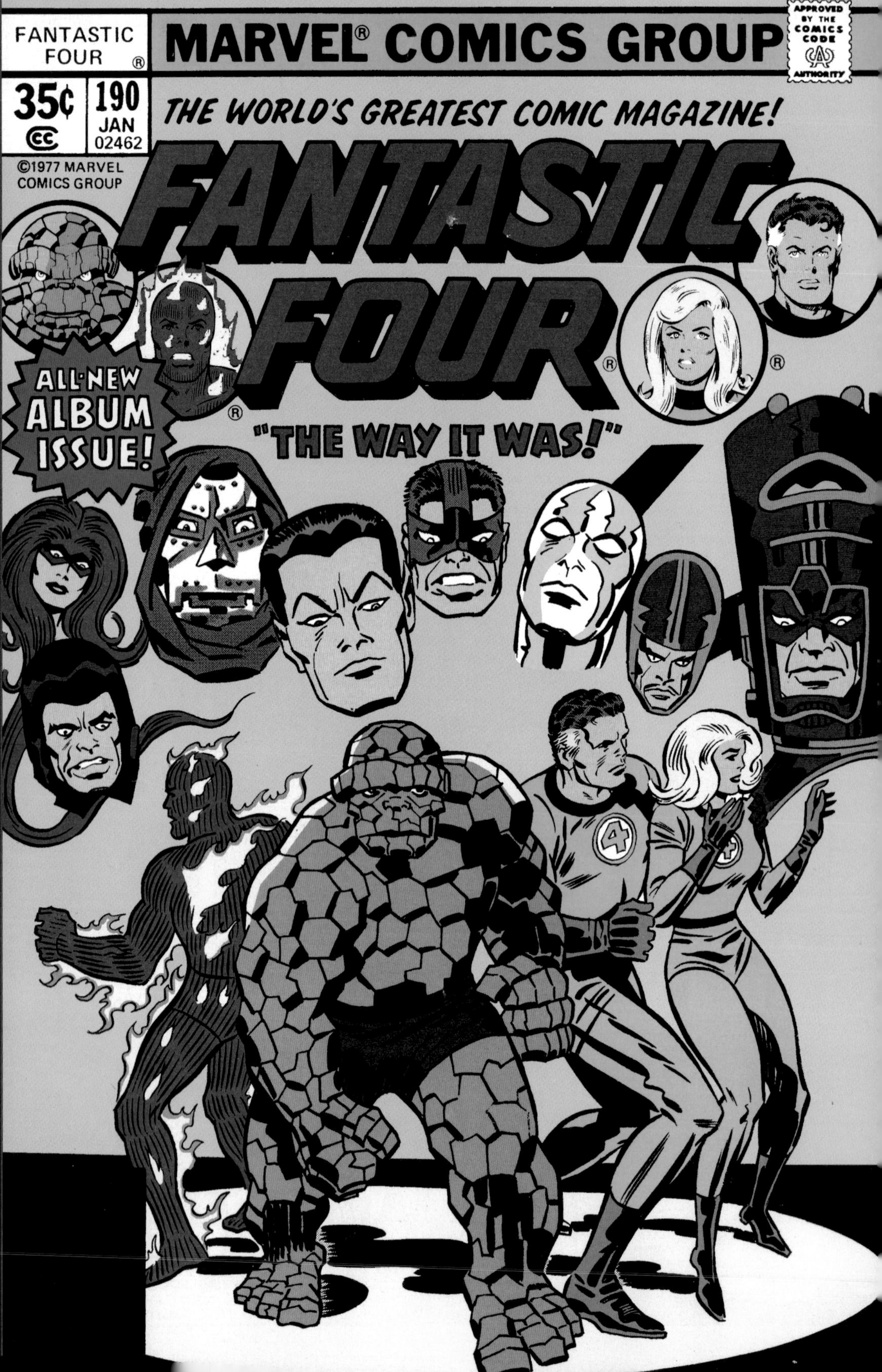
FANTASTIC FOUR ®
MARVEL® COMICS GROUP
APPROVED BY THE COMICS CODE AUTHORITY
35¢
190 JAN 02462
©1977 MARVEL COMICS GROUP
THE WORLD'S GREATEST COMIC MAGAZINE!
FANTASTIC FOUR ®
ALL-NEW ALBUM ISSUE!
"THE WAY IT WAS!"

A brilliant scientist— his best friend— the woman he loves— and her fiery-tempered kid brother! Together, they braved the unknown terrors of outer space, and were changed by cosmic rays into something more than merely human!
MR. FANTASTIC! THE THING! THE INVISIBLE GIRL! THE HUMAN TORCH! Now they are the FANTASTIC FOUR— and the world will never be the same again!

Stan Lee PRESENTS: THE FANTASTIC FOUR!™

MARV WOLFMAN / SAL BUSCEMA / TONY DEZUNIGA / J. COSTANZA, letterer / STAN LEE
WRITER / EDITOR LAYOUTS FINISHES GLYNIS WEIN, colorist INSPIRATION

THE WAY IT WAS

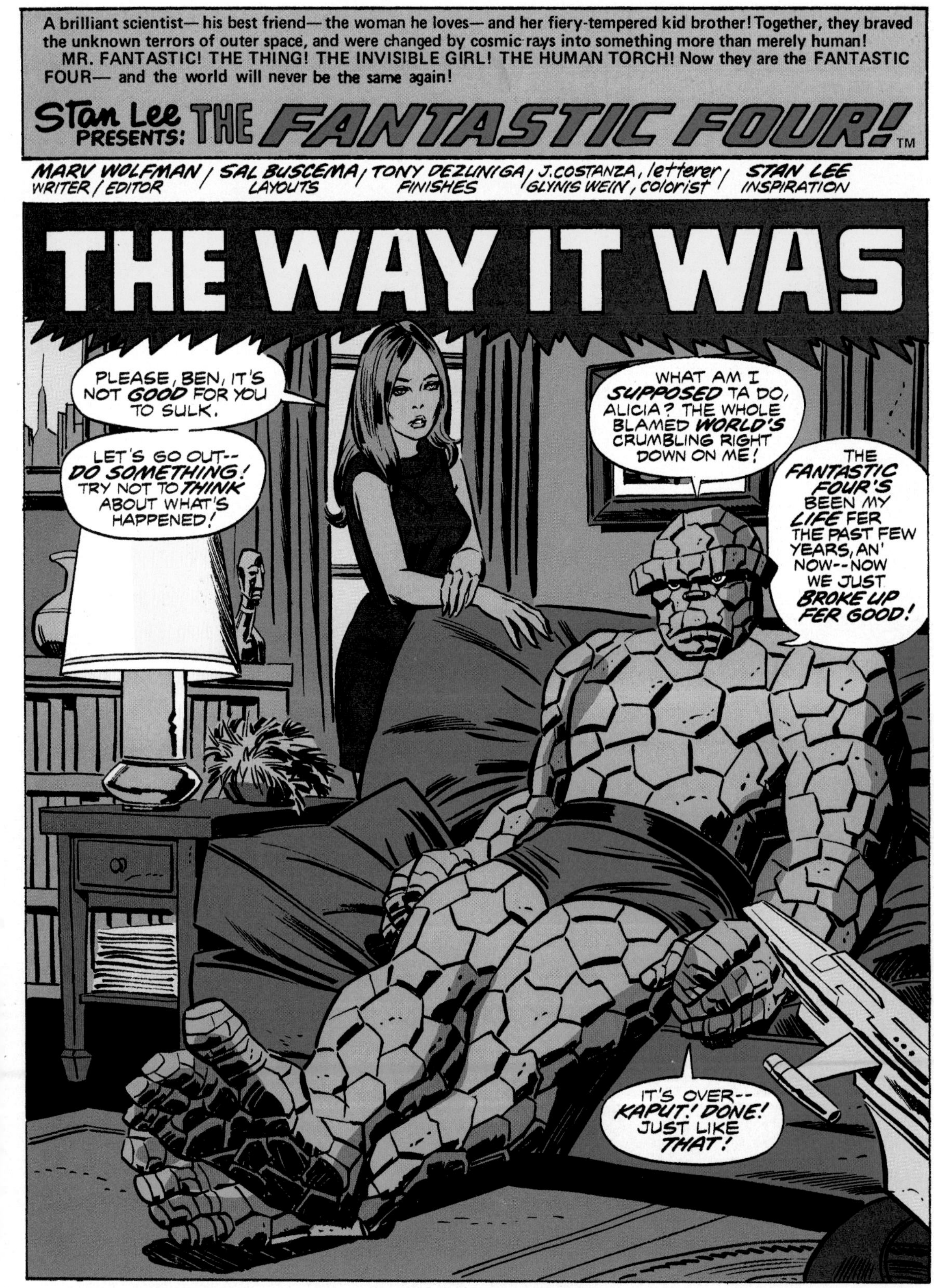
PLEASE, BEN, IT'S NOT GOOD FOR YOU TO SULK.
LET'S GO OUT-- DO SOMETHING! TRY NOT TO THINK ABOUT WHAT'S HAPPENED!
WHAT AM I SUPPOSED TA DO, ALICIA? THE WHOLE BLAMED WORLD'S CRUMBLING RIGHT DOWN ON ME!
THE FANTASTIC FOUR'S BEEN MY LIFE FER THE PAST FEW YEARS, AN' NOW--NOW WE JUST BROKE UP FER GOOD!
IT'S OVER-- KAPUT! DONE! JUST LIKE THAT!

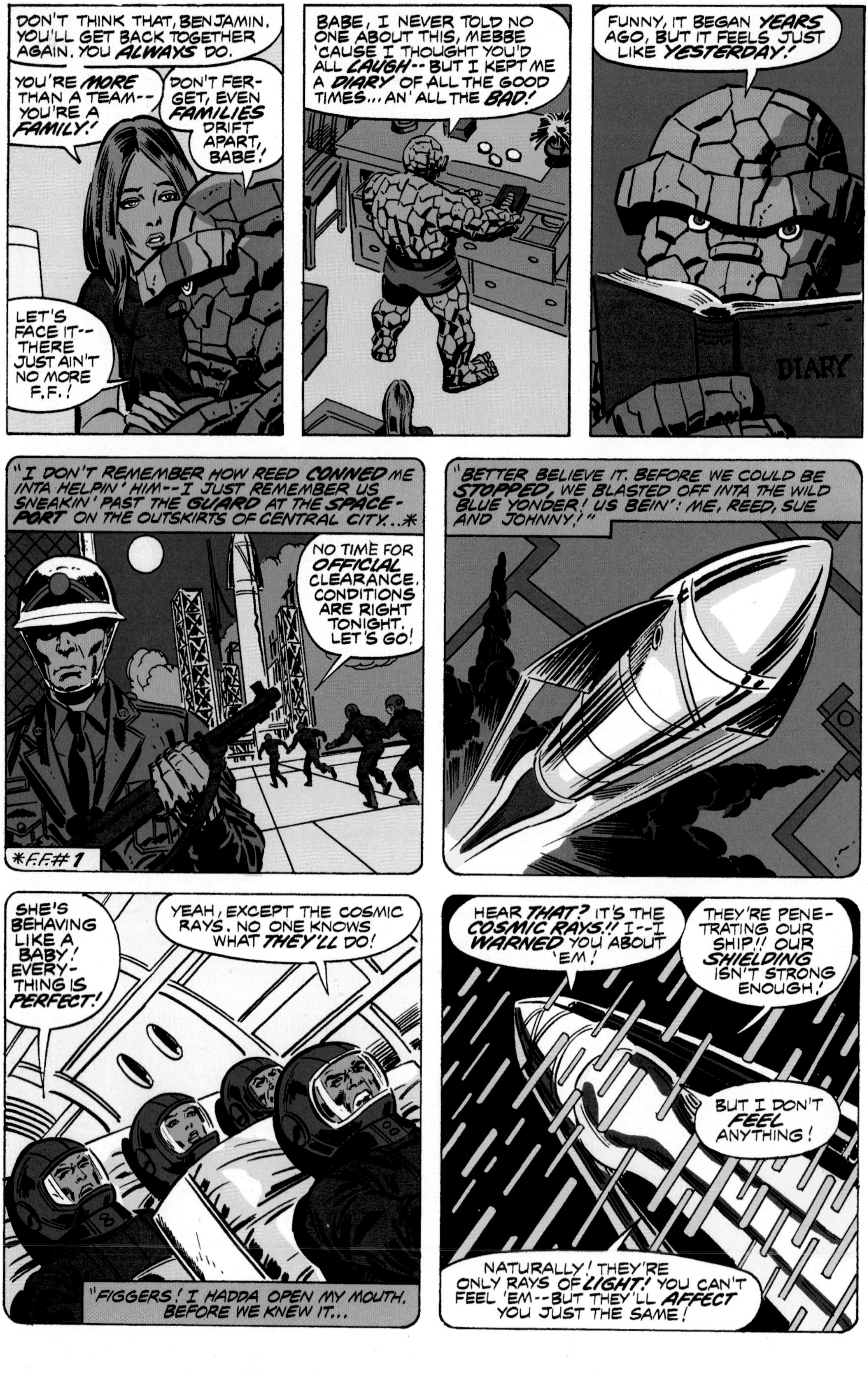
DON'T THINK THAT, BENJAMIN. YOU'LL GET BACK TOGETHER AGAIN. YOU ALWAYS DO.
YOU'RE MORE THAN A TEAM-- YOU'RE A FAMILY!
DON'T FER-GET, EVEN FAMILIES DRIFT APART, BABE!
LET'S FACE IT-- THERE JUST AIN'T NO MORE F.F.!
BABE, I NEVER TOLD NO ONE ABOUT THIS, MEBBE 'CAUSE I THOUGHT YOU'D ALL LAUGH-- BUT I KEPT ME A DIARY OF ALL THE GOOD TIMES... AN' ALL THE BAD!
FUNNY, IT BEGAN YEARS AGO, BUT IT FEELS JUST LIKE YESTERDAY!
DIARY
"I DON'T REMEMBER HOW REED CONNED ME INTA HELPIN' HIM-- I JUST REMEMBER US SNEAKIN' PAST THE GUARD AT THE SPACE-PORT ON THE OUTSKIRTS OF CENTRAL CITY...*
NO TIME FOR OFFICIAL CLEARANCE. CONDITIONS ARE RIGHT TONIGHT. LET'S GO!
*F.F.#1
"BETTER BELIEVE IT. BEFORE WE COULD BE STOPPED, WE BLASTED OFF INTA THE WILD BLUE YONDER! US BEIN': ME, REED, SUE AND JOHNNY!"
SHE'S BEHAVING LIKE A BABY! EVERY-THING IS PERFECT!
YEAH, EXCEPT THE COSMIC RAYS. NO ONE KNOWS WHAT THEY'LL DO!
"FIGGERS! I HADDA OPEN MY MOUTH. BEFORE WE KNEW IT...
HEAR THAT? IT'S THE COSMIC RAYS!! I--I WARNED YOU ABOUT 'EM!
THEY'RE PENE-TRATING OUR SHIP!! OUR SHIELDING ISN'T STRONG ENOUGH!
BUT I DON'T FEEL ANYTHING!
NATURALLY! THEY'RE ONLY RAYS OF LIGHT! YOU CAN'T FEEL 'EM--BUT THEY'LL AFFECT YOU JUST THE SAME!

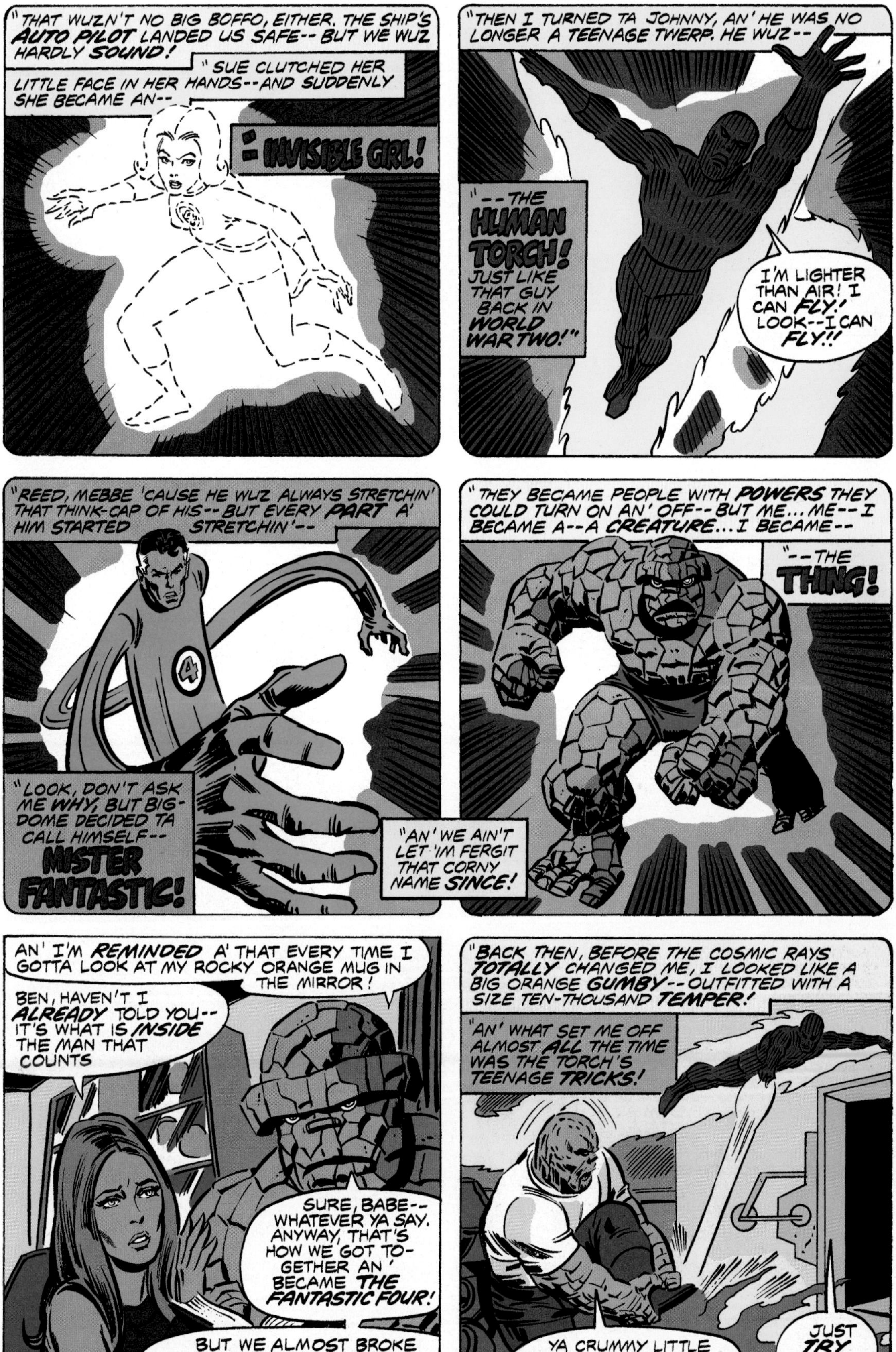
"THAT WUZN'T NO BIG BOFFO, EITHER. THE SHIP'S AUTO PILOT LANDED US SAFE-- BUT WE WUZ HARDLY SOUND!
"SUE CLUTCHED HER LITTLE FACE IN HER HANDS--AND SUDDENLY SHE BECAME AN--
--INVISIBLE GIRL!
"THEN I TURNED TA JOHNNY, AN' HE WAS NO LONGER A TEENAGE TWERP. HE WUZ--
"--THE HUMAN TORCH! JUST LIKE THAT GUY BACK IN WORLD WAR TWO!"
I'M LIGHTER THAN AIR! I CAN FLY! LOOK--I CAN FLY!!
"REED, MEBBE 'CAUSE HE WUZ ALWAYS STRETCHIN' THAT THINK-CAP OF HIS--BUT EVERY PART A' HIM STARTED STRETCHIN'--
"LOOK, DON'T ASK ME WHY, BUT BIG-DOME DECIDED TA CALL HIMSELF-- MISTER FANTASTIC!
"AN' WE AIN'T LET 'IM FERGIT THAT CORNY NAME SINCE!
"THEY BECAME PEOPLE WITH POWERS THEY COULD TURN ON AN' OFF--BUT ME... ME--I BECAME A--A CREATURE...I BECAME--
"--THE THING!
AN' I'M REMINDED A' THAT EVERY TIME I GOTTA LOOK AT MY ROCKY ORANGE MUG IN THE MIRROR!
BEN, HAVEN'T I ALREADY TOLD YOU-- IT'S WHAT IS INSIDE THE MAN THAT COUNTS
SURE, BABE-- WHATEVER YA SAY. ANYWAY, THAT'S HOW WE GOT TO-GETHER AN' BECAME THE FANTASTIC FOUR!
BUT WE ALMOST BROKE UP AT THE SAME TIME... JUST A LITTLE WHILE LATER!
"BACK THEN, BEFORE THE COSMIC RAYS TOTALLY CHANGED ME, I LOOKED LIKE A BIG ORANGE GUMBY--OUTFITTED WITH A SIZE TEN-THOUSAND TEMPER!
"AN' WHAT SET ME OFF ALMOST ALL THE TIME WAS THE TORCH'S TEENAGE TRICKS!
YA CRUMMY LITTLE PUNK, I'LL MASSACRE YA FER THAT!
JUST TRY IT, BIG MAN!

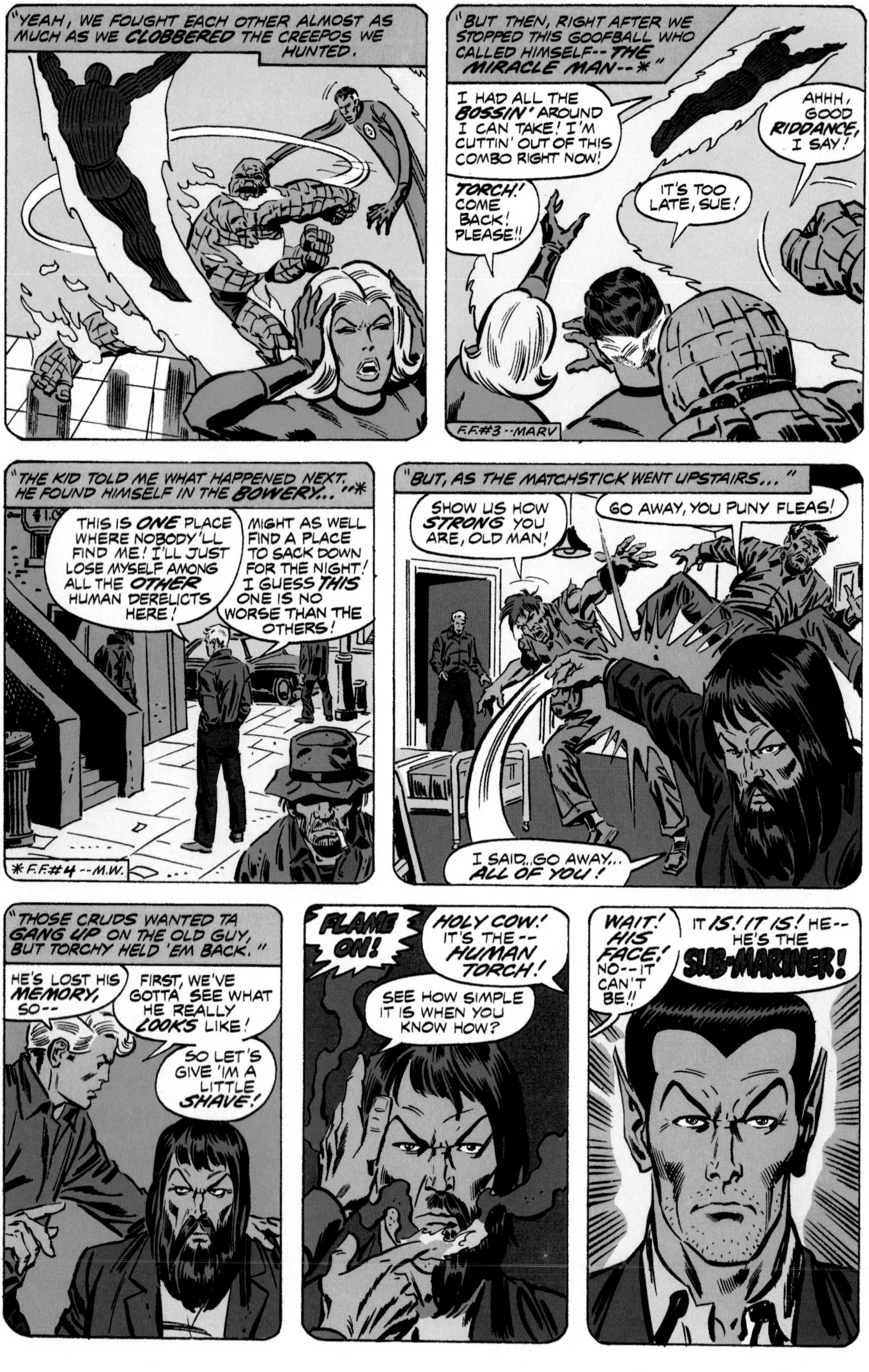

"YEAH, WE FOUGHT EACH OTHER ALMOST AS MUCH AS WE CLOBBERED THE CREEPOS WE HUNTED.
"BUT THEN, RIGHT AFTER WE STOPPED THIS GOOFBALL WHO CALLED HIMSELF--THE MIRACLE MAN--*"
I HAD ALL THE BOSSIN' AROUND I CAN TAKE! I'M CUTTIN' OUT OF THIS COMBO RIGHT NOW!
AHHH, GOOD RIDDANCE, I SAY!
TORCH! COME BACK! PLEASE!!
IT'S TOO LATE, SUE!
F.F.#3--MARV
"THE KID TOLD ME WHAT HAPPENED NEXT. HE FOUND HIMSELF IN THE BOWERY..."*
THIS IS ONE PLACE WHERE NOBODY'LL FIND ME! I'LL JUST LOSE MYSELF AMONG ALL THE OTHER HUMAN DERELICTS HERE!
MIGHT AS WELL FIND A PLACE TO SACK DOWN FOR THE NIGHT! I GUESS THIS ONE IS NO WORSE THAN THE OTHERS!
*F.F.#4--M.W.
"BUT, AS THE MATCHSTICK WENT UPSTAIRS..."
SHOW US HOW STRONG YOU ARE, OLD MAN!
GO AWAY, YOU PUNY FLEAS!
I SAID...GO AWAY... ALL OF YOU!
"THOSE CRUDS WANTED TA GANG UP ON THE OLD GUY, BUT TORCHY HELD 'EM BACK."
HE'S LOST HIS MEMORY, SO--
FIRST, WE'VE GOTTA SEE WHAT HE REALLY LOOKS LIKE!
SO LET'S GIVE 'IM A LITTLE SHAVE!
FLAME ON!
HOLY COW! IT'S THE--HUMAN TORCH!
SEE HOW SIMPLE IT IS WHEN YOU KNOW HOW?
WAIT! HIS FACE! NO--IT CAN'T BE!!
IT IS! IT IS! HE--HE'S THE SUB-MARINER!

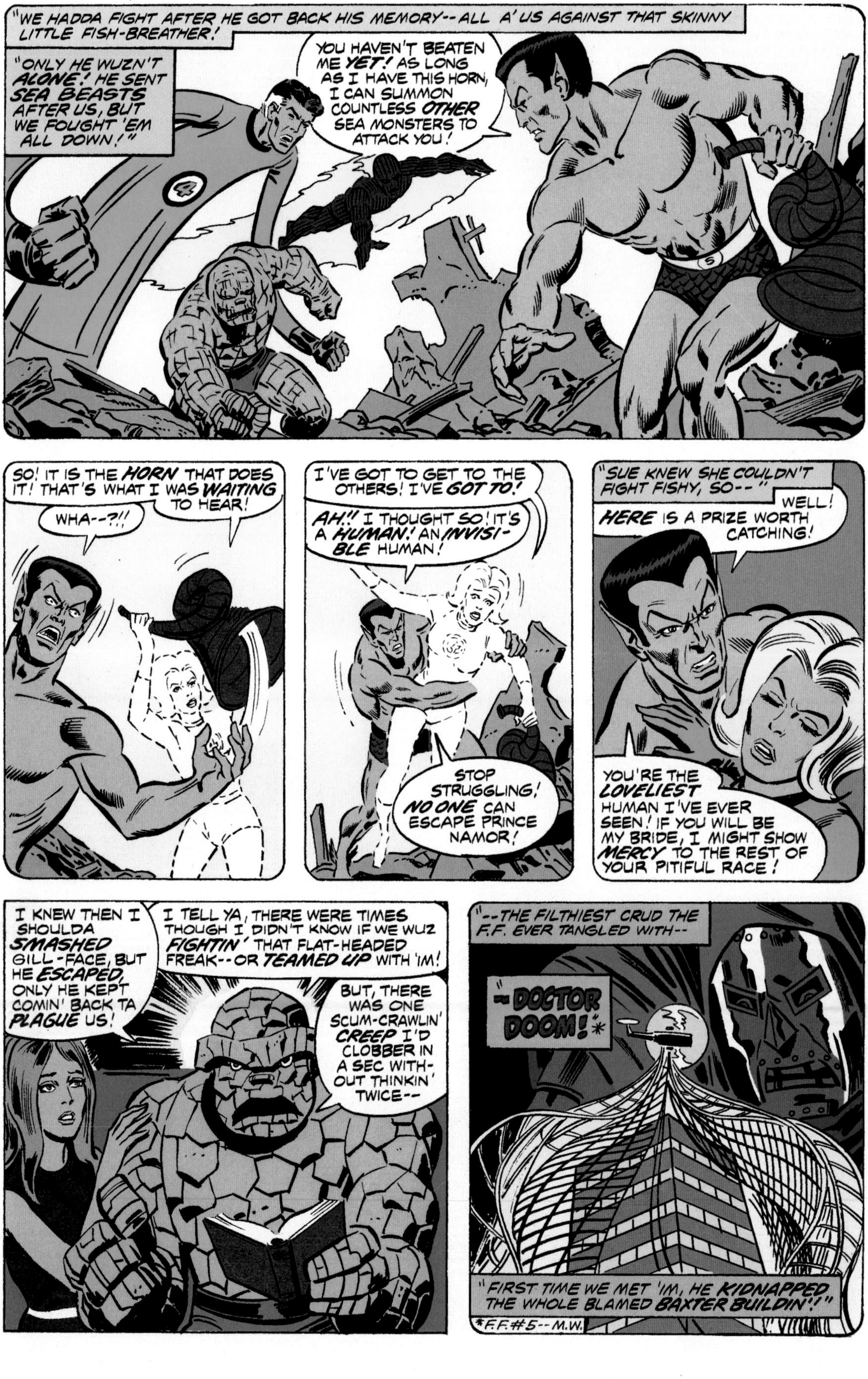
"WE HADDA FIGHT AFTER HE GOT BACK HIS MEMORY--ALL A' US AGAINST THAT SKINNY LITTLE FISH-BREATHER!
"ONLY HE WUZN'T ALONE! HE SENT SEA BEASTS AFTER US, BUT WE FOUGHT 'EM ALL DOWN!"
YOU HAVEN'T BEATEN ME YET! AS LONG AS I HAVE THIS HORN, I CAN SUMMON COUNTLESS OTHER SEA MONSTERS TO ATTACK YOU!
SO! IT IS THE HORN THAT DOES IT! THAT'S WHAT I WAS WAITING TO HEAR!
WHA--?!!
I'VE GOT TO GET TO THE OTHERS! I'VE GOT TO!
AH!! I THOUGHT SO! IT'S A HUMAN! AN INVISIBLE HUMAN!
STOP STRUGGLING! NO ONE CAN ESCAPE PRINCE NAMOR!
"SUE KNEW SHE COULDN'T FIGHT FISHY, SO--"
WELL! HERE IS A PRIZE WORTH CATCHING!
YOU'RE THE LOVELIEST HUMAN I'VE EVER SEEN! IF YOU WILL BE MY BRIDE, I MIGHT SHOW MERCY TO THE REST OF YOUR PITIFUL RACE!
I KNEW THEN I SHOULDA SMASHED GILL-FACE, BUT HE ESCAPED, ONLY HE KEPT COMIN' BACK TA PLAGUE US!
I TELL YA, THERE WERE TIMES THOUGH I DIDN'T KNOW IF WE WUZ FIGHTIN' THAT FLAT-HEADED FREAK--OR TEAMED UP WITH 'IM!
BUT, THERE WAS ONE SCUM-CRAWLIN' CREEP I'D CLOBBER IN A SEC WITHOUT THINKIN' TWICE--
"--THE FILTHIEST CRUD THE F.F. EVER TANGLED WITH--
"--DOCTOR DOOM!"*
"FIRST TIME WE MET 'IM, HE KIDNAPPED THE WHOLE BLAMED BAXTER BUILDIN'!"
*F.F. #5--M.W.

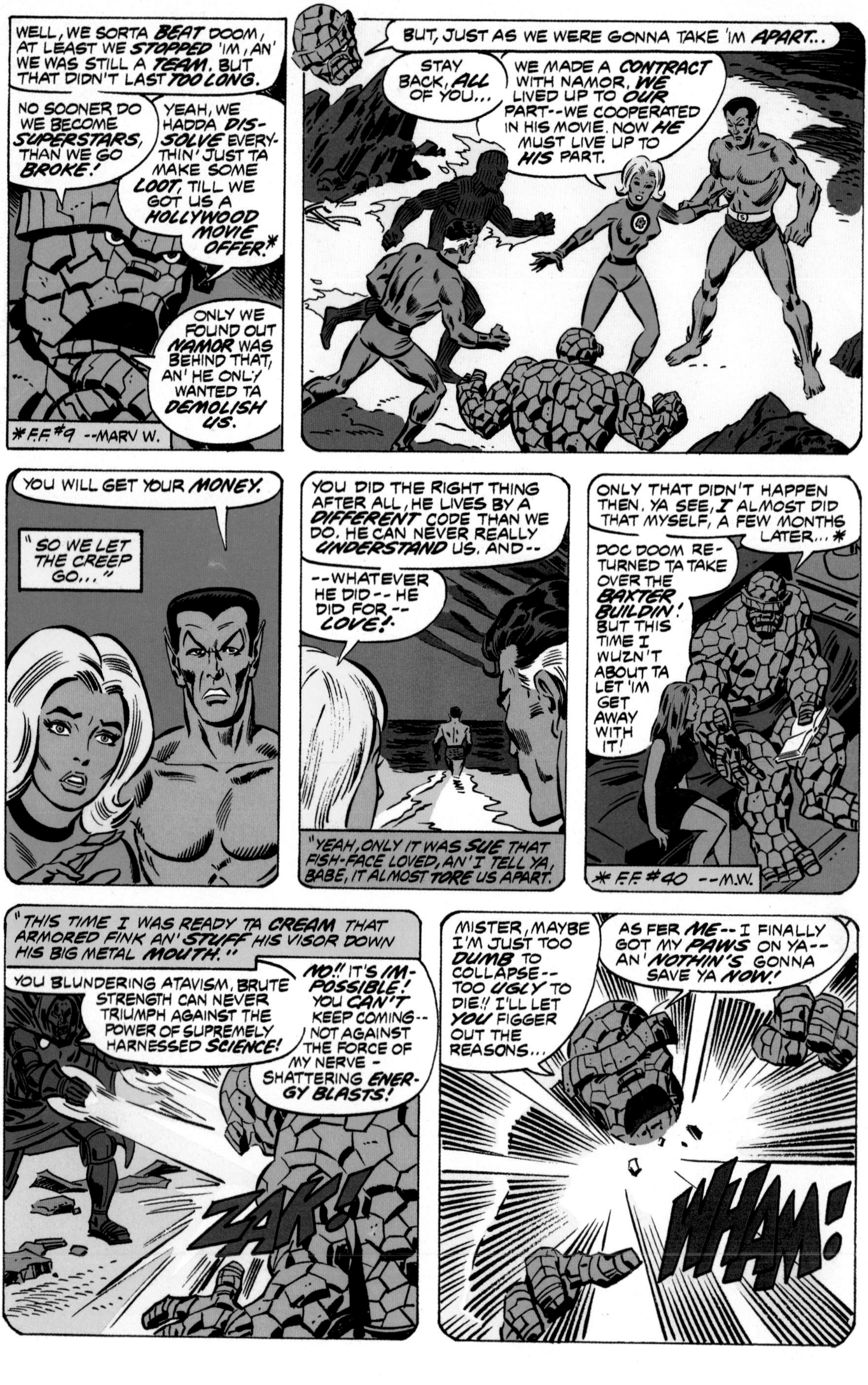

WELL, WE SORTA BEAT DOOM, AT LEAST WE STOPPED 'IM, AN' WE WAS STILL A TEAM. BUT THAT DIDN'T LAST TOO LONG.
NO SOONER DO WE BECOME SUPERSTARS, THAN WE GO BROKE!
YEAH, WE HADDA DIS-SOLVE EVERY-THIN' JUST TA MAKE SOME LOOT, TILL WE GOT US A HOLLYWOOD MOVIE OFFER.*
ONLY WE FOUND OUT NAMOR WAS BEHIND THAT, AN' HE ONLY WANTED TA DEMOLISH US.
*F.F. #9 --MARV W.
BUT, JUST AS WE WERE GONNA TAKE 'IM APART...
STAY BACK, ALL OF YOU...
WE MADE A CONTRACT WITH NAMOR, WE LIVED UP TO OUR PART--WE COOPERATED IN HIS MOVIE. NOW HE MUST LIVE UP TO HIS PART.
YOU WILL GET YOUR MONEY.
"SO WE LET THE CREEP GO..."
YOU DID THE RIGHT THING AFTER ALL, HE LIVES BY A DIFFERENT CODE THAN WE DO. HE CAN NEVER REALLY UNDERSTAND US. AND--
--WHATEVER HE DID--HE DID FOR--LOVE!
"YEAH, ONLY IT WAS SUE THAT FISH-FACE LOVED, AN' I TELL YA, BABE, IT ALMOST TORE US APART.
ONLY THAT DIDN'T HAPPEN THEN, YA SEE, I ALMOST DID THAT MYSELF, A FEW MONTHS LATER...*
DOC DOOM RE-TURNED TA TAKE OVER THE BAXTER BUILDIN'! BUT THIS TIME I WUZN'T ABOUT TA LET 'IM GET AWAY WITH IT!
*F.F. #40 --M.W.
"THIS TIME I WAS READY TA CREAM THAT ARMORED FINK AN' STUFF HIS VISOR DOWN HIS BIG METAL MOUTH."
YOU BLUNDERING ATAVISM, BRUTE STRENGTH CAN NEVER TRIUMPH AGAINST THE POWER OF SUPREMELY HARNESSED SCIENCE!
NO!! IT'S IM-POSSIBLE! YOU CAN'T KEEP COMING--NOT AGAINST THE FORCE OF MY NERVE-SHATTERING ENER-GY BLASTS!
ZAK!!
MISTER, MAYBE I'M JUST TOO DUMB TO COLLAPSE--TOO UGLY TO DIE!! I'LL LET YOU FIGGER OUT THE REASONS...
AS FER ME--I FINALLY GOT MY PAWS ON YA--AN' NOTHIN'S GONNA SAVE YA NOW!
WHAM!

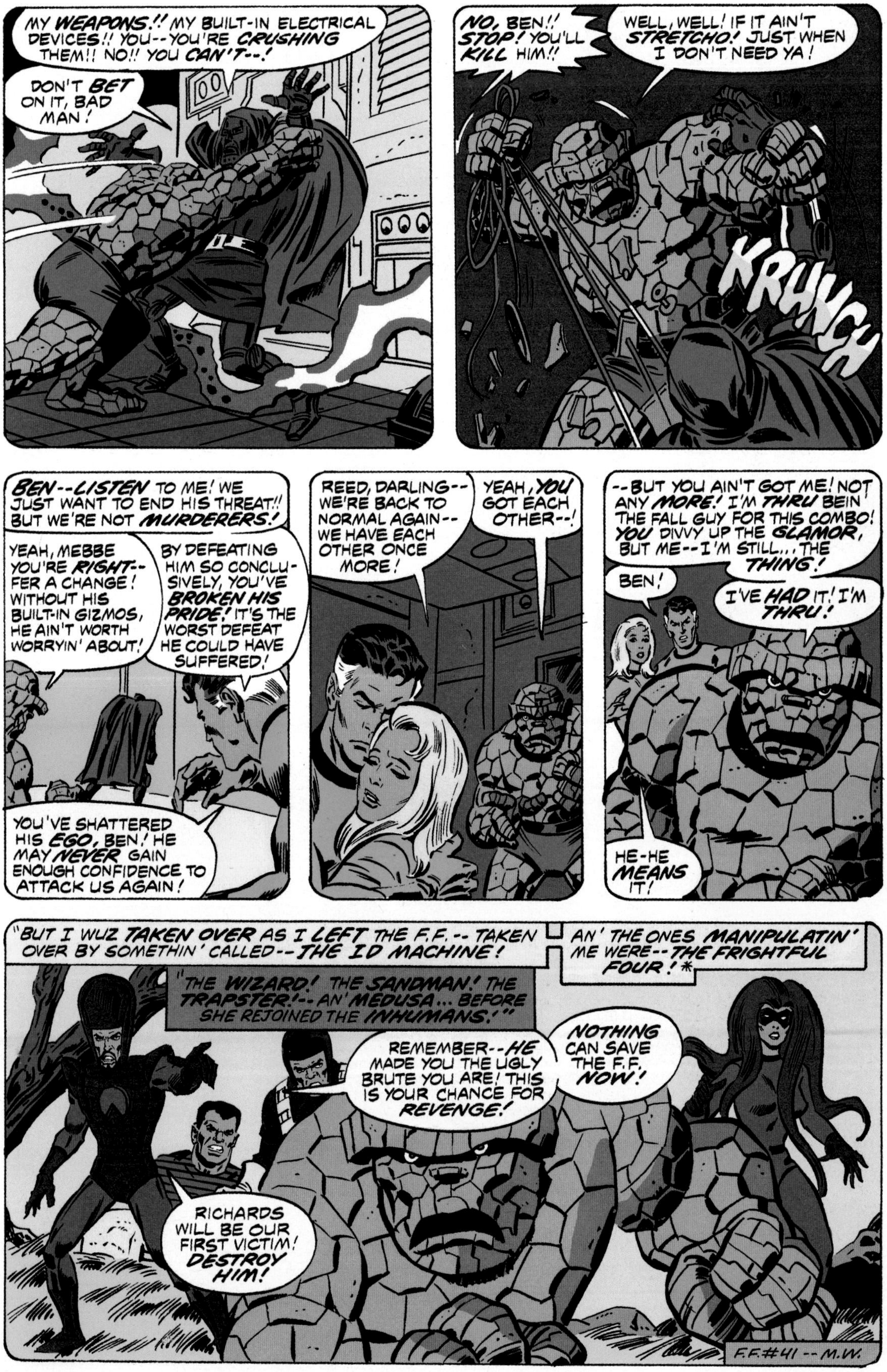
MY WEAPONS!! MY BUILT-IN ELECTRICAL DEVICES!! YOU--YOU'RE CRUSHING THEM!! NO!! YOU CAN'T--!
DON'T BET ON IT, BAD MAN!
NO, BEN!! STOP! YOU'LL KILL HIM!!
WELL, WELL! IF IT AIN'T STRETCHO! JUST WHEN I DON'T NEED YA!
KRUNCH
BEN--LISTEN TO ME! WE JUST WANT TO END HIS THREAT!! BUT WE'RE NOT MURDERERS!
YEAH, MEBBE YOU'RE RIGHT--FER A CHANGE! WITHOUT HIS BUILT-IN GIZMOS, HE AIN'T WORTH WORRYIN' ABOUT!
BY DEFEATING HIM SO CONCLUSIVELY, YOU'VE BROKEN HIS PRIDE! IT'S THE WORST DEFEAT HE COULD HAVE SUFFERED!
YOU'VE SHATTERED HIS EGO, BEN! HE MAY NEVER GAIN ENOUGH CONFIDENCE TO ATTACK US AGAIN!
REED, DARLING--WE'RE BACK TO NORMAL AGAIN--WE HAVE EACH OTHER ONCE MORE!
YEAH, YOU GOT EACH OTHER--!
--BUT YOU AIN'T GOT ME! NOT ANY MORE! I'M THRU BEIN' THE FALL GUY FOR THIS COMBO! YOU DIVVY UP THE GLAMOR, BUT ME--I'M STILL... THE THING!
BEN!
I'VE HAD IT! I'M THRU!
HE-HE MEANS IT!
"BUT I WUZ TAKEN OVER AS I LEFT THE F.F.--TAKEN OVER BY SOMETHIN' CALLED--THE ID MACHINE!
AN' THE ONES MANIPULATIN' ME WERE--THE FRIGHTFUL FOUR!*
"THE WIZARD! THE SANDMAN! THE TRAPSTER!--AN' MEDUSA... BEFORE SHE REJOINED THE INHUMANS!"
REMEMBER--HE MADE YOU THE UGLY BRUTE YOU ARE! THIS IS YOUR CHANCE FOR REVENGE!
NOTHING CAN SAVE THE F.F. NOW!
RICHARDS WILL BE OUR FIRST VICTIM! DESTROY HIM!
F.F.#41--M.W.

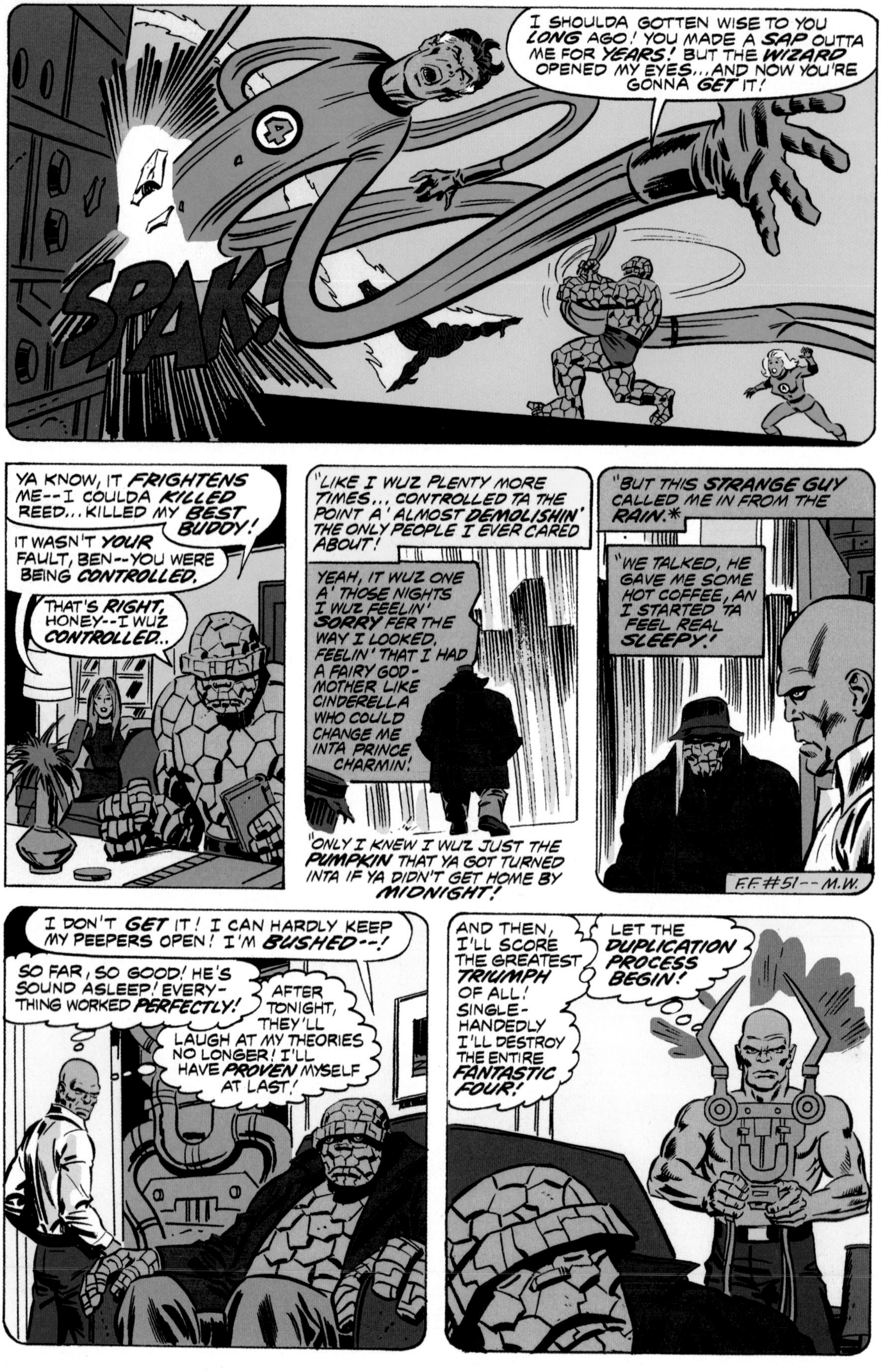
I SHOULDA GOTTEN WISE TO YOU LONG AGO! YOU MADE A SAP OUTTA ME FOR YEARS! BUT THE WIZARD OPENED MY EYES...AND NOW YOU'RE GONNA GET IT!
SPAK!
YA KNOW, IT FRIGHTENS ME--I COULDA KILLED REED... KILLED MY BEST BUDDY!
IT WASN'T YOUR FAULT, BEN--YOU WERE BEING CONTROLLED.
THAT'S RIGHT, HONEY--I WUZ CONTROLLED...
"LIKE I WUZ PLENTY MORE TIMES... CONTROLLED TA THE POINT A' ALMOST DEMOLISHIN' THE ONLY PEOPLE I EVER CARED ABOUT!
YEAH, IT WUZ ONE A' THOSE NIGHTS I WUZ FEELIN' SORRY FER THE WAY I LOOKED, FEELIN' THAT I HAD A FAIRY GOD-MOTHER LIKE CINDERELLA WHO COULD CHANGE ME INTA PRINCE CHARMIN'.
"ONLY I KNEW I WUZ JUST THE PUMPKIN THAT YA GOT TURNED INTA IF YA DIDN'T GET HOME BY MIDNIGHT!
"BUT THIS STRANGE GUY CALLED ME IN FROM THE RAIN.*
"WE TALKED, HE GAVE ME SOME HOT COFFEE, AN I STARTED TA FEEL REAL SLEEPY!
F.F. #51--M.W.
I DON'T GET IT! I CAN HARDLY KEEP MY PEEPERS OPEN! I'M BUSHED--!
SO FAR, SO GOOD! HE'S SOUND ASLEEP! EVERY-THING WORKED PERFECTLY!
AFTER TONIGHT, THEY'LL LAUGH AT MY THEORIES NO LONGER! I'LL HAVE PROVEN MYSELF AT LAST!
AND THEN, I'LL SCORE THE GREATEST TRIUMPH OF ALL! SINGLE-HANDEDLY I'LL DESTROY THE ENTIRE FANTASTIC FOUR!
LET THE DUPLICATION PROCESS BEGIN!

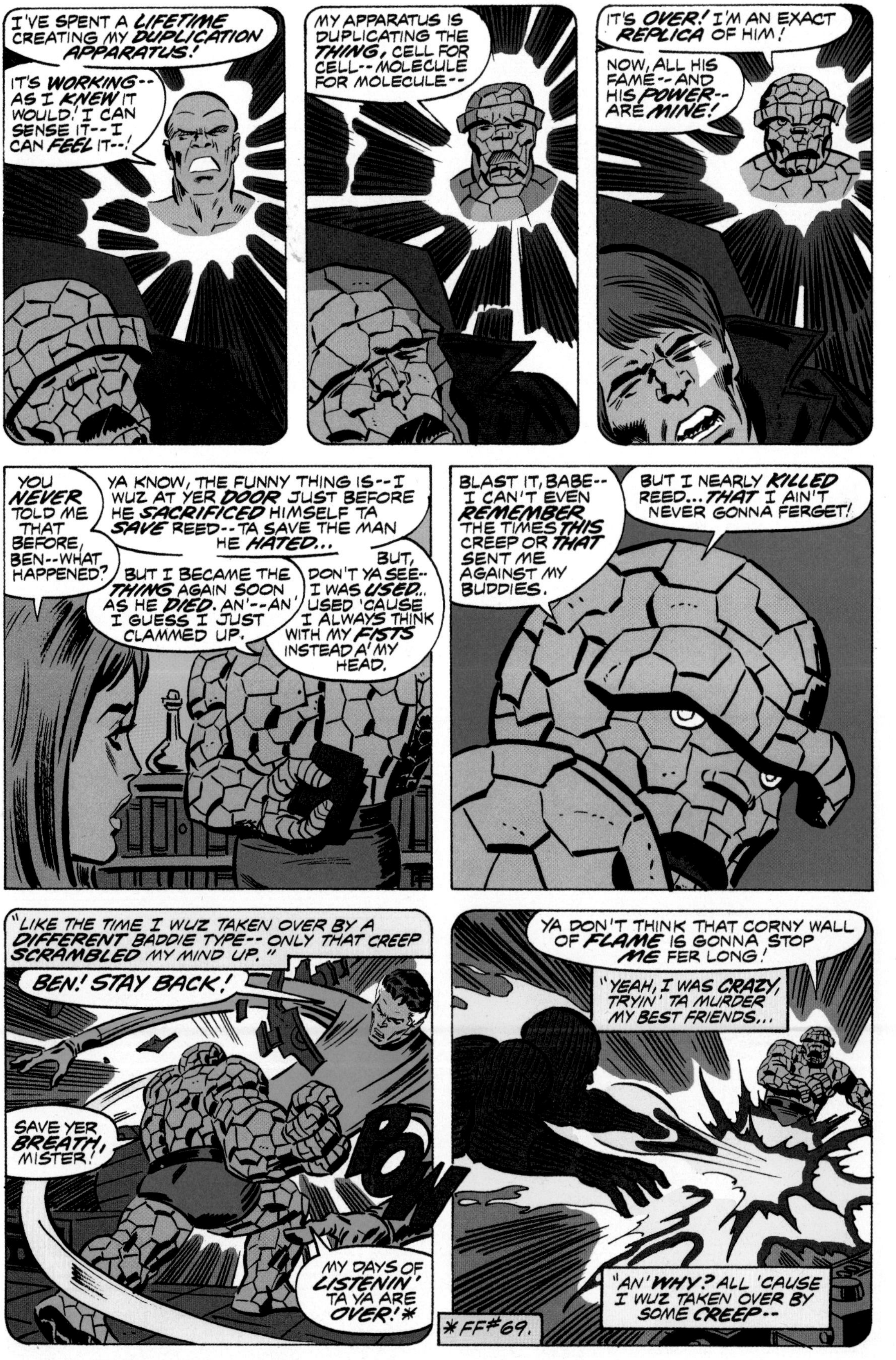
I'VE SPENT A LIFETIME CREATING MY DUPLICATION APPARATUS!
IT'S WORKING-- AS I KNEW IT WOULD! I CAN SENSE IT-- I CAN FEEL IT--!
MY APPARATUS IS DUPLICATING THE THING, CELL FOR CELL-- MOLECULE FOR MOLECULE--
IT'S OVER! I'M AN EXACT REPLICA OF HIM!
NOW, ALL HIS FAME-- AND HIS POWER-- ARE MINE!
YOU NEVER TOLD ME THAT BEFORE, BEN--WHAT HAPPENED?
YA KNOW, THE FUNNY THING IS--I WUZ AT YER DOOR JUST BEFORE HE SACRIFICED HIMSELF TA SAVE REED--TA SAVE THE MAN HE HATED...
BUT I BECAME THE THING AGAIN SOON AS HE DIED. AN'--AN' I GUESS I JUST CLAMMED UP.
BUT, DON'T YA SEE-- I WAS USED... USED 'CAUSE I ALWAYS THINK WITH MY FISTS INSTEAD A' MY HEAD.
BLAST IT, BABE-- I CAN'T EVEN REMEMBER THE TIMES THIS CREEP OR THAT SENT ME AGAINST MY BUDDIES.
BUT I NEARLY KILLED REED... THAT I AIN'T NEVER GONNA FERGET!
"LIKE THE TIME I WUZ TAKEN OVER BY A DIFFERENT BADDIE TYPE-- ONLY THAT CREEP SCRAMBLED MY MIND UP."
BEN! STAY BACK!
SAVE YER BREATH, MISTER!
BOW
MY DAYS OF LISTENIN' TA YA ARE OVER!*
*FF#69.
YA DON'T THINK THAT CORNY WALL OF FLAME IS GONNA STOP ME FER LONG!
"YEAH, I WAS CRAZY, TRYIN' TA MURDER MY BEST FRIENDS...
"AN' WHY? ALL 'CAUSE I WUZ TAKEN OVER BY SOME CREEP--

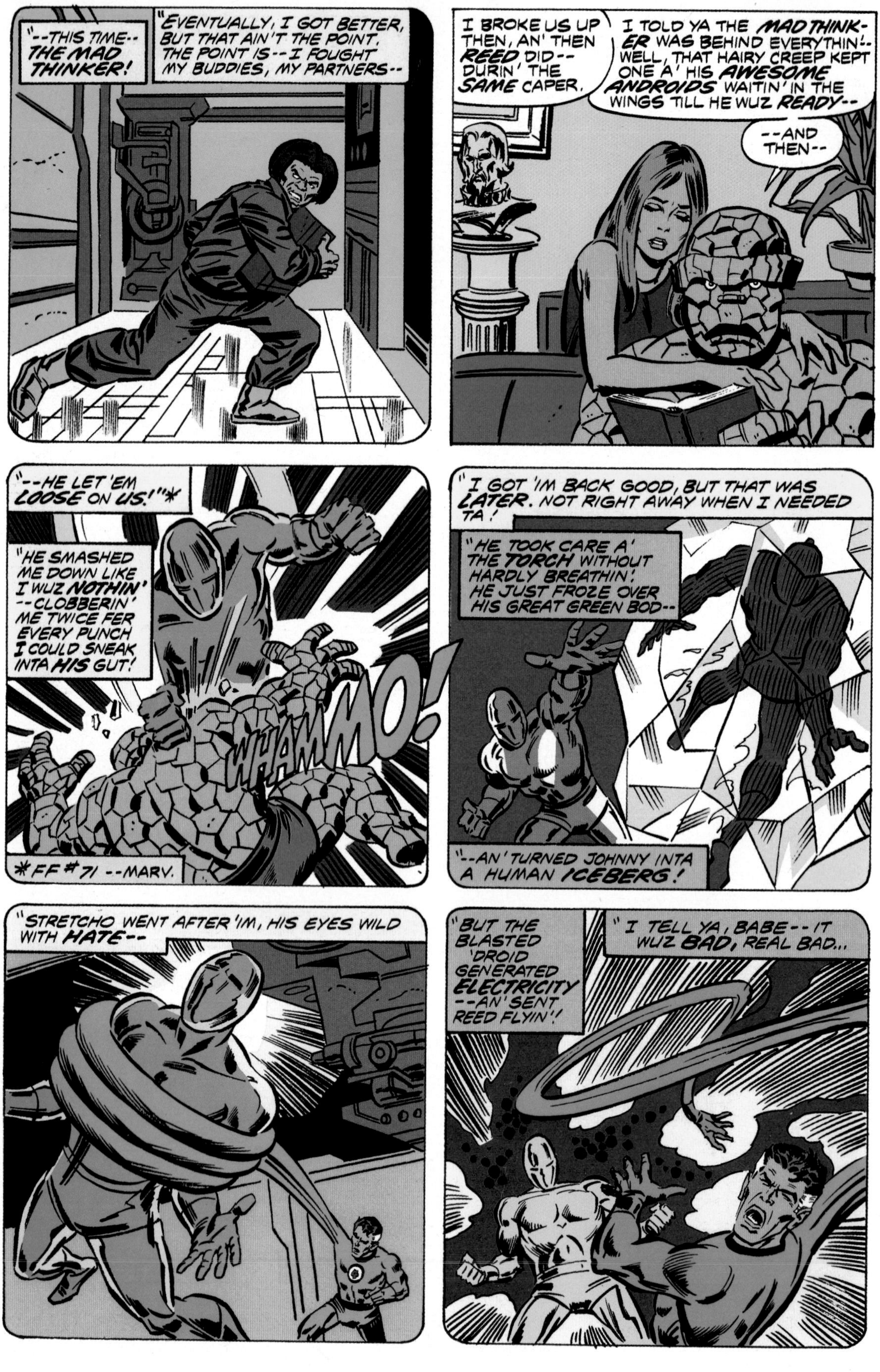
"--THIS TIME--
THE MAD THINKER!
"EVENTUALLY, I GOT BETTER, BUT THAT AIN'T THE POINT. THE POINT IS--I FOUGHT MY BUDDIES, MY PARTNERS--
I BROKE US UP THEN, AN' THEN REED DID--DURIN' THE SAME CAPER.
I TOLD YA THE MAD THINK-ER WAS BEHIND EVERYTHIN'--WELL, THAT HAIRY CREEP KEPT ONE A' HIS AWESOME ANDROIDS WAITIN' IN THE WINGS TILL HE WUZ READY--
--AND THEN--
"--HE LET 'EM LOOSE ON US!"*
"HE SMASHED ME DOWN LIKE I WUZ NOTHIN' --CLOBBERIN' ME TWICE FER EVERY PUNCH I COULD SNEAK INTA HIS GUT!
WHAMMO!
*FF #71 --MARV.
"I GOT 'IM BACK GOOD, BUT THAT WAS LATER. NOT RIGHT AWAY WHEN I NEEDED TA!
"HE TOOK CARE A' THE TORCH WITHOUT HARDLY BREATHIN'! HE JUST FROZE OVER HIS GREAT GREEN BOD--
"--AN' TURNED JOHNNY INTA A HUMAN ICEBERG!
"STRETCHO WENT AFTER 'IM, HIS EYES WILD WITH HATE--
"BUT THE BLASTED 'DROID GENERATED ELECTRICITY --AN' SENT REED FLYIN'!
"I TELL YA, BABE--IT WUZ BAD, REAL BAD...

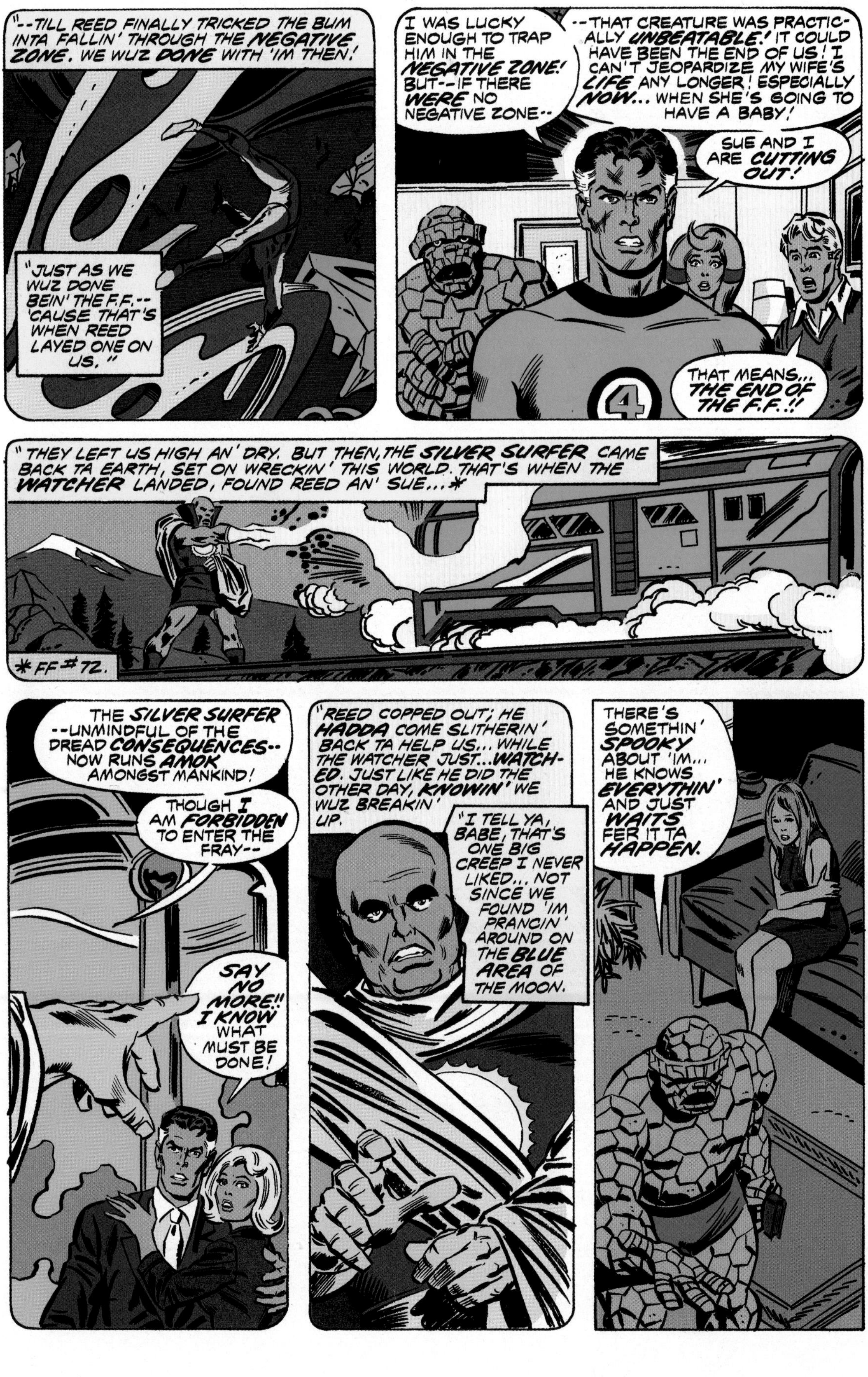
"--TILL REED FINALLY TRICKED THE BUM INTA FALLIN' THROUGH THE NEGATIVE ZONE. WE WUZ DONE WITH 'IM THEN!
"JUST AS WE WUZ DONE BEIN' THE F.F.--'CAUSE THAT'S WHEN REED LAYED ONE ON US."
I WAS LUCKY ENOUGH TO TRAP HIM IN THE NEGATIVE ZONE! BUT--IF THERE WERE NO NEGATIVE ZONE--
--THAT CREATURE WAS PRACTICALLY UNBEATABLE! IT COULD HAVE BEEN THE END OF US! I CAN'T JEOPARDIZE MY WIFE'S LIFE ANY LONGER! ESPECIALLY NOW... WHEN SHE'S GOING TO HAVE A BABY!
SUE AND I ARE CUTTING OUT!
THAT MEANS... THE END OF THE F.F.!!
"THEY LEFT US HIGH AN' DRY. BUT THEN, THE SILVER SURFER CAME BACK TA EARTH, SET ON WRECKIN' THIS WORLD. THAT'S WHEN THE WATCHER LANDED, FOUND REED AN' SUE...*
*FF #72.
THE SILVER SURFER --UNMINDFUL OF THE DREAD CONSEQUENCES-- NOW RUNS AMOK AMONGST MANKIND!
THOUGH I AM FORBIDDEN TO ENTER THE FRAY--
SAY NO MORE!! I KNOW WHAT MUST BE DONE!
"REED COPPED OUT; HE HADDA COME SLITHERIN' BACK TA HELP US... WHILE THE WATCHER JUST...WATCHED. JUST LIKE HE DID THE OTHER DAY, KNOWIN' WE WUZ BREAKIN' UP.
"I TELL YA, BABE, THAT'S ONE BIG CREEP I NEVER LIKED... NOT SINCE WE FOUND 'IM PRANCIN' AROUND ON THE BLUE AREA OF THE MOON.
THERE'S SOMETHIN' SPOOKY ABOUT 'IM... HE KNOWS EVERYTHIN' AND JUST WAITS FER IT TA HAPPEN.

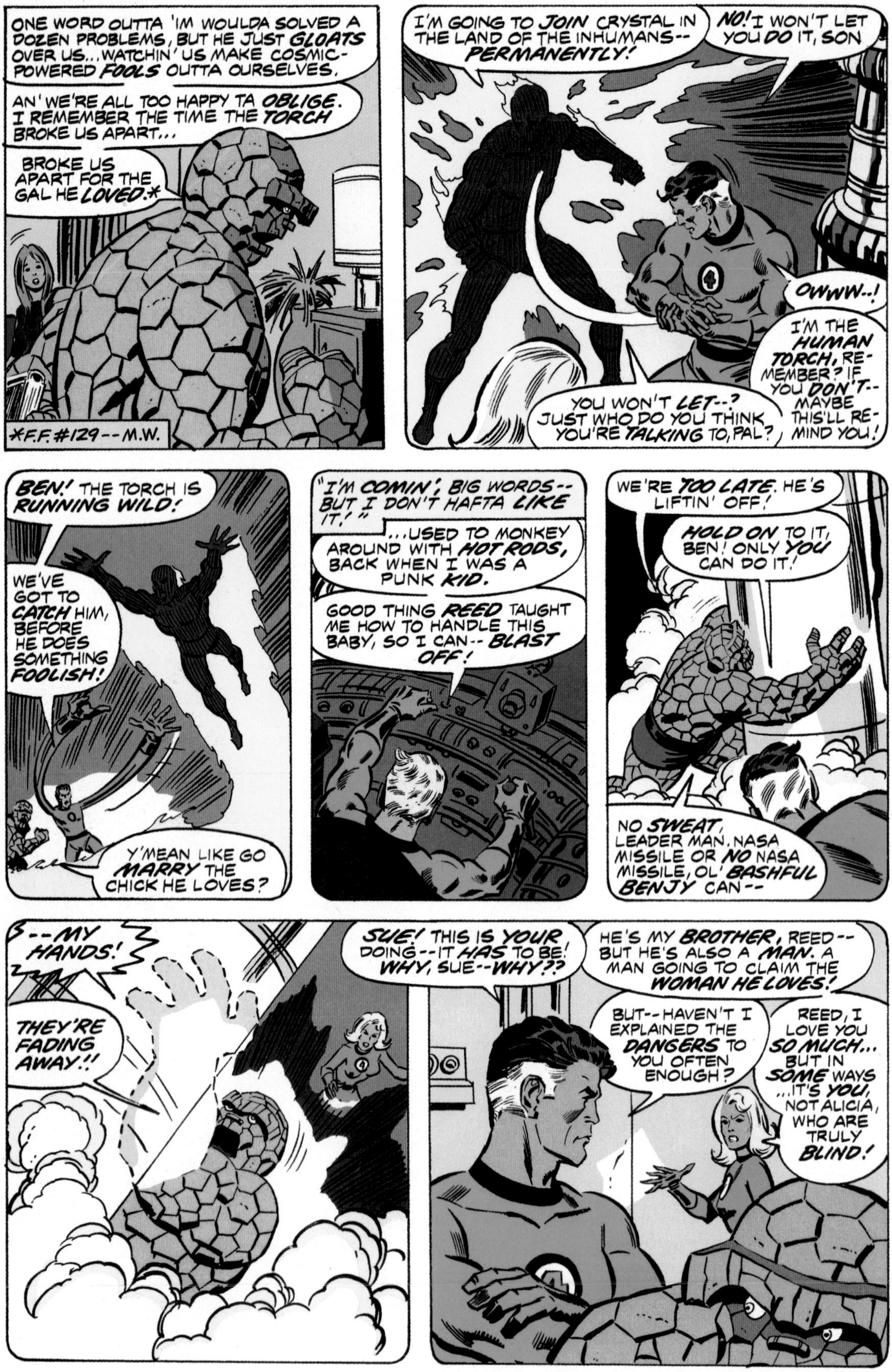
ONE WORD OUTTA 'IM WOULDA SOLVED A DOZEN PROBLEMS, BUT HE JUST GLOATS OVER US... WATCHIN' US MAKE COSMIC-POWERED FOOLS OUTTA OURSELVES.
AN' WE'RE ALL TOO HAPPY TA OBLIGE. I REMEMBER THE TIME THE TORCH BROKE US APART...
BROKE US APART FOR THE GAL HE LOVED.*
*F.F. #129--M.W.
I'M GOING TO JOIN CRYSTAL IN THE LAND OF THE INHUMANS-- PERMANENTLY!
NO! I WON'T LET YOU DO IT, SON
OWWW--!
I'M THE HUMAN TORCH, RE-MEMBER? IF YOU DON'T-- MAYBE THIS'LL RE-MIND YOU!
YOU WON'T LET--? JUST WHO DO YOU THINK YOU'RE TALKING TO, PAL?
BEN! THE TORCH IS RUNNING WILD!
WE'VE GOT TO CATCH HIM, BEFORE HE DOES SOMETHING FOOLISH!
Y'MEAN LIKE GO MARRY THE CHICK HE LOVES?
"I'M COMIN', BIG WORDS-- BUT I DON'T HAFTA LIKE IT!"
...USED TO MONKEY AROUND WITH HOT RODS, BACK WHEN I WAS A PUNK KID.
GOOD THING REED TAUGHT ME HOW TO HANDLE THIS BABY, SO I CAN-- BLAST OFF!
WE'RE TOO LATE. HE'S LIFTIN' OFF!
HOLD ON TO IT, BEN! ONLY YOU CAN DO IT!
NO SWEAT, LEADER MAN. NASA MISSILE OR NO NASA MISSILE, OL' BASHFUL BENJY CAN--
--MY HANDS!
THEY'RE FADING AWAY!!
SUE! THIS IS YOUR DOING--IT HAS TO BE! WHY, SUE--WHY??
HE'S MY BROTHER, REED-- BUT HE'S ALSO A MAN. A MAN GOING TO CLAIM THE WOMAN HE LOVES!
BUT--HAVEN'T I EXPLAINED THE DANGERS TO YOU OFTEN ENOUGH?
REED, I LOVE YOU SO MUCH... BUT IN SOME WAYS ...IT'S YOU, NOT ALICIA, WHO ARE TRULY BLIND!

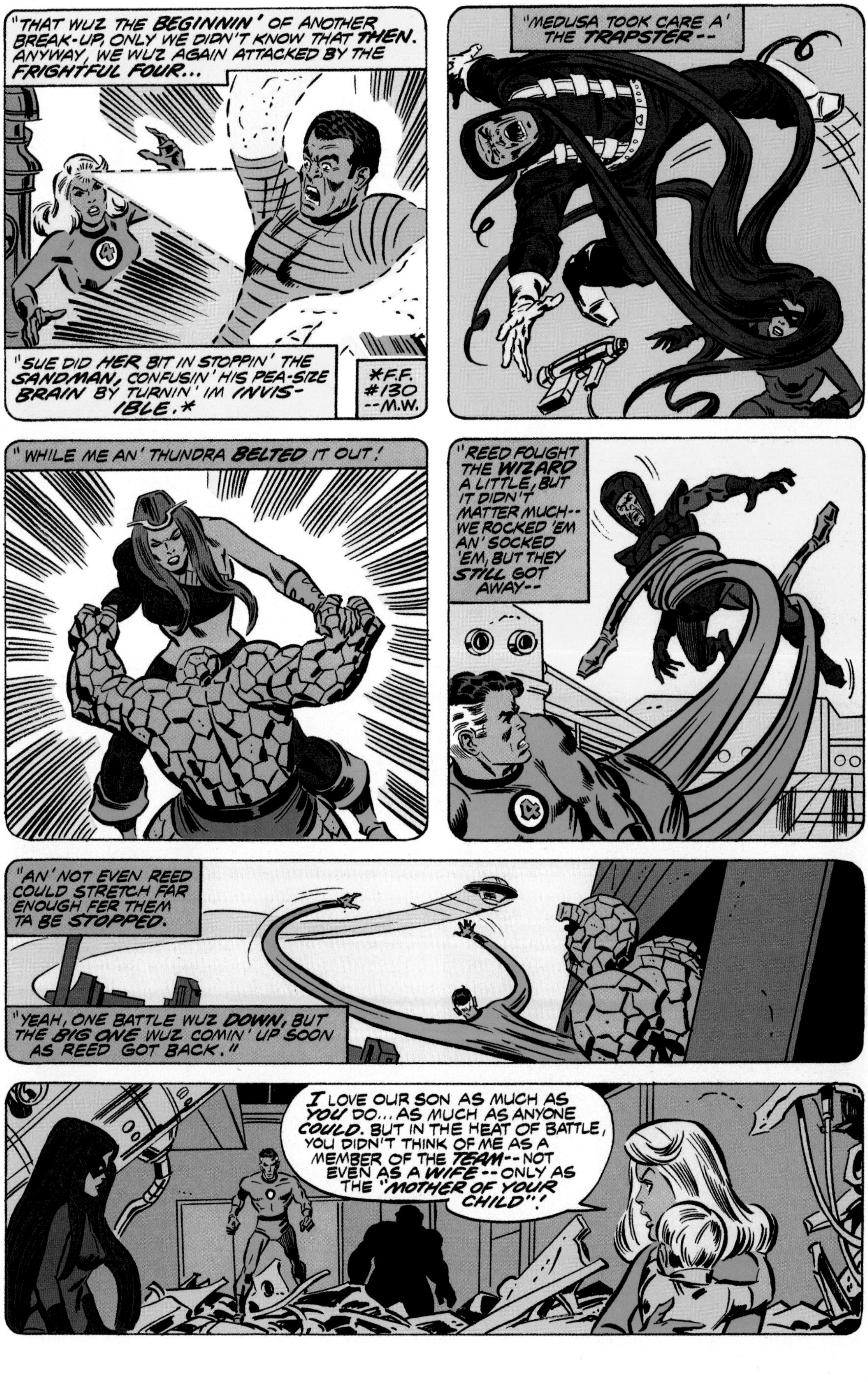
"THAT WUZ THE BEGINNIN' OF ANOTHER BREAK-UP, ONLY WE DIDN'T KNOW THAT THEN. ANYWAY, WE WUZ AGAIN ATTACKED BY THE FRIGHTFUL FOUR...
"SUE DID HER BIT IN STOPPIN' THE SANDMAN, CONFUSIN' HIS PEA-SIZE BRAIN BY TURNIN' IM INVIS-IBLE.*
*F.F. #130 --M.W.
"MEDUSA TOOK CARE A' THE TRAPSTER--
"WHILE ME AN' THUNDRA BELTED IT OUT!
"REED FOUGHT THE WIZARD A LITTLE, BUT IT DIDN'T MATTER MUCH-- WE ROCKED 'EM AN' SOCKED 'EM, BUT THEY STILL GOT AWAY--
"AN' NOT EVEN REED COULD STRETCH FAR ENOUGH FER THEM TA BE STOPPED.
"YEAH, ONE BATTLE WUZ DOWN, BUT THE BIG ONE WUZ COMIN' UP SOON AS REED GOT BACK."
I LOVE OUR SON AS MUCH AS YOU DO... AS MUCH AS ANYONE COULD. BUT IN THE HEAT OF BATTLE, YOU DIDN'T THINK OF ME AS A MEMBER OF THE TEAM--NOT EVEN AS A WIFE--ONLY AS THE "MOTHER OF YOUR CHILD"!

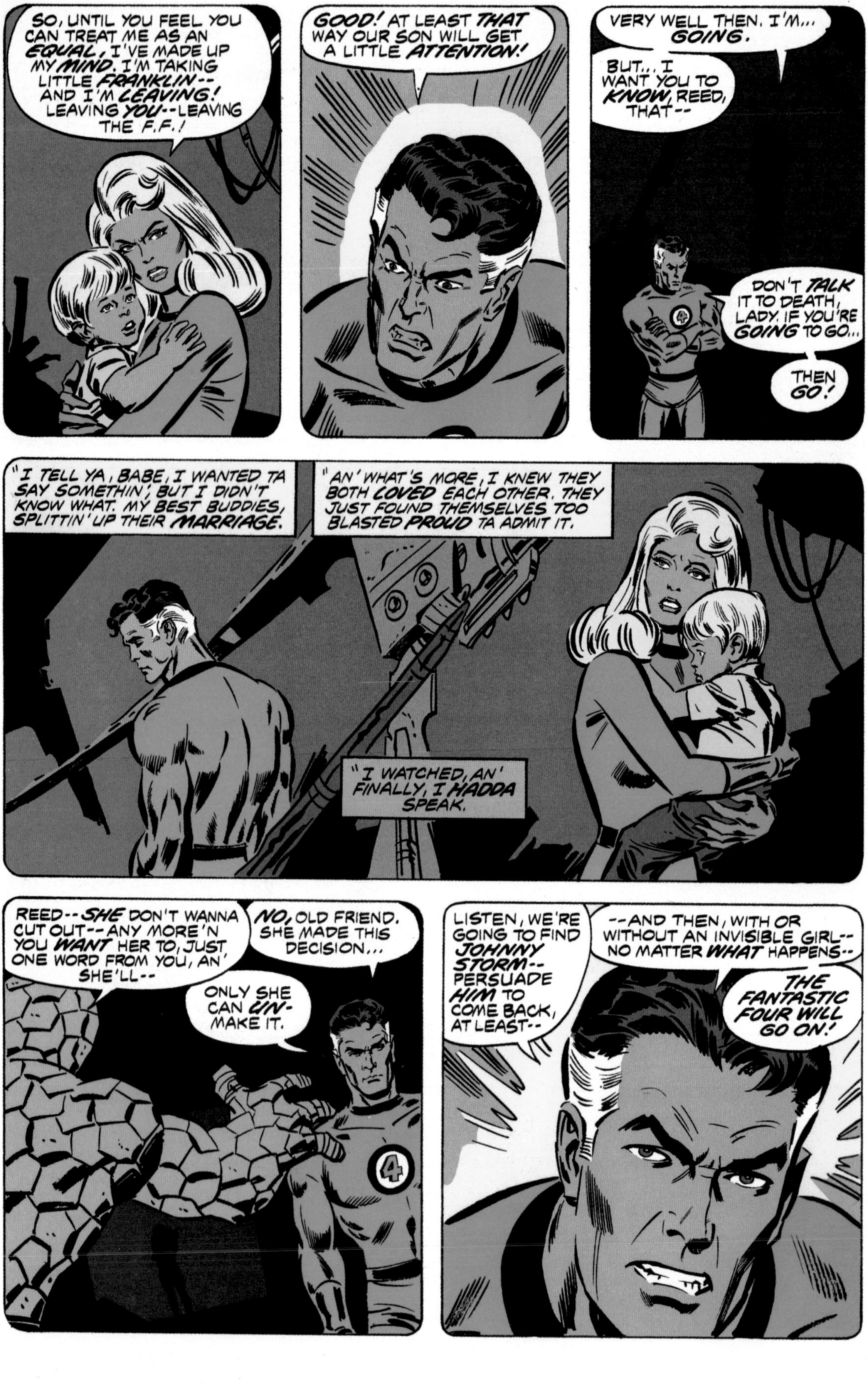
SO, UNTIL YOU FEEL YOU CAN TREAT ME AS AN EQUAL, I'VE MADE UP MY MIND. I'M TAKING LITTLE FRANKLIN-- AND I'M LEAVING! LEAVING YOU--LEAVING THE F.F.!
GOOD! AT LEAST THAT WAY OUR SON WILL GET A LITTLE ATTENTION!
VERY WELL THEN. I'M... GOING.
BUT... I WANT YOU TO KNOW, REED, THAT--
DON'T TALK IT TO DEATH, LADY. IF YOU'RE GOING TO GO...
THEN GO!
"I TELL YA, BABE, I WANTED TA SAY SOMETHIN', BUT I DIDN'T KNOW WHAT. MY BEST BUDDIES, SPLITTIN' UP THEIR MARRIAGE.
"AN' WHAT'S MORE, I KNEW THEY BOTH LOVED EACH OTHER. THEY JUST FOUND THEMSELVES TOO BLASTED PROUD TA ADMIT IT.
"I WATCHED, AN' FINALLY, I HADDA SPEAK.
REED--SHE DON'T WANNA CUT OUT--ANY MORE 'N YOU WANT HER TO, JUST ONE WORD FROM YOU, AN' SHE'LL--
NO, OLD FRIEND. SHE MADE THIS DECISION...
ONLY SHE CAN UN-MAKE IT.
LISTEN, WE'RE GOING TO FIND JOHNNY STORM-- PERSUADE HIM TO COME BACK, AT LEAST--
--AND THEN, WITH OR WITHOUT AN INVISIBLE GIRL-- NO MATTER WHAT HAPPENS--
THE FANTASTIC FOUR WILL GO ON!

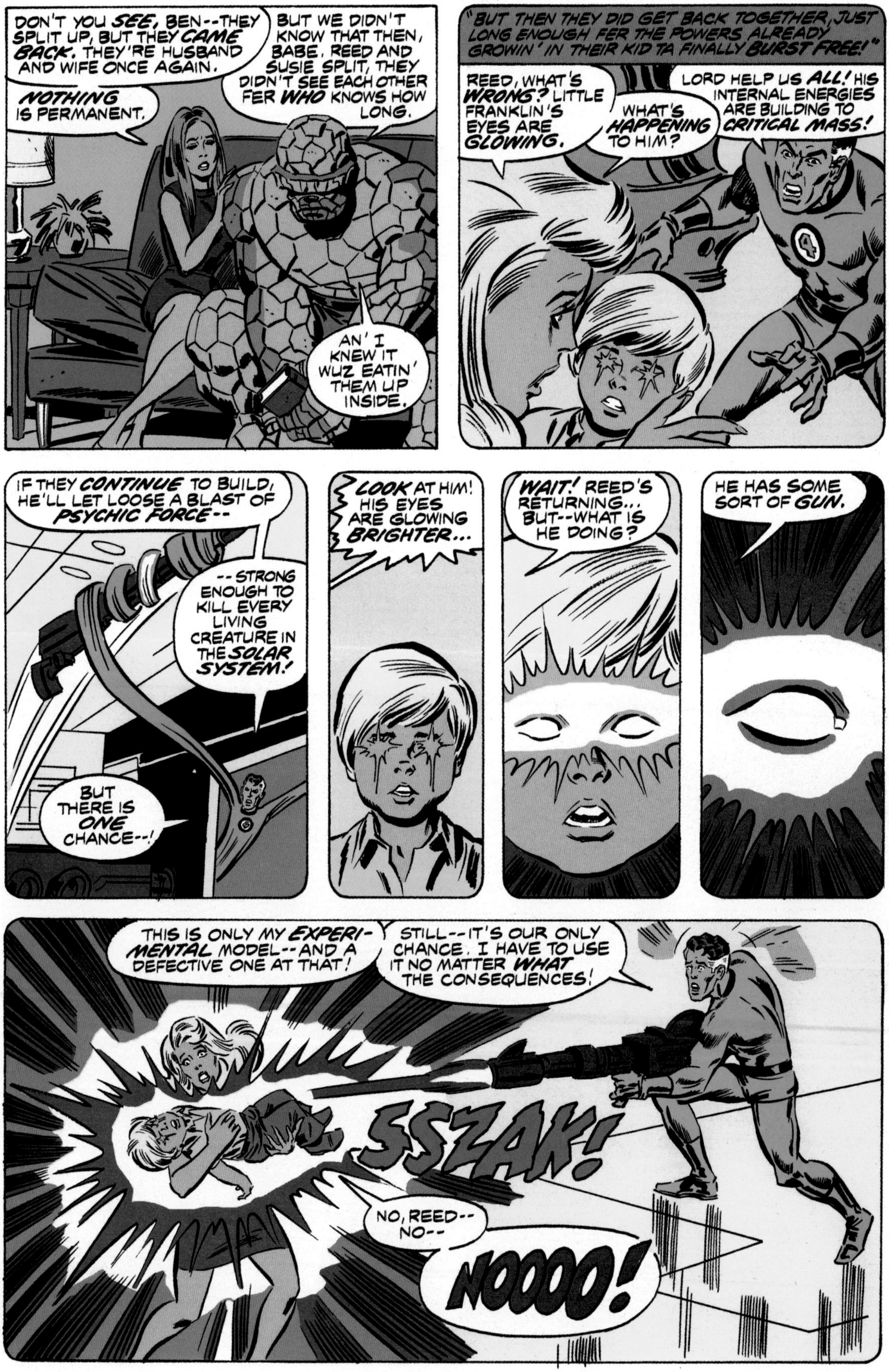
DON'T YOU SEE, BEN--THEY SPLIT UP, BUT THEY CAME BACK. THEY'RE HUSBAND AND WIFE ONCE AGAIN.
NOTHING IS PERMANENT.
BUT WE DIDN'T KNOW THAT THEN, BABE. REED AND SUSIE SPLIT, THEY DIDN'T SEE EACH OTHER FER WHO KNOWS HOW LONG.
AN' I KNEW IT WUZ EATIN' THEM UP INSIDE.
"BUT THEN THEY DID GET BACK TOGETHER, JUST LONG ENOUGH FER THE POWERS ALREADY GROWIN' IN THEIR KID TA FINALLY BURST FREE!"
REED, WHAT'S WRONG? LITTLE FRANKLIN'S EYES ARE GLOWING.
WHAT'S HAPPENING TO HIM?
LORD HELP US ALL! HIS INTERNAL ENERGIES ARE BUILDING TO CRITICAL MASS!
IF THEY CONTINUE TO BUILD, HE'LL LET LOOSE A BLAST OF PSYCHIC FORCE--
--STRONG ENOUGH TO KILL EVERY LIVING CREATURE IN THE SOLAR SYSTEM!
BUT THERE IS ONE CHANCE--!
LOOK AT HIM! HIS EYES ARE GLOWING BRIGHTER...
WAIT! REED'S RETURNING... BUT--WHAT IS HE DOING?
HE HAS SOME SORT OF GUN.
THIS IS ONLY MY EXPERIMENTAL MODEL--AND A DEFECTIVE ONE AT THAT!
STILL--IT'S OUR ONLY CHANCE. I HAVE TO USE IT NO MATTER WHAT THE CONSEQUENCES!
SSZAK!
NO, REED--NO--
NOOOO!

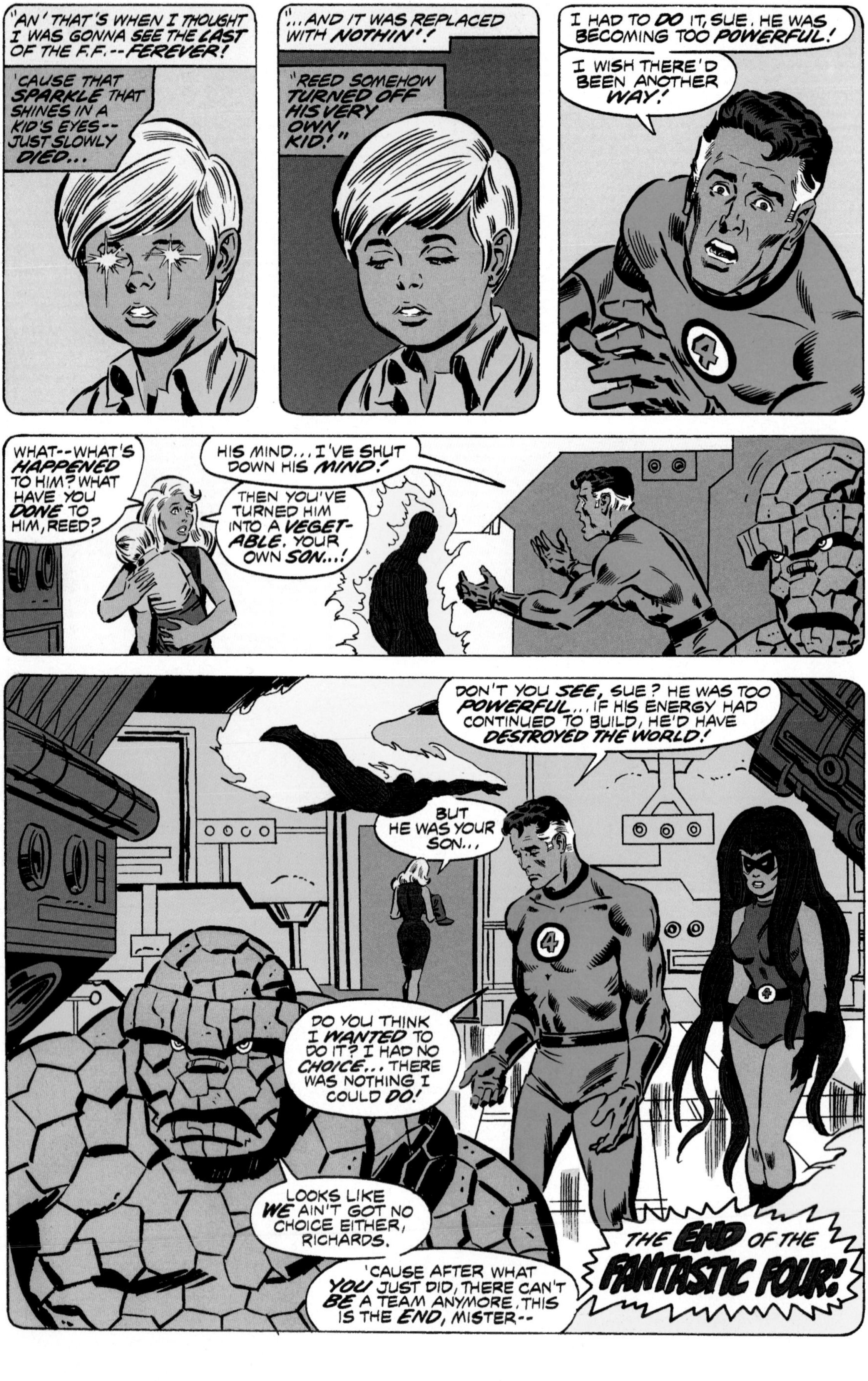
"AN' THAT'S WHEN I THOUGHT I WAS GONNA SEE THE LAST OF THE F.F.--FEREVER!
'CAUSE THAT SPARKLE THAT SHINES IN A KID'S EYES--JUST SLOWLY DIED...
"...AND IT WAS REPLACED WITH NOTHIN'!
"REED SOMEHOW TURNED OFF HIS VERY OWN KID!"
I HAD TO DO IT, SUE. HE WAS BECOMING TOO POWERFUL!
I WISH THERE'D BEEN ANOTHER WAY!
WHAT--WHAT'S HAPPENED TO HIM? WHAT HAVE YOU DONE TO HIM, REED?
HIS MIND... I'VE SHUT DOWN HIS MIND!
THEN YOU'VE TURNED HIM INTO A VEGETABLE. YOUR OWN SON...!
DON'T YOU SEE, SUE? HE WAS TOO POWERFUL... IF HIS ENERGY HAD CONTINUED TO BUILD, HE'D HAVE DESTROYED THE WORLD!
BUT HE WAS YOUR SON...
DO YOU THINK I WANTED TO DO IT? I HAD NO CHOICE... THERE WAS NOTHING I COULD DO!
LOOKS LIKE WE AIN'T GOT NO CHOICE EITHER, RICHARDS.
'CAUSE AFTER WHAT YOU JUST DID, THERE CAN'T BE A TEAM ANYMORE. THIS IS THE END, MISTER--
THE END OF THE FANTASTIC FOUR!

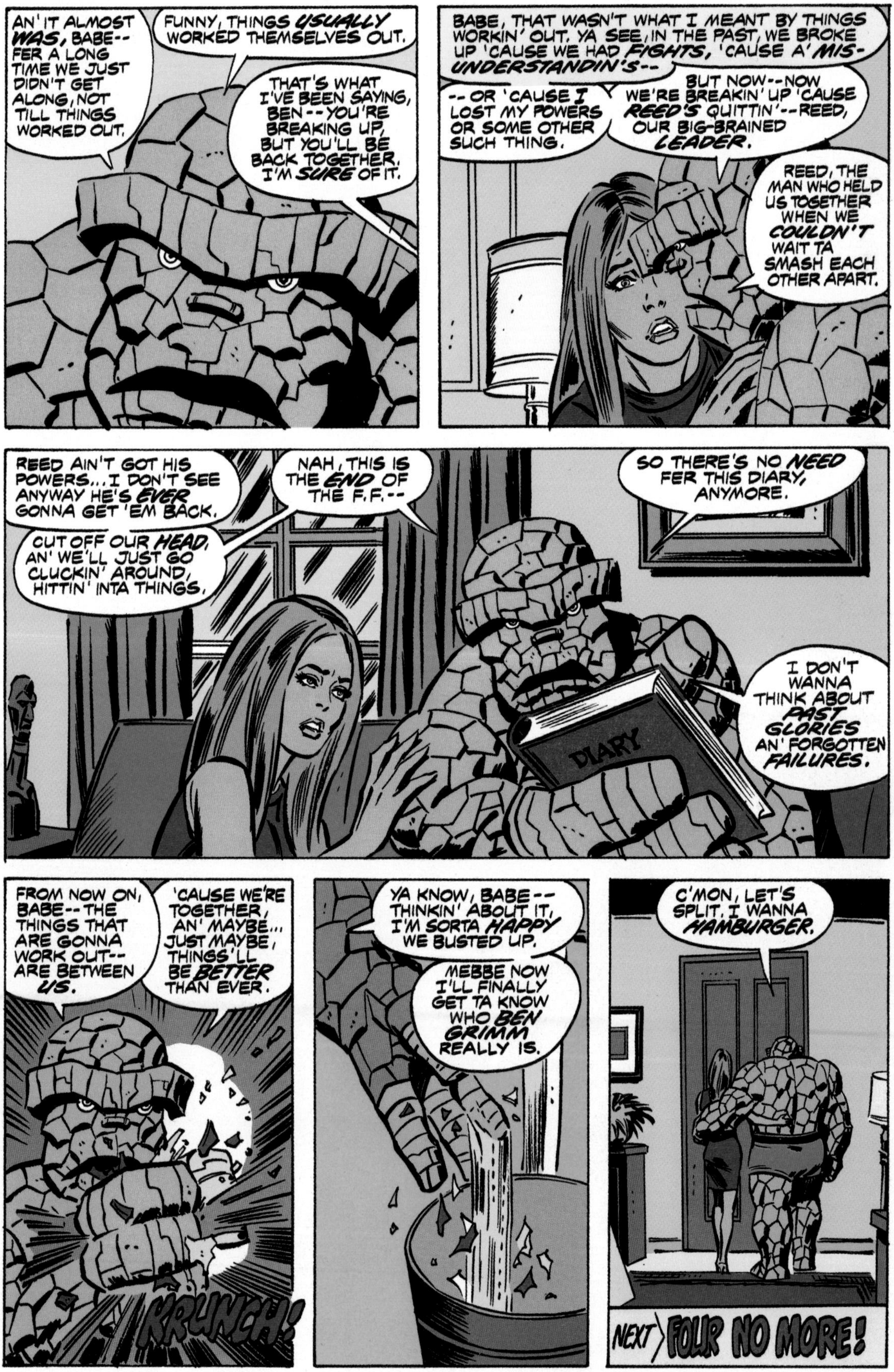
AN' IT ALMOST WAS, BABE-- FER A LONG TIME WE JUST DIDN'T GET ALONG, NOT TILL THINGS WORKED OUT.
FUNNY, THINGS USUALLY WORKED THEMSELVES OUT.
THAT'S WHAT I'VE BEEN SAYING, BEN--YOU'RE BREAKING UP, BUT YOU'LL BE BACK TOGETHER. I'M SURE OF IT.
BABE, THAT WASN'T WHAT I MEANT BY THINGS WORKIN' OUT. YA SEE, IN THE PAST, WE BROKE UP 'CAUSE WE HAD FIGHTS, 'CAUSE A' MIS-UNDERSTANDIN'S--
--OR 'CAUSE I LOST MY POWERS OR SOME OTHER SUCH THING.
BUT NOW--NOW WE'RE BREAKIN' UP 'CAUSE REED'S QUITTIN'--REED, OUR BIG-BRAINED LEADER.
REED, THE MAN WHO HELD US TOGETHER WHEN WE COULDN'T WAIT TA SMASH EACH OTHER APART.
REED AIN'T GOT HIS POWERS... I DON'T SEE ANYWAY HE'S EVER GONNA GET 'EM BACK.
CUT OFF OUR HEAD, AN' WE'LL JUST GO CLUCKIN' AROUND, HITTIN' INTA THINGS.
NAH, THIS IS THE END OF THE F.F.--
SO THERE'S NO NEED FER THIS DIARY, ANYMORE.
DIARY
I DON'T WANNA THINK ABOUT PAST GLORIES AN' FORGOTTEN FAILURES.
FROM NOW ON, BABE--THE THINGS THAT ARE GONNA WORK OUT--ARE BETWEEN US.
'CAUSE WE'RE TOGETHER, AN' MAYBE... JUST MAYBE, THINGS'LL BE BETTER THAN EVER.
KRUNCH!
YA KNOW, BABE-- THINKIN' ABOUT IT, I'M SORTA HAPPY WE BUSTED UP.
MEBBE NOW I'LL FINALLY GET TA KNOW WHO BEN GRIMM REALLY IS.
C'MON, LET'S SPLIT. I WANNA HAMBURGER.
NEXT
FOUR NO MORE!

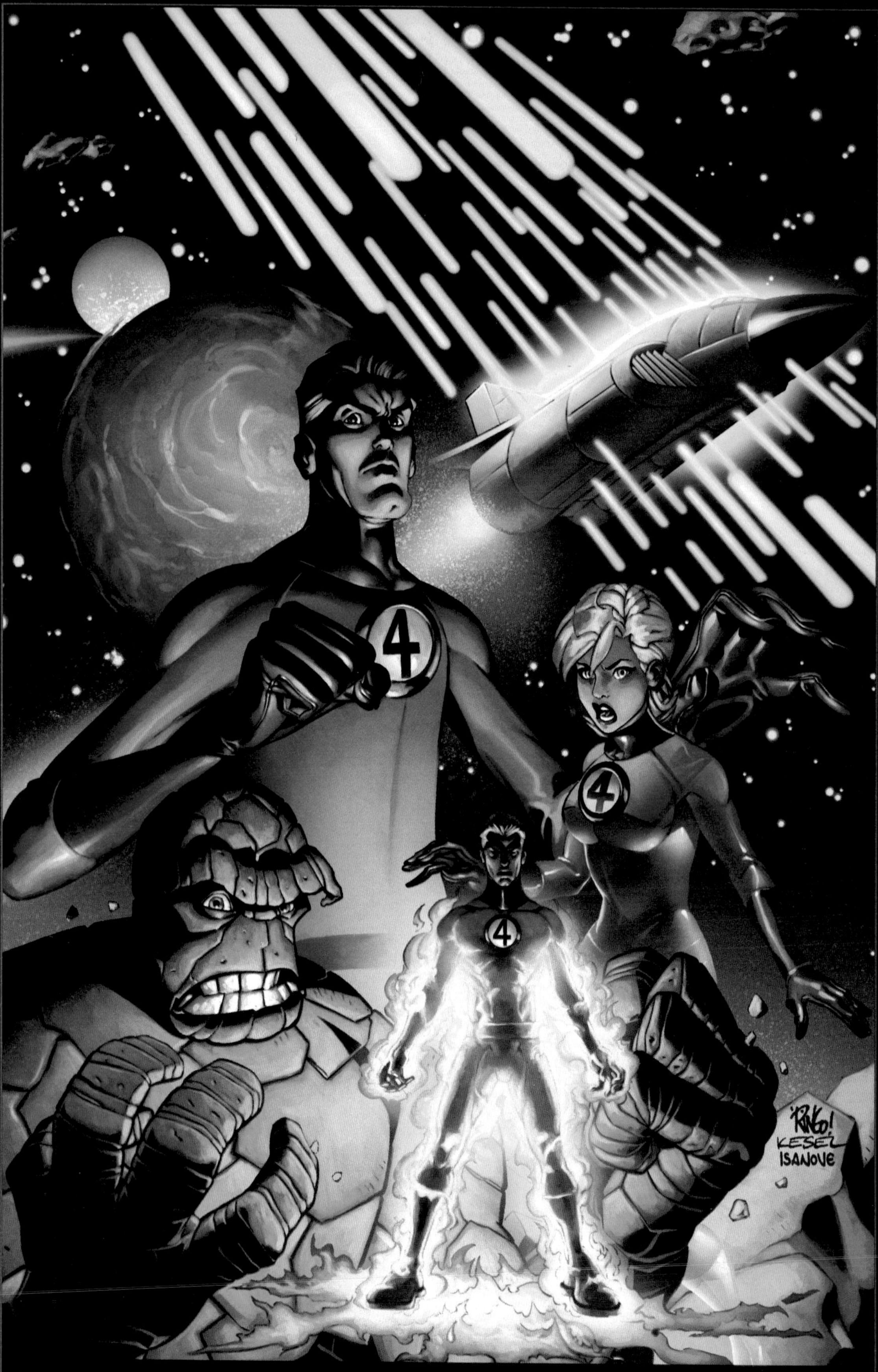
RINGO!
KESEL
ISANOVE

FANTASTIC FOUR #60

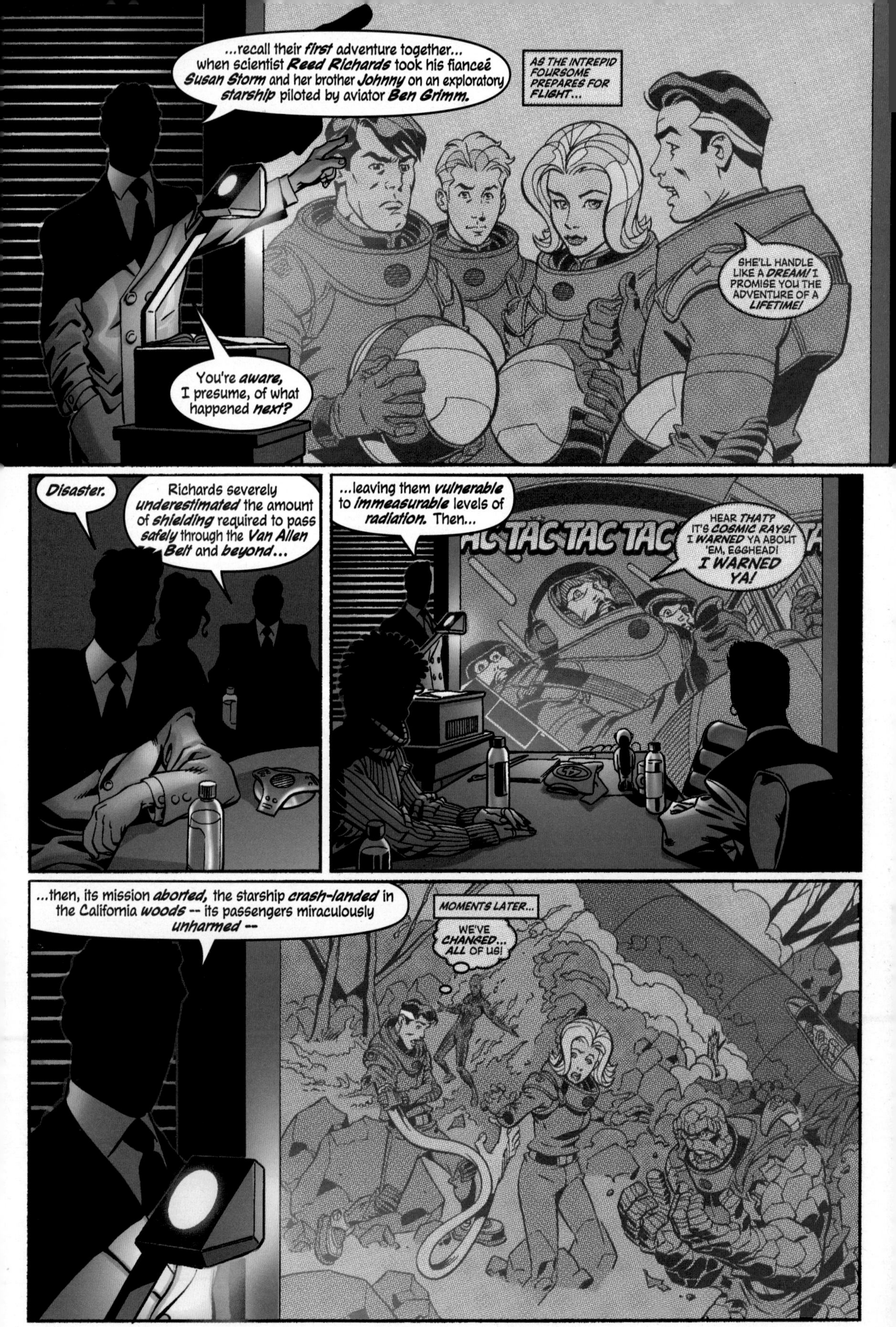

...recall their first adventure together... when scientist Reed Richards took his fianceé Susan Storm and her brother Johnny on an exploratory starship piloted by aviator Ben Grimm.
AS THE INTREPID FOURSOME PREPARES FOR FLIGHT...
SHE'LL HANDLE LIKE A DREAM! I PROMISE YOU THE ADVENTURE OF A LIFETIME!
You're aware, I presume, of what happened next?
Disaster.
Richards severely underestimated the amount of shielding required to pass safely through the Van Allen Belt and beyond...
...leaving them vulnerable to immeasurable levels of radiation. Then...
TAC TAC TAC TAC
HEAR THAT? IT'S COSMIC RAYS! I WARNED YA ABOUT 'EM, EGGHEAD! I WARNED YA!
...then, its mission aborted, the starship crash-landed in the California woods -- its passengers miraculously unharmed --
MOMENTS LATER...
WE'VE CHANGED... ALL OF US!

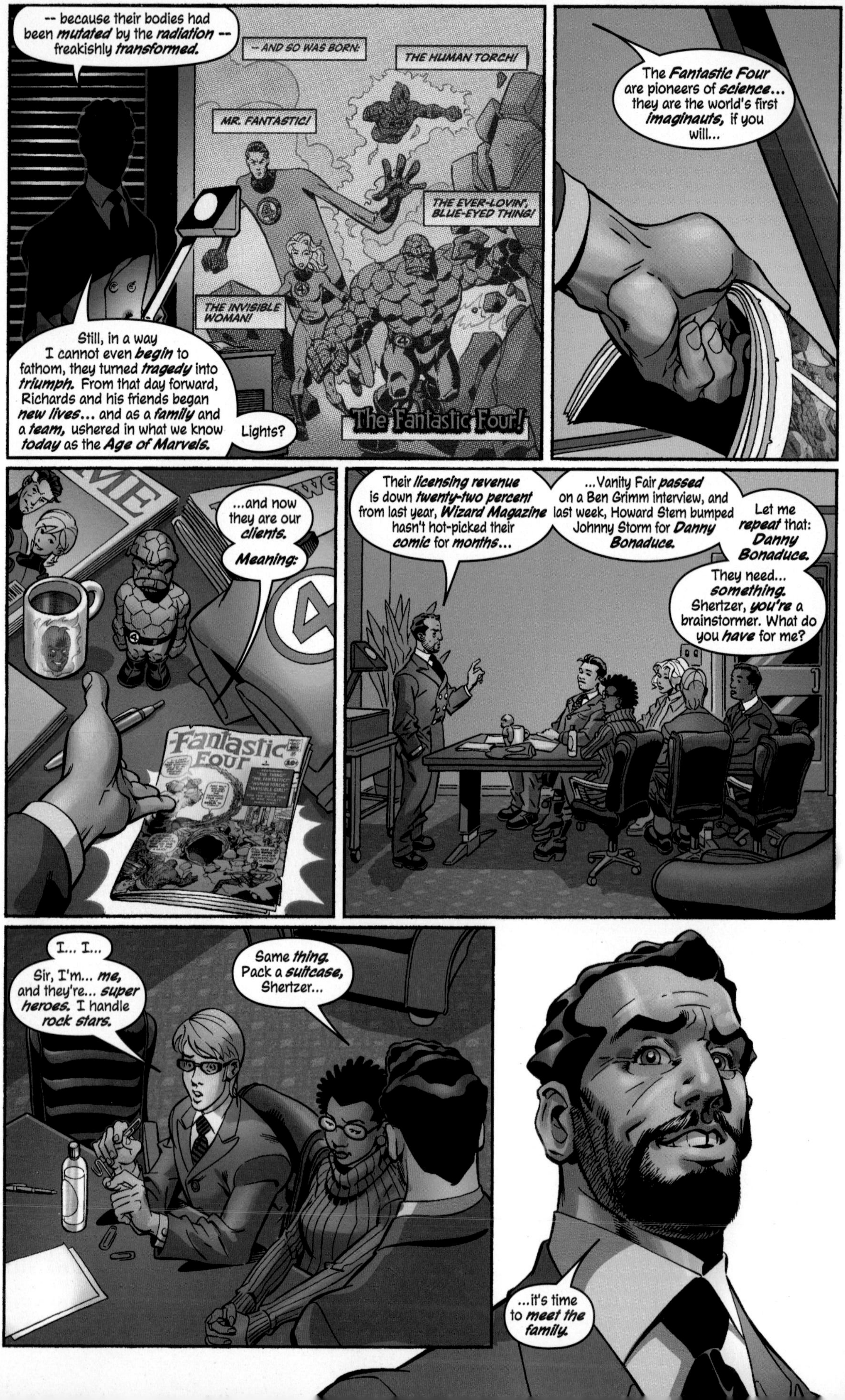

-- because their bodies had been mutated by the radiation -- freakishly transformed.
-- AND SO WAS BORN:
THE HUMAN TORCH!
MR. FANTASTIC!
THE EVER-LOVIN', BLUE-EYED THING!
THE INVISIBLE WOMAN!
Still, in a way I cannot even begin to fathom, they turned tragedy into triumph. From that day forward, Richards and his friends began new lives... and as a family and a team, ushered in what we know today as the Age of Marvels.
Lights?
The Fantastic Four!
The Fantastic Four are pioneers of science... they are the world's first imaginauts, if you will...
...and now they are our clients.
Meaning:
Fantastic Four
Their licensing revenue is down twenty-two percent from last year, Wizard Magazine hasn't hot-picked their comic for months...
...Vanity Fair passed on a Ben Grimm interview, and last week, Howard Stern bumped Johnny Storm for Danny Bonaduce.
Let me repeat that: Danny Bonaduce.
They need... something. Shertzer, you're a brainstormer. What do you have for me?
I... I...
Sir, I'm... me, and they're... super heroes. I handle rock stars.
Same thing. Pack a suitcase, Shertzer...
...it's time to meet the family.

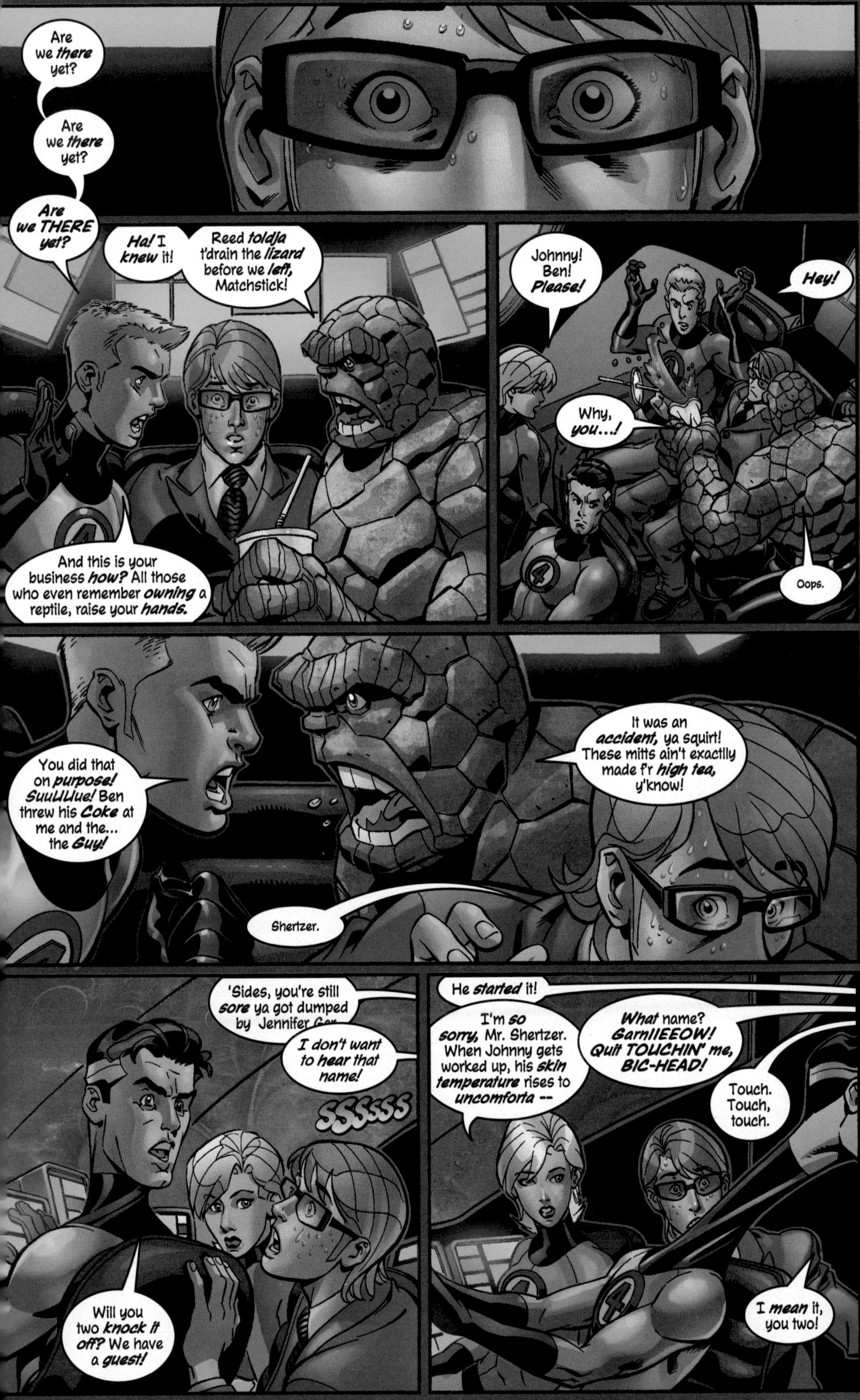
Are we *there* yet?
Are we *there* yet?
Are we THERE yet?
Ha! I *knew* it!
Reed *toldja* t'drain the *lizard* before we *left,* Matchstick!
And this is your business *how?* All those who even remember *owning* a reptile, raise your *hands.*
Johnny! Ben! *Please!*
Hey!
Why, *you...!*
Oops.
You did that on *purpose! SuuUUue!* Ben threw his *Coke* at me and the... the *Guy!*
It was an *accident,* ya squirt! These mitts ain't exactlly made f'r *high tea,* y'know!
Shertzer.
'Sides, you're still *sore* ya got dumped by Jennifer Gar--
I don't want to hear that name!
SSSsss
Will you two *knock it off?* We have a *guest!*
He *started* it!
I'm *so sorry,* Mr. Shertzer. When Johnny gets worked up, his *skin temperature* rises to *uncomforta --*
What name? *GarnIIEEOW! Quit TOUCHIN' me, BIG-HEAD!*
Touch. Touch, touch.
I *mean* it, you two!

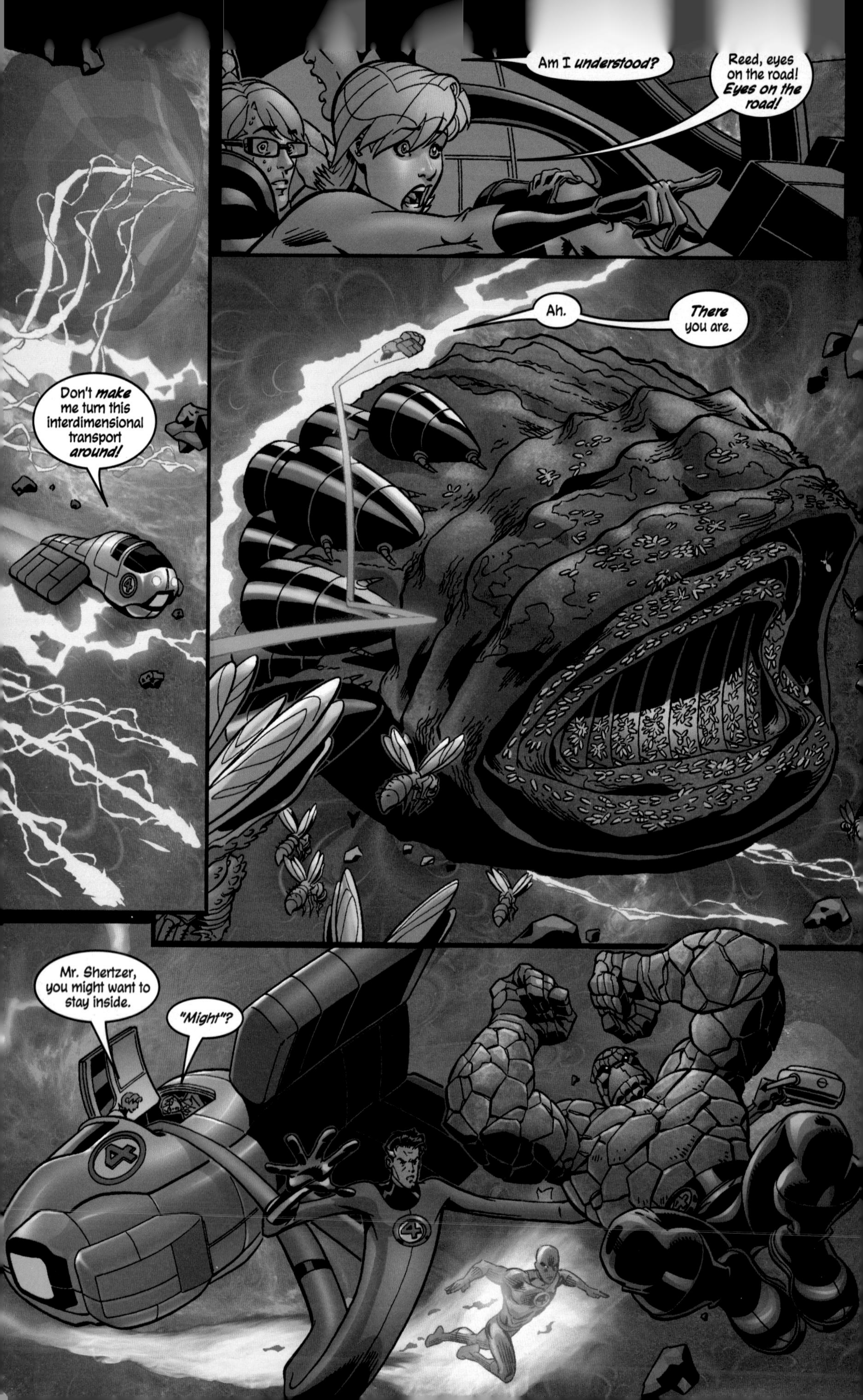

Am I *understood?*
Reed, eyes on the road! ***Eyes on the road!***
Don't ***make*** me turn this interdimensional transport ***around!***
Ah.
There you are.
Mr. Shertzer, you might want to stay inside.
"Might"?

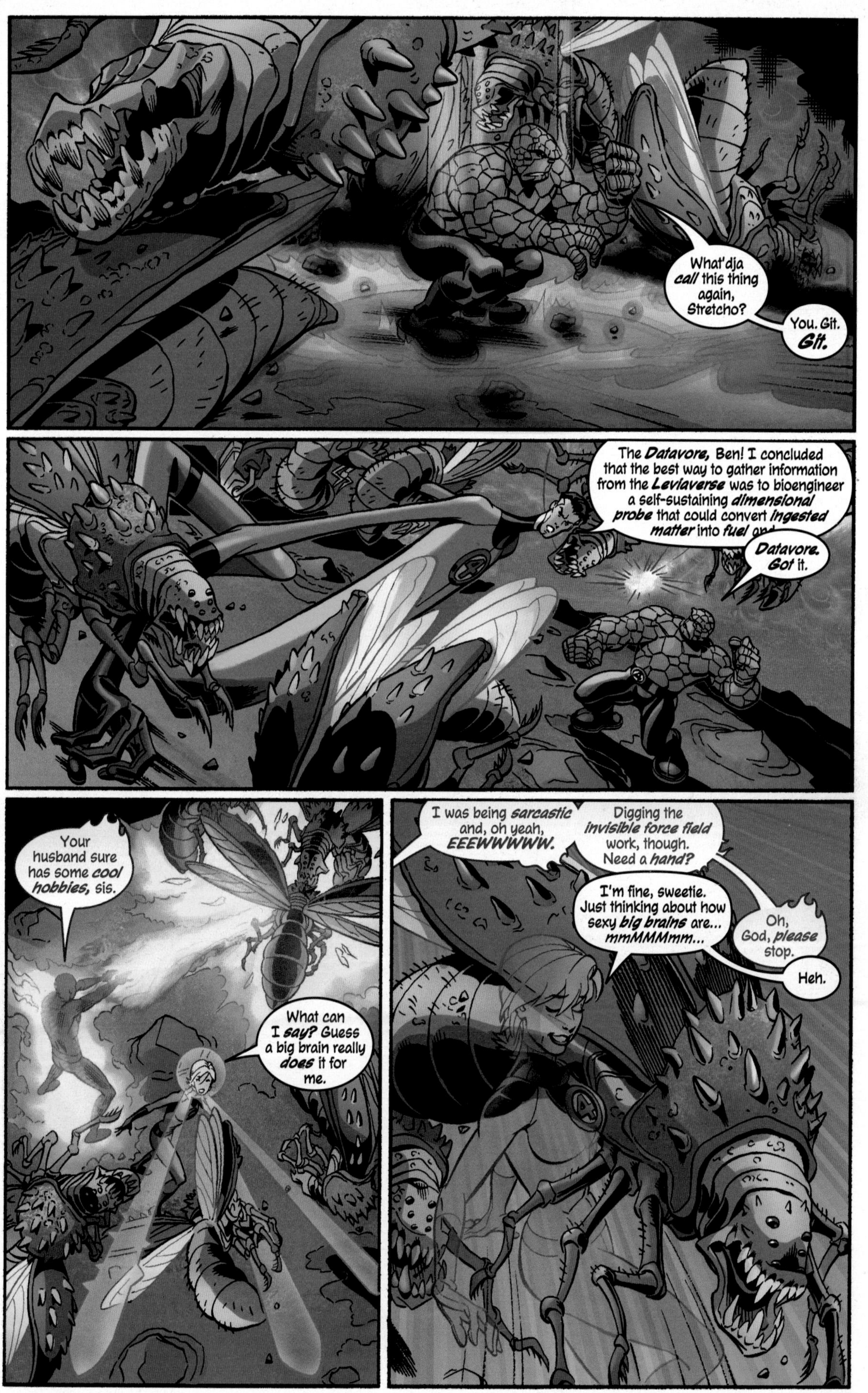

What'dja call this thing again, Stretcho?
You. Git. Git.
The Datavore, Ben! I concluded that the best way to gather information from the Leviaverse was to bioengineer a self-sustaining dimensional probe that could convert ingested matter into fuel
Datavore. Got it.
Your husband sure has some cool hobbies, sis.
What can I say? Guess a big brain really does it for me.
I was being sarcastic and, oh yeah, EEEWWWWW.
Digging the invisible force field work, though. Need a hand?
I'm fine, sweetie. Just thinking about how sexy big brains are... mmMMMmm...
Oh, God, please stop.
Heh.

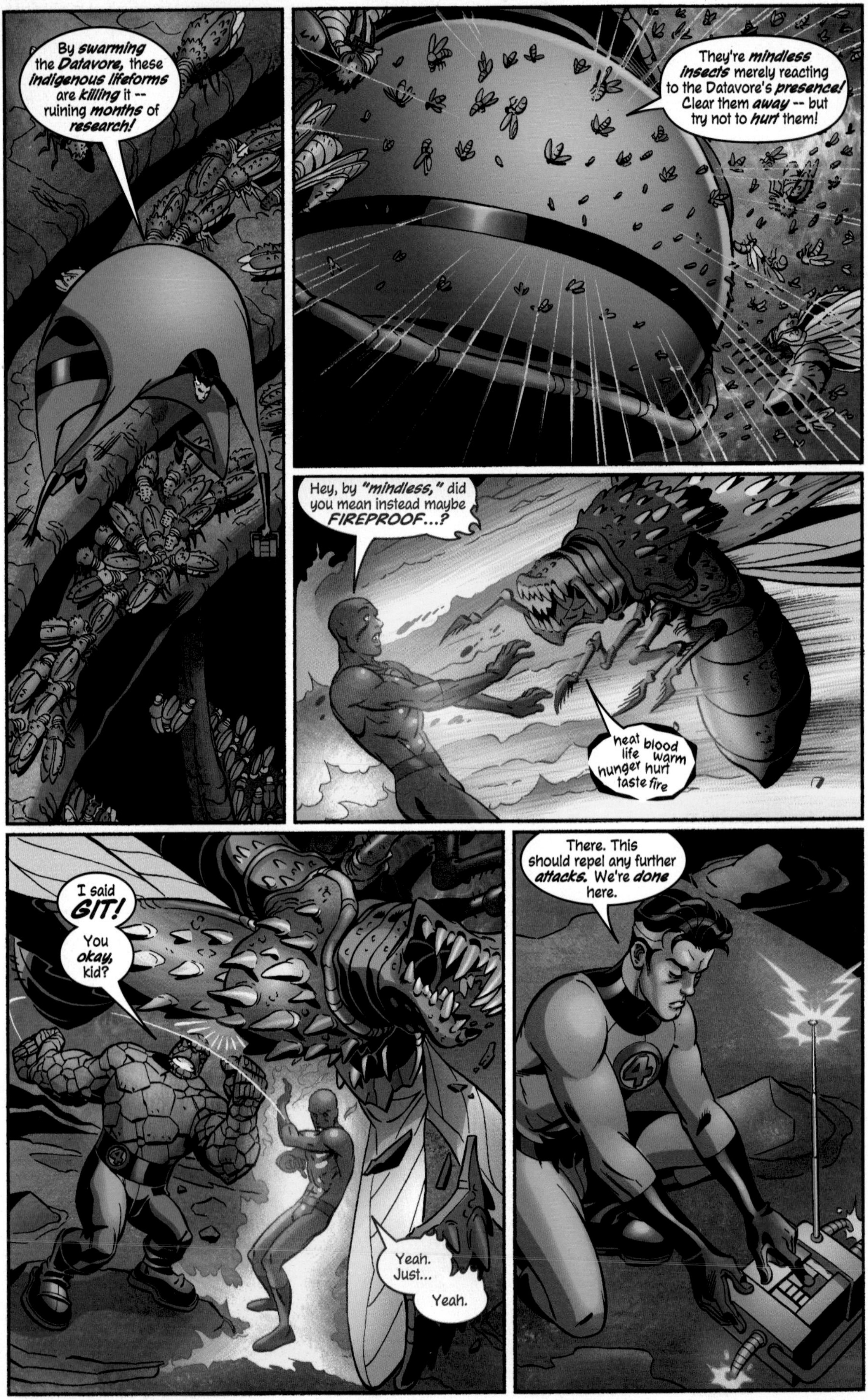
By swarming the Datavore, these indigenous lifeforms are killing it -- ruining months of research!
They're mindless insects merely reacting to the Datavore's presence! Clear them away -- but try not to hurt them!
Hey, by "mindless," did you mean instead maybe FIREPROOF...?
heat blood life warm hunger hurt taste fire
I said GIT!
You okay, kid?
Yeah. Just...
Yeah.
There. This should repel any further attacks. We're done here.

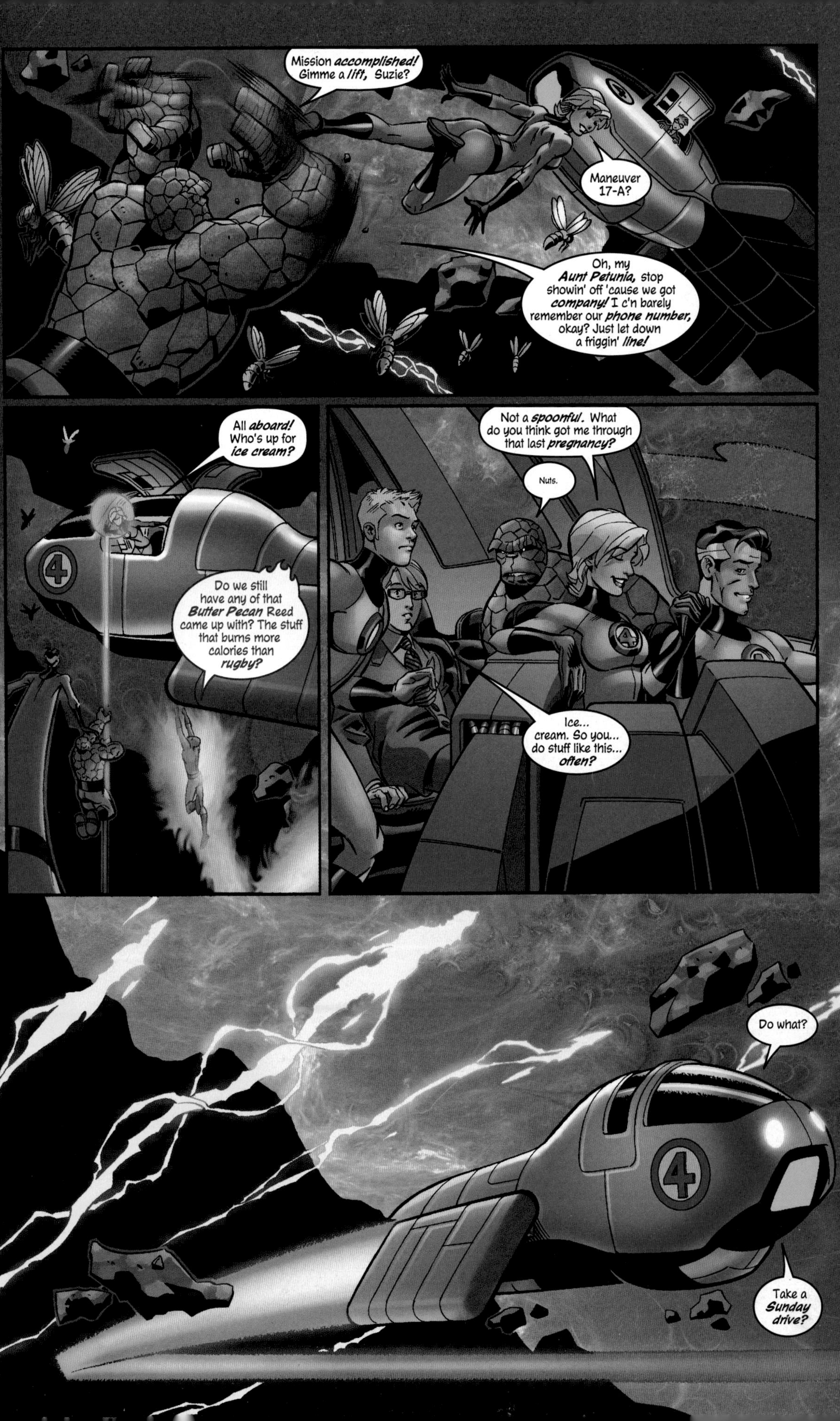

Mission *accomplished!* Gimme a *lift,* Suzie?
Maneuver 17-A?
Oh, my *Aunt Petunia,* stop showin' off 'cause we got *company!* I c'n barely remember our *phone number,* okay? Just let down a friggin' *line!*
All *aboard!* Who's up for *ice cream?*
Do we still have any of that *Butter Pecan* Reed came up with? The stuff that burns more calories than *rugby?*
Not a *spoonful.* What do you think got me through that last *pregnancy?*
Nuts.
Ice... cream. So you... do stuff like this... *often?*
Do what?
Take a *Sunday drive?*

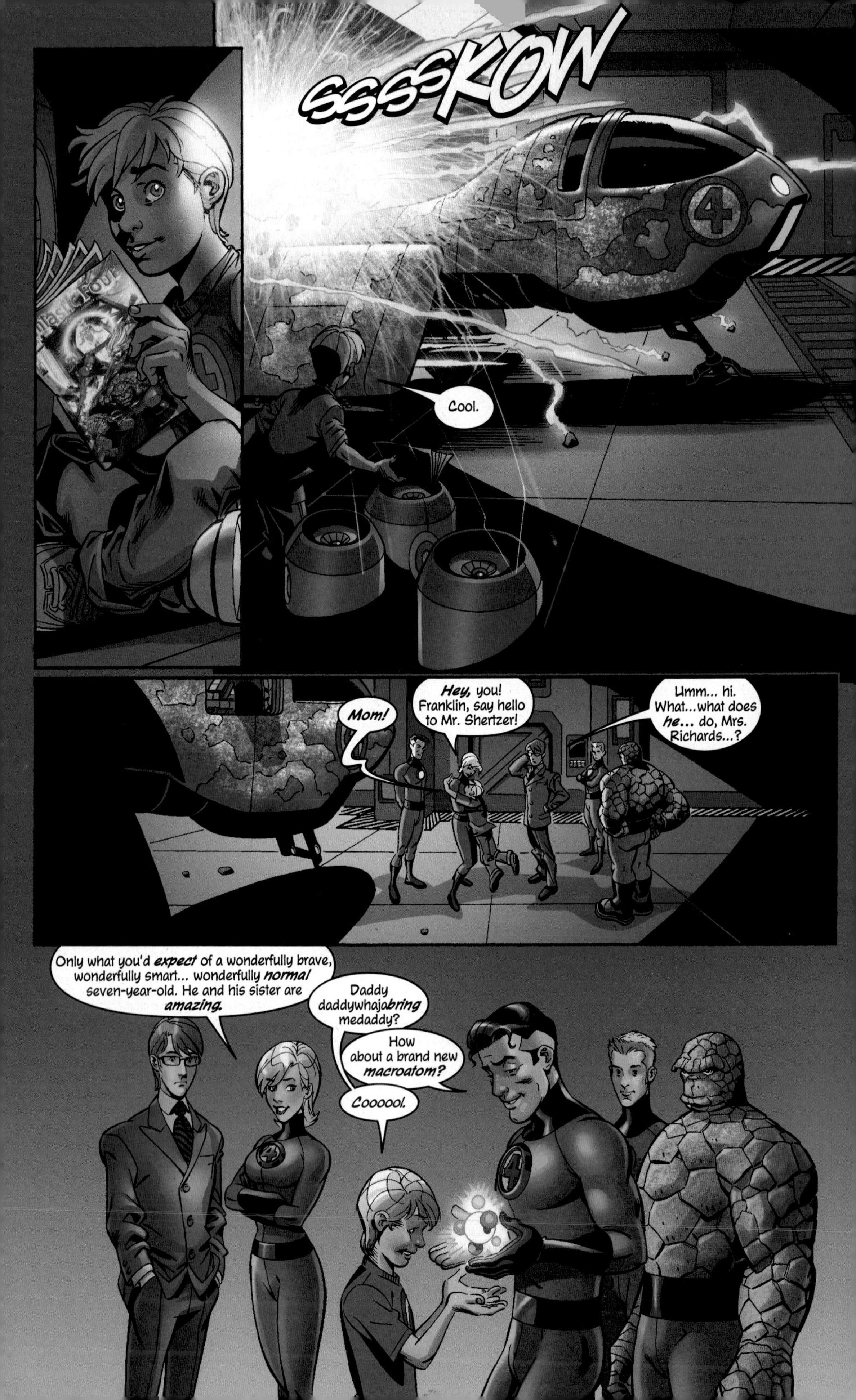
SSSSKOW
Cool.
Mom!
Hey, you! Franklin, say hello to Mr. Shertzer!
Umm... hi. What...what does he... do, Mrs. Richards...?
Only what you'd expect of a wonderfully brave, wonderfully smart... wonderfully normal seven-year-old. He and his sister are amazing.
Daddy daddywhajabring medaddy?
How about a brand new macroatom?
Coooool.

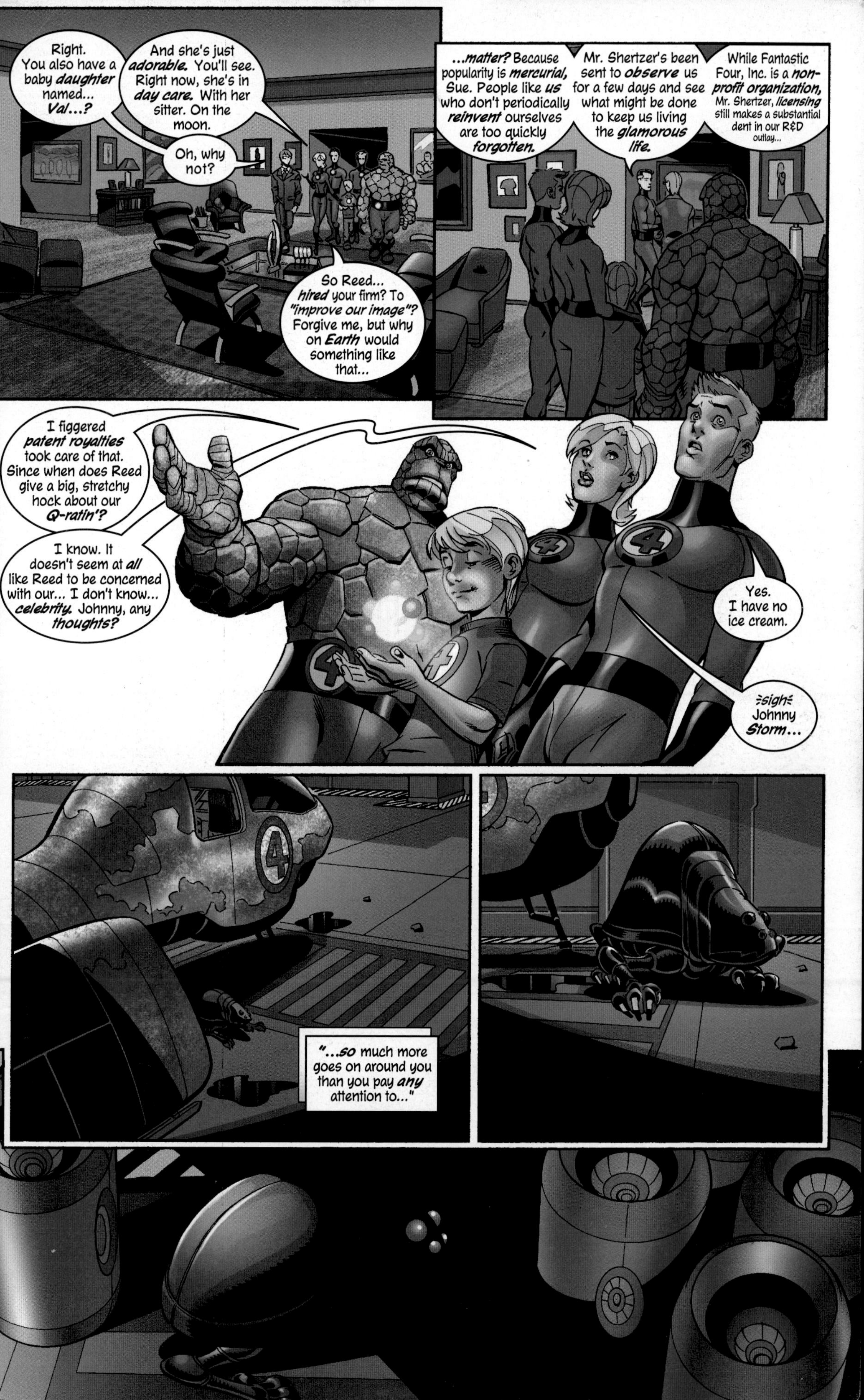
Right. You also have a baby *daughter* named... *Val...?*
And she's just *adorable.* You'll see. Right now, she's in *day care.* With her sitter. On the moon.
Oh, why not?
So Reed... *hired* your firm? To *"improve our image"*? Forgive me, but why on *Earth* would something like that...
...matter? Because popularity is *mercurial,* Sue. People like *us* who don't periodically *reinvent* ourselves are too quickly *forgotten.*
Mr. Shertzer's been sent to *observe* us for a few days and see what might be done to keep us living the *glamorous life.*
While Fantastic Four, Inc. is a *non-profit organization,* Mr. Shertzer, *licensing* still makes a substantial dent in our R&D outlay...
I figgered *patent royalties* took care of that. Since when does Reed give a big, stretchy hock about our *Q-ratin'?*
I know. It doesn't seem at *all* like Reed to be concerned with our... I don't know... *celebrity.* Johnny, any *thoughts?*
Yes. I have no ice cream.
sigh Johnny *Storm...*
"...so much more goes on around you than you pay *any* attention to..."

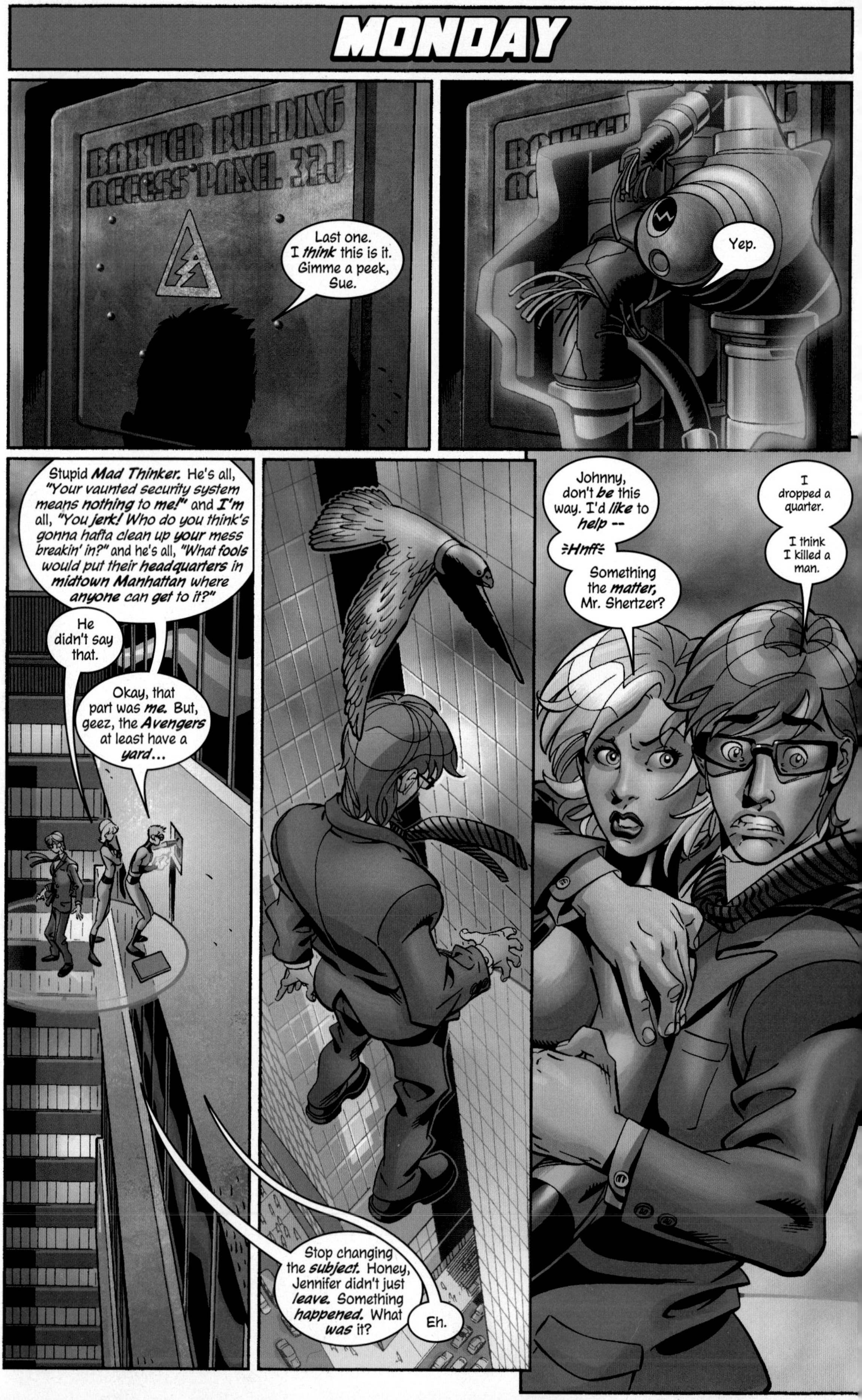
MONDAY
BAXTER BUILDING ACCESS PANEL 32J
Last one. I think this is it. Gimme a peek, Sue.
Yep.
Stupid Mad Thinker. He's all, "Your vaunted security system means nothing to me!" and I'm all, "You jerk! Who do you think's gonna hafta clean up your mess breakin' in?" and he's all, "What fools would put their headquarters in midtown Manhattan where anyone can get to it?"
He didn't say that.
Okay, that part was me. But, geez, the Avengers at least have a yard...
Stop changing the subject. Honey, Jennifer didn't just leave. Something happened. What was it?
Eh.
Johnny, don't be this way. I'd like to help --
Hnff
Something the matter, Mr. Shertzer?
I dropped a quarter.
I think I killed a man.

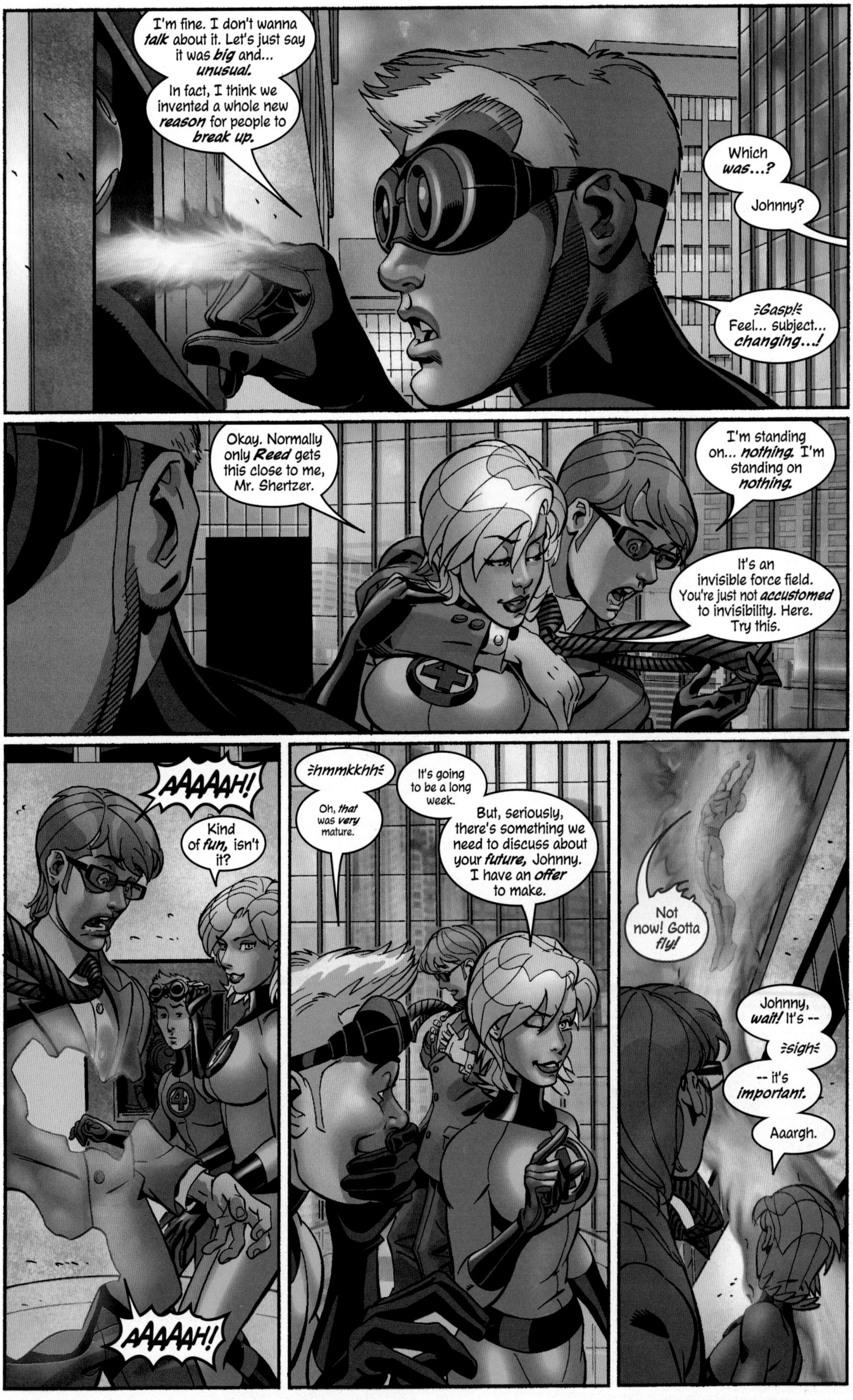
I'm fine. I don't wanna talk about it. Let's just say it was big and... unusual.
In fact, I think we invented a whole new reason for people to break up.
Which was...?
Johnny?
Gasp! Feel... subject... changing...!
Okay. Normally only Reed gets this close to me, Mr. Shertzer.
I'm standing on... nothing. I'm standing on nothing.
It's an invisible force field. You're just not accustomed to invisibility. Here. Try this.
AAAAAH!
Kind of fun, isn't it?
AAAAAH!
hmmkkhh
Oh, that was very mature.
It's going to be a long week.
But, seriously, there's something we need to discuss about your future, Johnny. I have an offer to make.
Not now! Gotta fly!
Johnny, wait! It's --
sigh
-- it's important.
Aaargh.

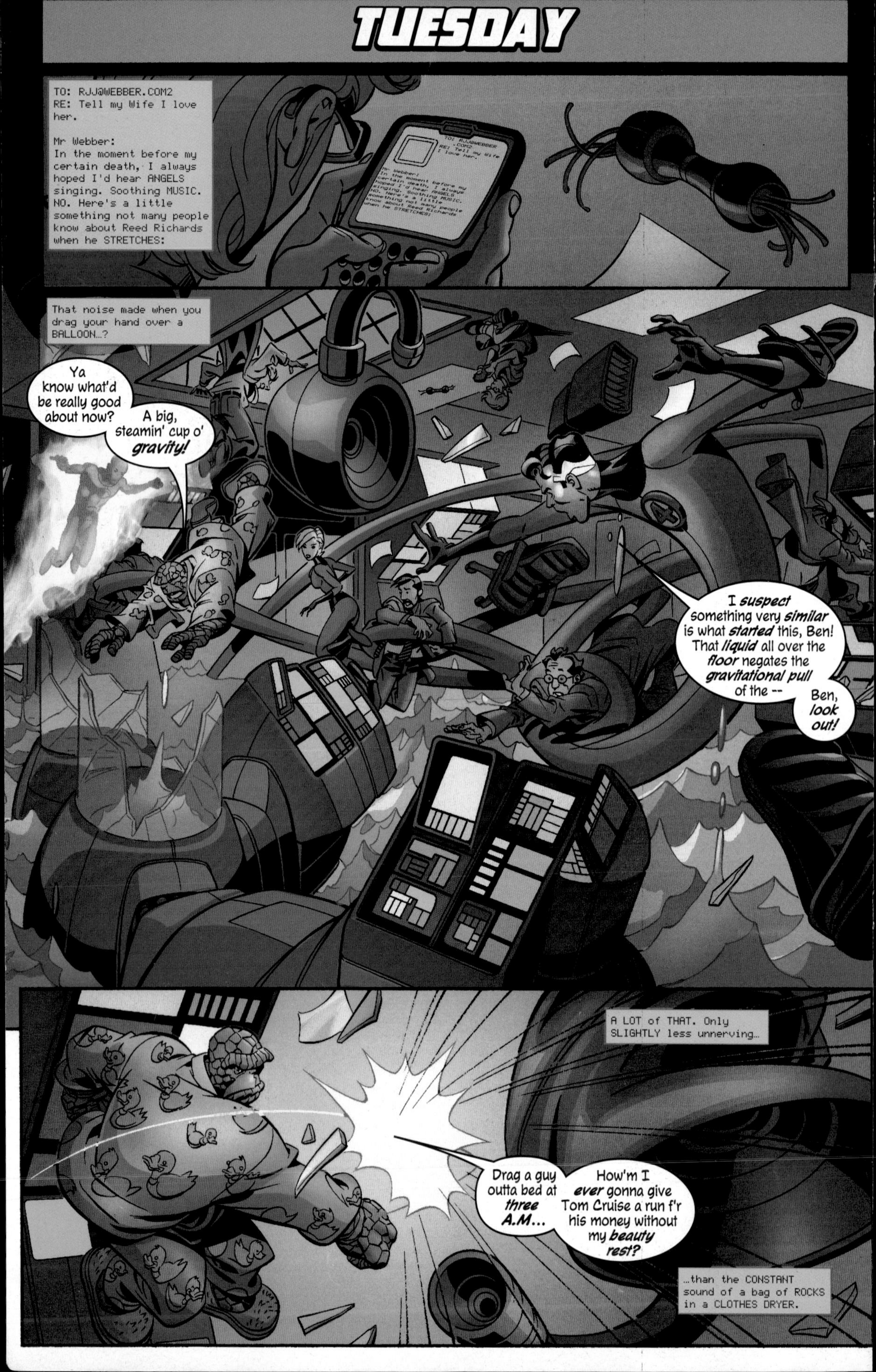
TUESDAY
TO: RJJ@WEBBER.COM2
RE: Tell my Wife I love her.
Mr Webber:
In the moment before my certain death, I always hoped I'd hear ANGELS singing. Soothing MUSIC. NO. Here's a little something not many people know about Reed Richards when he STRETCHES:
That noise made when you drag your hand over a BALLOON...?
Ya know what'd be really good about now?
A big, steamin' cup o' *gravity!*
I *suspect* something very *similar* is what *started* this, Ben! That *liquid* all over the *floor* negates the *gravitational pull* of the --
Ben, *look out!*
A LOT of THAT. Only SLIGHTLY less unnerving...
Drag a guy outta bed at *three A.M...*
How'm I *ever* gonna give Tom Cruise a run f'r his money without my *beauty rest?*
...than the CONSTANT sound of a bag of ROCKS in a CLOTHES DRYER.

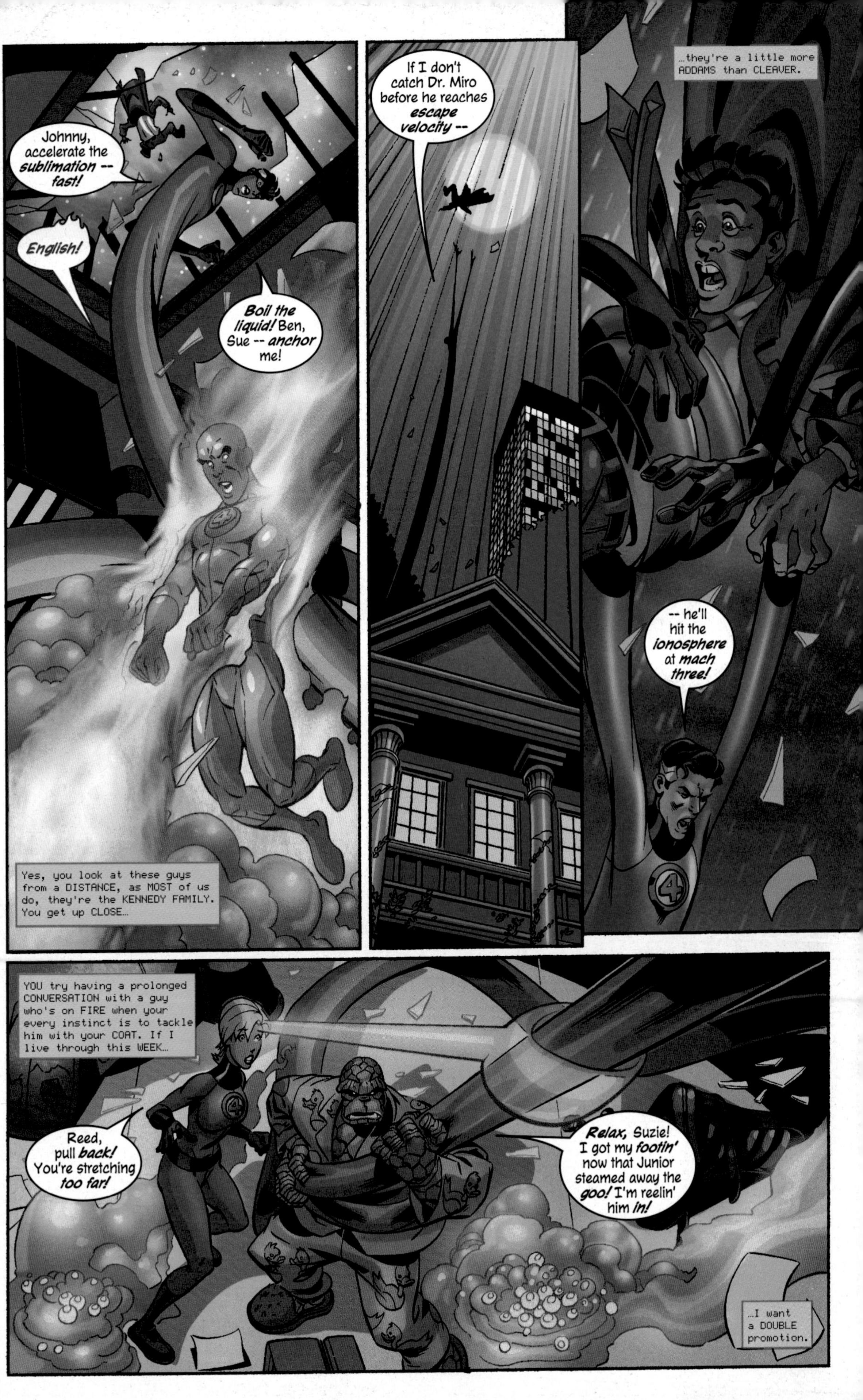
Johnny, accelerate the sublimation -- fast!
English!
Boil the liquid! Ben, Sue -- anchor me!
Yes, you look at these guys from a DISTANCE, as MOST of us do, they're the KENNEDY FAMILY. You get up CLOSE...
If I don't catch Dr. Miro before he reaches escape velocity --
...they're a little more ADDAMS than CLEAVER.
-- he'll hit the ionosphere at mach three!
YOU try having a prolonged CONVERSATION with a guy who's on FIRE when your every instinct is to tackle him with your COAT. If I live through this WEEK...
Reed, pull back! You're stretching too far!
Relax, Suzie! I got my footin' now that Junior steamed away the goo! I'm reelin' him in!
...I want a DOUBLE promotion.

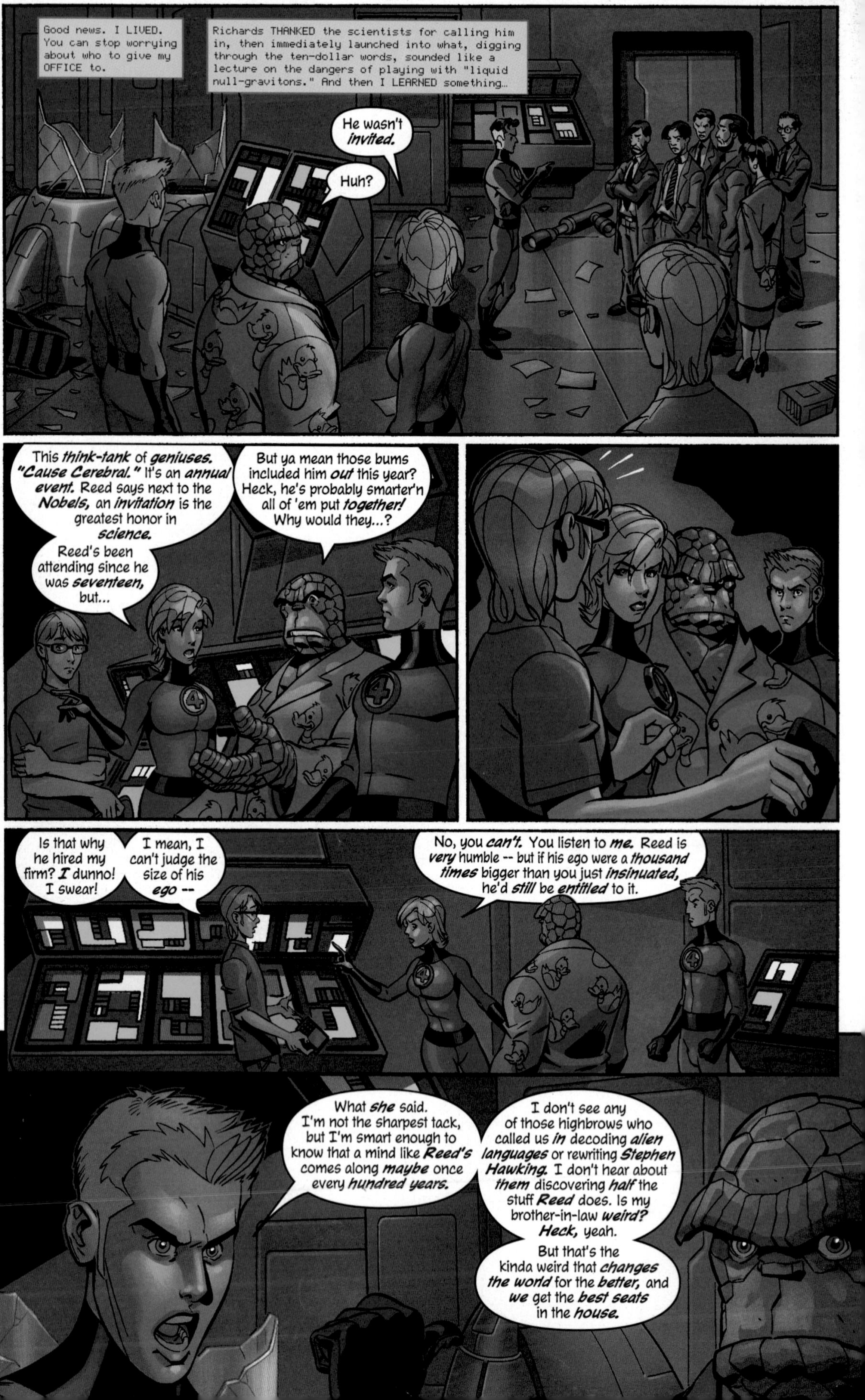

Good news. I LIVED. You can stop worrying about who to give my OFFICE to.
Richards THANKED the scientists for calling him in, then immediately launched into what, digging through the ten-dollar words, sounded like a lecture on the dangers of playing with "liquid null-gravitons." And then I LEARNED something...
He wasn't *invited.*
Huh?
This *think-tank* of *geniuses.* *"Cause Cerebral."* It's an *annual event.* Reed says next to the *Nobels,* an *invitation* is the greatest honor in *science.*
Reed's been attending since he was *seventeen,* but...
But ya mean those bums included him *out* this year? Heck, he's probably smarter'n all of 'em put *together!* Why would they...?
Is that why he hired my firm? *I* dunno! I swear!
I mean, I can't judge the size of his *ego* --
No, you *can't.* You listen to *me.* Reed is *very* humble -- but if his ego were a *thousand times* bigger than you just *insinuated,* he'd *still* be *entitled* to it.
What *she* said. I'm not the sharpest tack, but I'm smart enough to know that a mind like *Reed's* comes along *maybe* once every *hundred years.*
I don't see any of those highbrows who called us *in* decoding *alien languages* or rewriting *Stephen Hawking.* I don't hear about *them* discovering *half* the stuff *Reed* does. Is my brother-in-law *weird?* *Heck,* yeah.
But that's the kinda weird that *changes the world* for the *better,* and *we* get the *best seats* in the *house.*

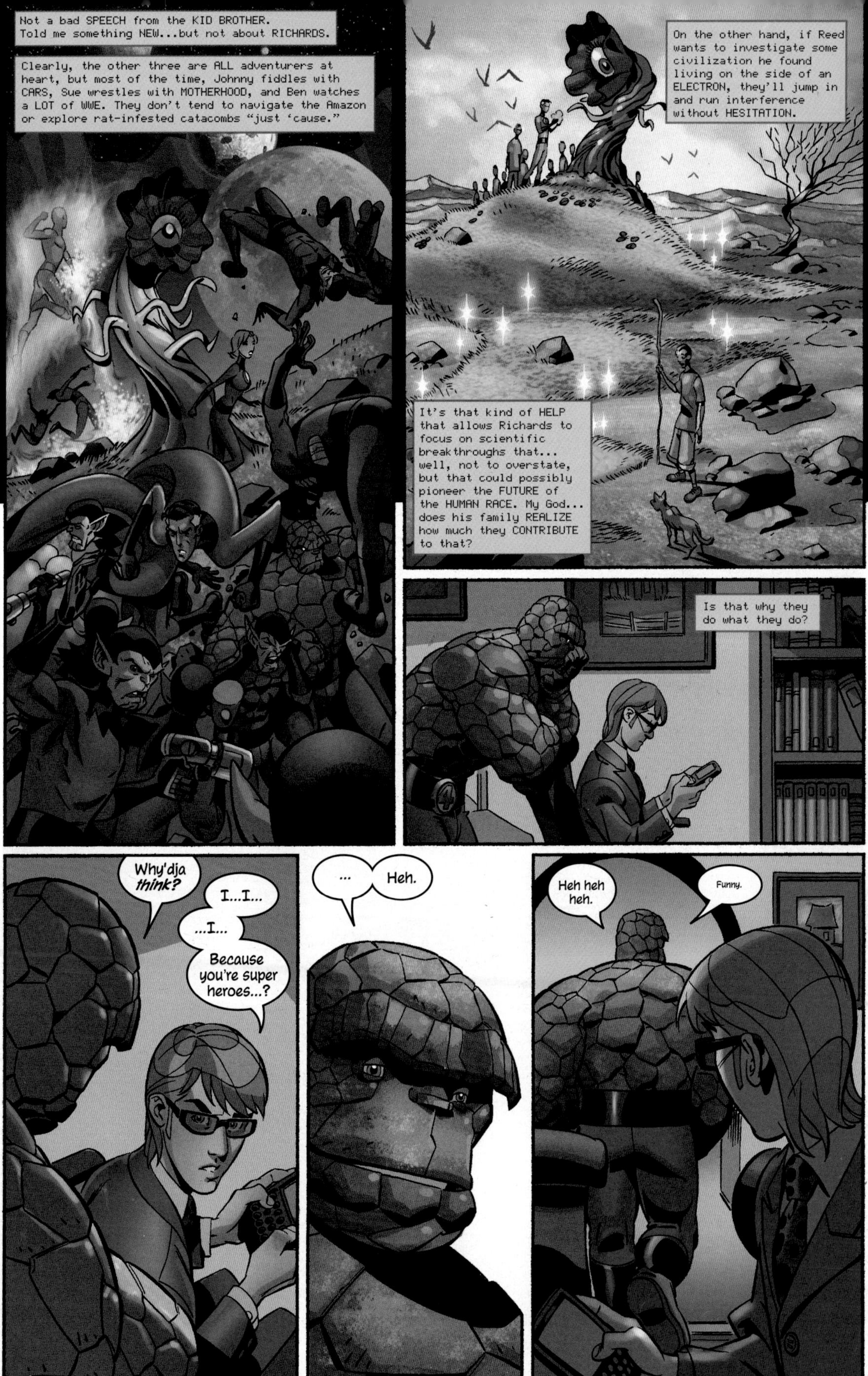

Not a bad SPEECH from the KID BROTHER. Told me something NEW...but not about RICHARDS.
Clearly, the other three are ALL adventurers at heart, but most of the time, Johnny fiddles with CARS, Sue wrestles with MOTHERHOOD, and Ben watches a LOT of WWE. They don't tend to navigate the Amazon or explore rat-infested catacombs "just 'cause."
On the other hand, if Reed wants to investigate some civilization he found living on the side of an ELECTRON, they'll jump in and run interference without HESITATION.
It's that kind of HELP that allows Richards to focus on scientific breakthroughs that... well, not to overstate, but that could possibly pioneer the FUTURE of the HUMAN RACE. My God... does his family REALIZE how much they CONTRIBUTE to that?
Is that why they do what they do?
Why'dja *think?*
I...I...
...I...
Because you're super heroes...?
...
Heh.
Heh heh heh.
Funny.

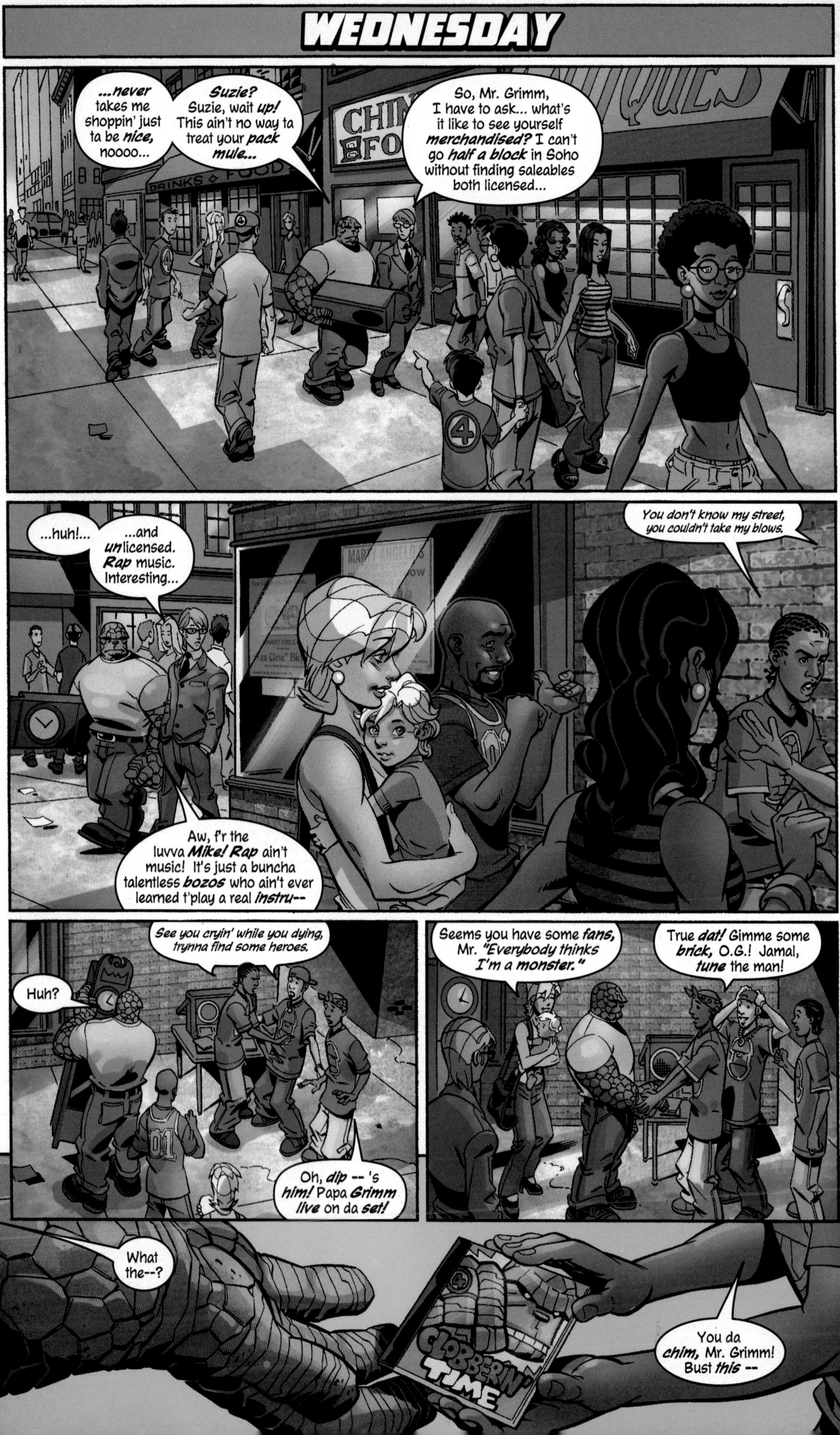
WEDNESDAY
...never takes me shoppin' just ta be nice, noooo...
Suzie? Suzie, wait up! This ain't no way ta treat your pack mule...
So, Mr. Grimm, I have to ask... what's it like to see yourself merchandised? I can't go half a block in Soho without finding saleables both licensed...
...huh!...
...and unlicensed. Rap music. Interesting...
You don't know my street, you couldn't take my blows.
Aw, f'r the luvva Mike! Rap ain't music! It's just a buncha talentless bozos who ain't ever learned t'play a real instru--
See you cryin' while you dying, trynna find some heroes.
Huh?
Oh, dip -- 's him! Papa Grimm live on da set!
Seems you have some fans, Mr. "Everybody thinks I'm a monster."
True dat! Gimme some brick, O.G.! Jamal, tune the man!
What the--?
CLOBBERIN' TIME
You da chim, Mr. Grimm! Bust this --

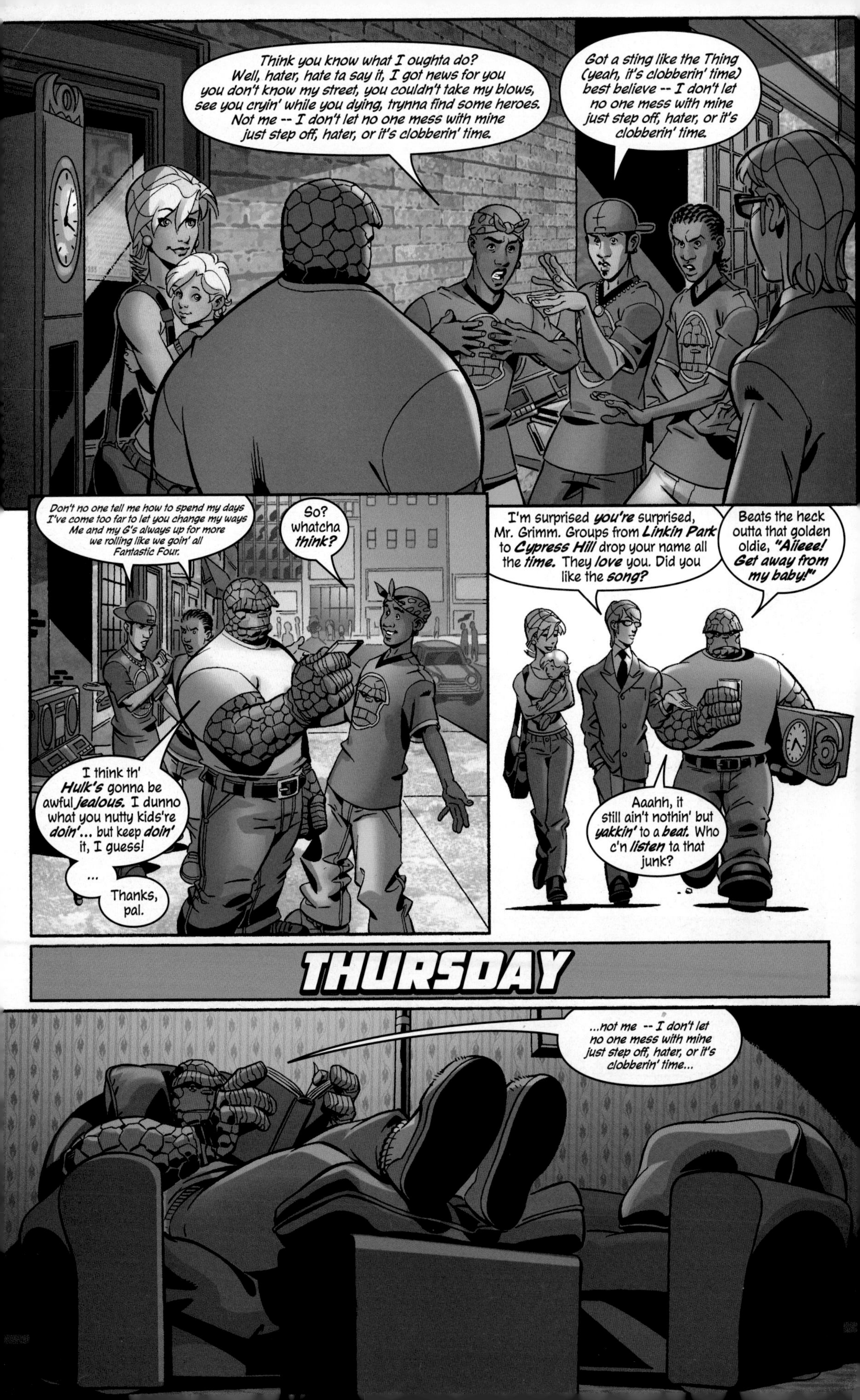
Think you know what I oughta do? Well, hater, hate ta say it, I got news for you you don't know my street, you couldn't take my blows, see you cryin' while you dying, trynna find some heroes. Not me -- I don't let no one mess with mine just step off, hater, or it's clobberin' time.
Got a sting like the Thing (yeah, it's clobberin' time) best believe -- I don't let no one mess with mine just step off, hater, or it's clobberin' time.
Don't no one tell me how to spend my days I've come too far to let you change my ways Me and my G's always up for more we rolling like we goin' all Fantastic Four.
So? whatcha think?
I think th' Hulk's gonna be awful jealous. I dunno what you nutty kids're doin'... but keep doin' it, I guess!
... Thanks, pal.
I'm surprised you're surprised, Mr. Grimm. Groups from Linkin Park to Cypress Hill drop your name all the time. They love you. Did you like the song?
Beats the heck outta that golden oldie, "Aiieee! Get away from my baby!"
Aaahh, it still ain't nothin' but yakkin' to a beat. Who c'n listen ta that junk?
THURSDAY
...not me -- I don't let no one mess with mine just step off, hater, or it's clobberin' time...

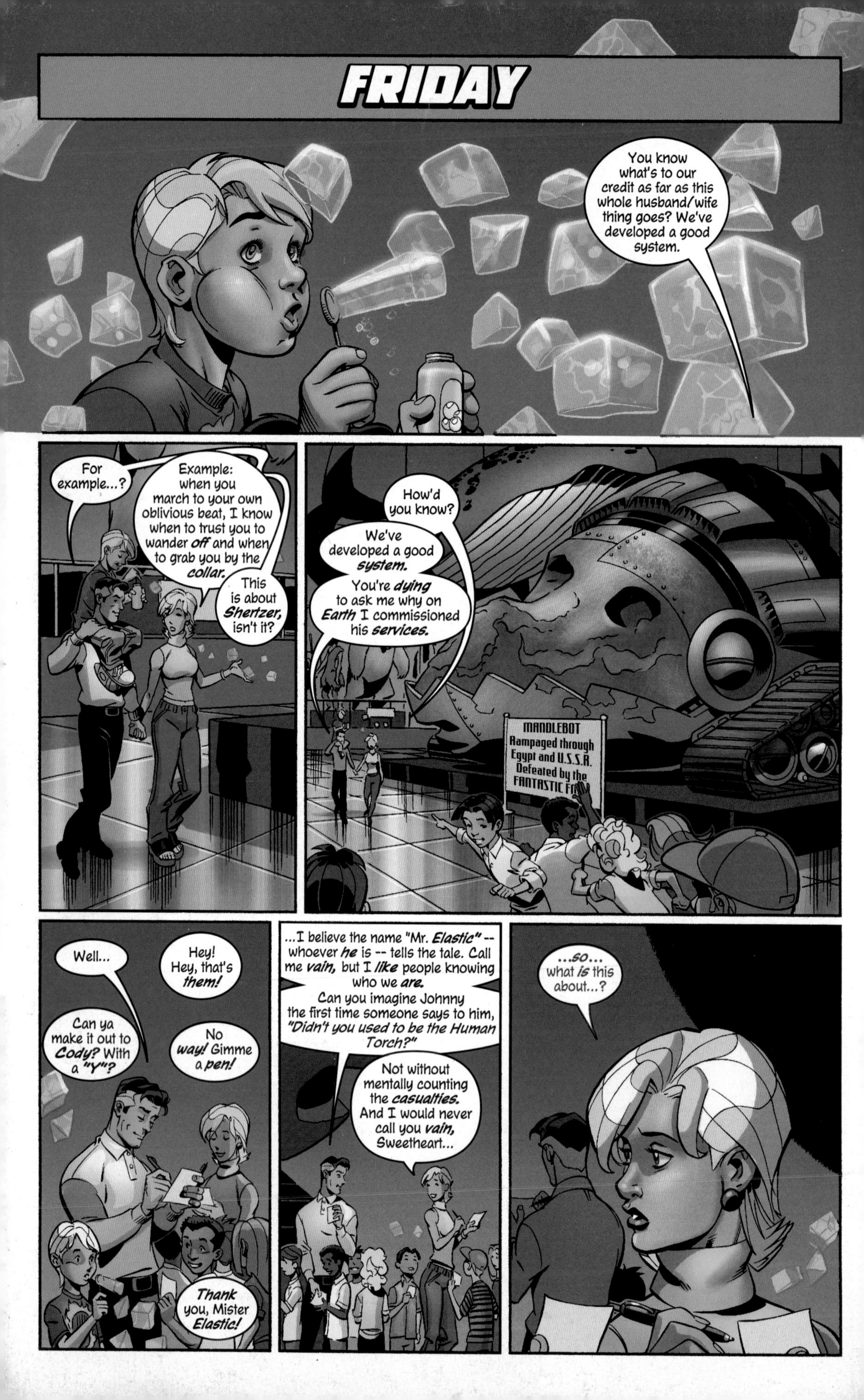
FRIDAY
You know what's to our credit as far as this whole husband/wife thing goes? We've developed a good system.
For example...?
Example: when you march to your own oblivious beat, I know when to trust you to wander off and when to grab you by the collar.
This is about Shertzer, isn't it?
How'd you know?
We've developed a good system.
You're dying to ask me why on Earth I commissioned his services.
MANDLEBOT Rampaged through Egypt and U.S.S.R. Defeated by the FANTASTIC FO
Well...
Hey! Hey, that's them!
Can ya make it out to Cody? With a "Y"?
No way! Gimme a pen!
Thank you, Mister Elastic!
...I believe the name "Mr. Elastic" -- whoever he is -- tells the tale. Call me vain, but I like people knowing who we are.
Can you imagine Johnny the first time someone says to him, "Didn't you used to be the Human Torch?"
Not without mentally counting the casualties. And I would never call you vain, Sweetheart...
...so... what is this about...?

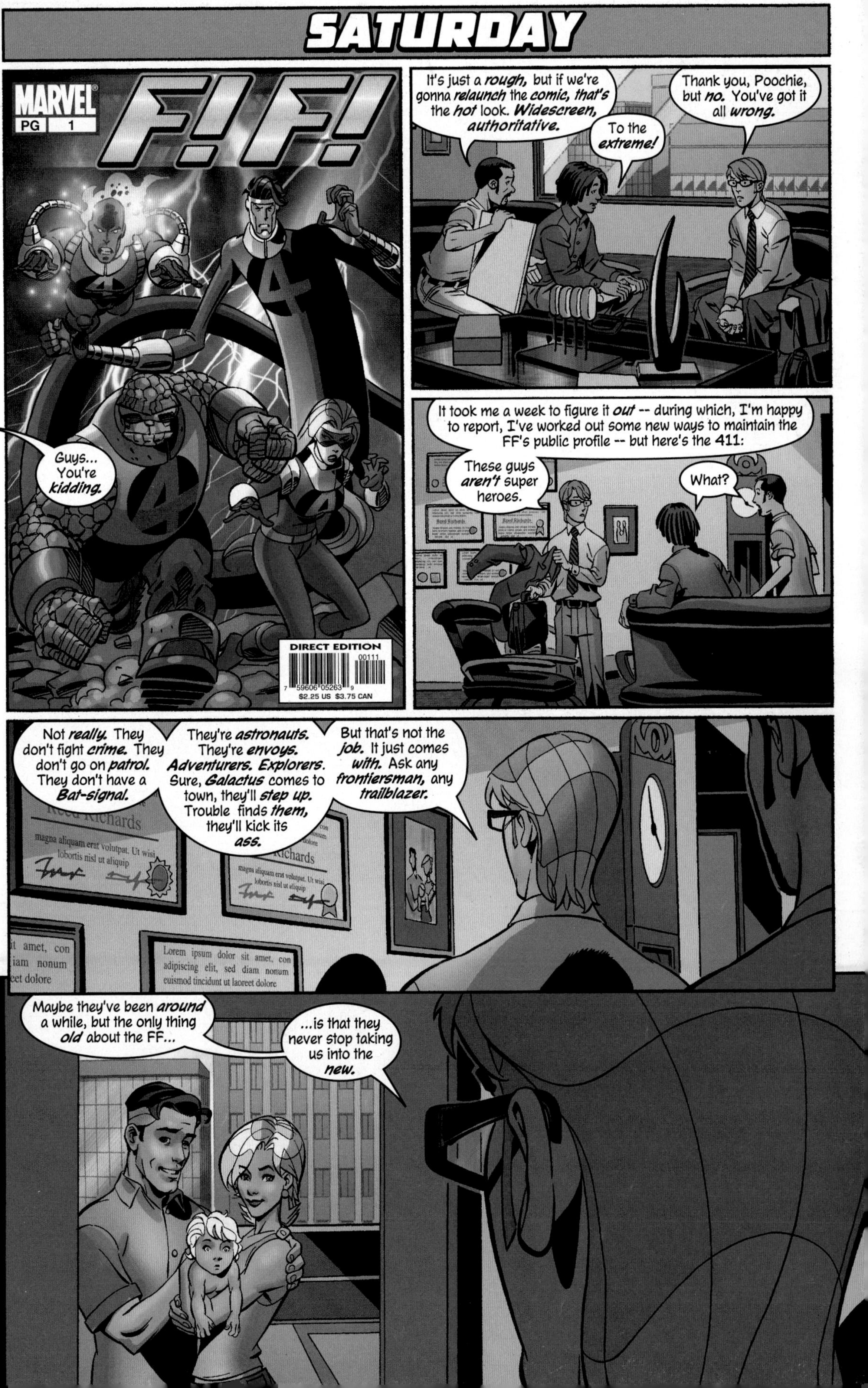

SATURDAY
MARVEL
PG 1
F!F!
Guys... You're *kidding.*
DIRECT EDITION
$2.25 US $3.75 CAN
It's just a *rough,* but if we're gonna *relaunch* the *comic, that's* the *hot* look. *Widescreen, authoritative.*
To the *extreme!*
Thank you, Poochie, but *no.* You've got it all *wrong.*
It took me a week to figure it *out* -- during which, I'm happy to report, I've worked out some new ways to maintain the FF's public profile -- but here's the 411:
These guys *aren't* super heroes.
What?
Not *really.* They don't fight *crime.* They don't go on *patrol.* They don't have a *Bat-signal.*
They're *astronauts.* They're *envoys. Adventurers. Explorers.* Sure, *Galactus* comes to town, they'll *step up.* Trouble finds *them,* they'll kick its *ass.*
But that's not the *job.* It just comes *with.* Ask any *frontiersman,* any *trailblazer.*
Reed Richards
magna aliquam erat volutpat. Ut wisi lobortis nisl ut aliquip
Richards
magna aliquam erat volutpat. Ut wisi lobortis nisl ut aliquip
Lorem ipsum dolor sit amet, con adipiscing elit, sed diam nonum euismod tincidunt ut laoreet dolore
Maybe they've been *around* a while, but the only thing *old* about the FF...
...is that they never stop taking us into the *new.*

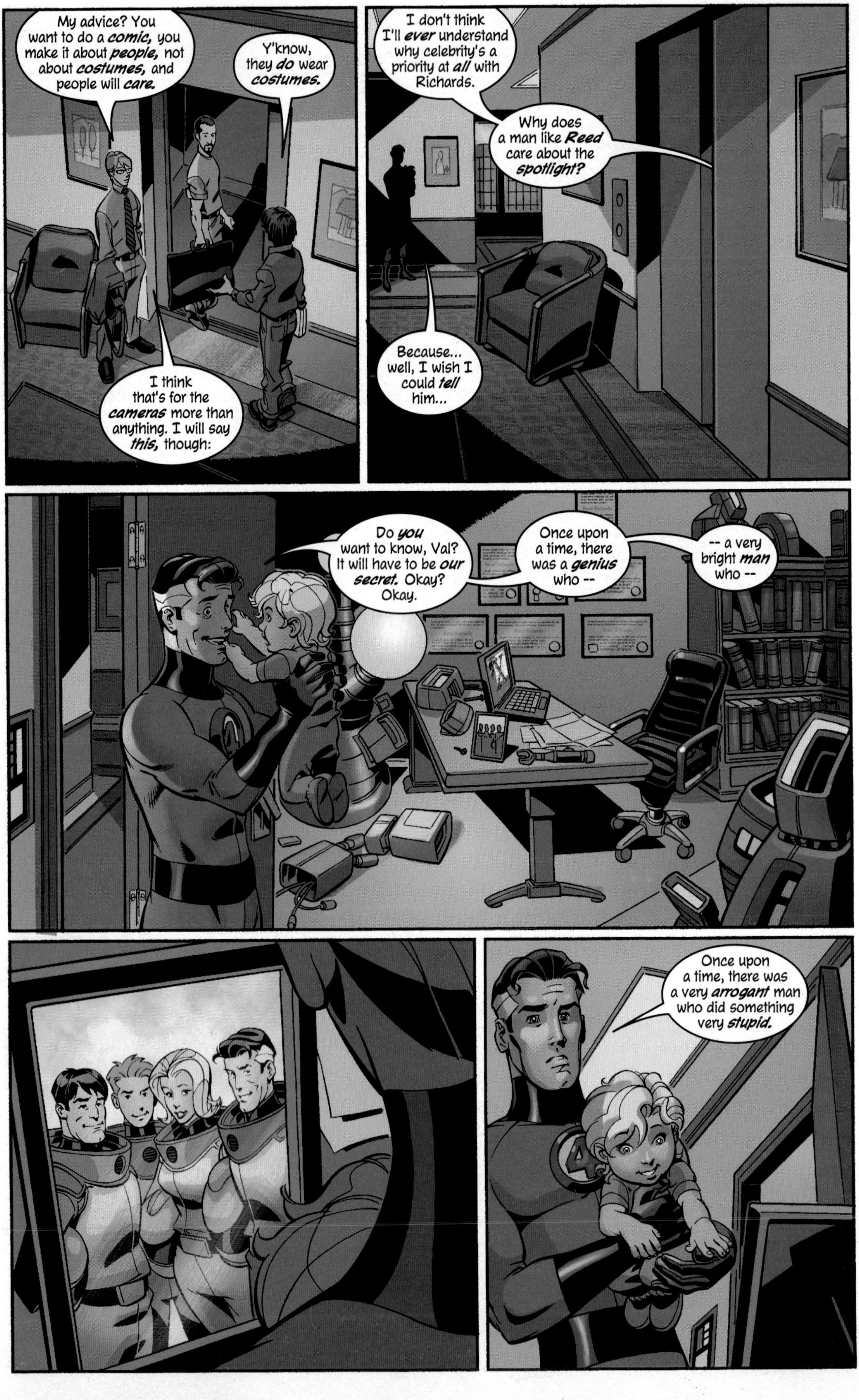
My advice? You want to do a *comic,* you make it about *people,* not about *costumes,* and people will *care.*
Y'know, they *do* wear *costumes.*
I think that's for the *cameras* more than anything. I will say *this,* though:
I don't think I'll *ever* understand why celebrity's a priority at *all* with Richards.
Why does a man like *Reed* care about the *spotlight?*
Because... well, I wish I could *tell* him...
Do *you* want to know, Val? It will have to be *our secret.* Okay? Okay.
Once upon a time, there was a *genius* who --
-- a very bright *man* who --
Once upon a time, there was a very *arrogant* man who did something very *stupid.*

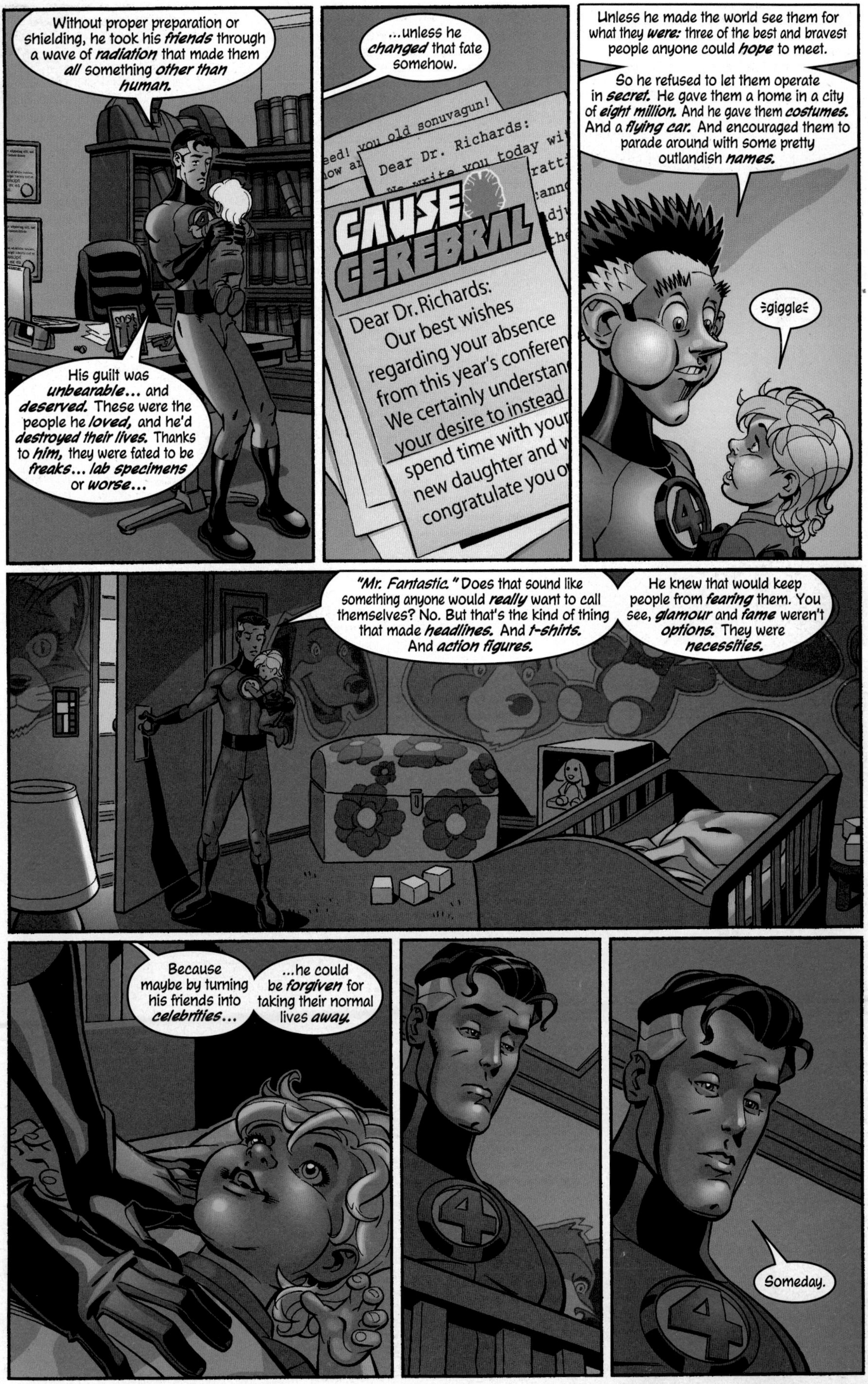
Without proper preparation or shielding, he took his *friends* through a wave of *radiation* that made them *all* something *other than human.*
His guilt was *unbearable...* and *deserved.* These were the people he *loved,* and he'd *destroyed their lives.* Thanks to *him,* they were fated to be *freaks... lab specimens* or *worse...*
...unless he *changed* that fate somehow.
you old sonuvagun!
Dear Dr. Richards:
CAUSE CEREBRAL
Dear Dr. Richards:
Our best wishes
regarding your absence
from this year's conferen
We certainly understan
your desire to instead
spend time with your
new daughter and w
congratulate you o
Unless he made the world see them for what they *were:* three of the best and bravest people anyone could *hope* to meet.
So he refused to let them operate in *secret.* He gave them a home in a city of *eight million.* And he gave them *costumes.* And a *flying car.* And encouraged them to parade around with some pretty outlandish *names.*
giggle
"Mr. Fantastic." Does that sound like something anyone would *really* want to call themselves? No. But that's the kind of thing that made *headlines.* And *t-shirts.* And *action figures.*
He knew that would keep people from *fearing* them. You see, *glamour* and *fame* weren't *options.* They were *necessities.*
Because maybe by turning his friends into *celebrities...*
...he could be *forgiven* for taking their normal lives *away.*
Someday.

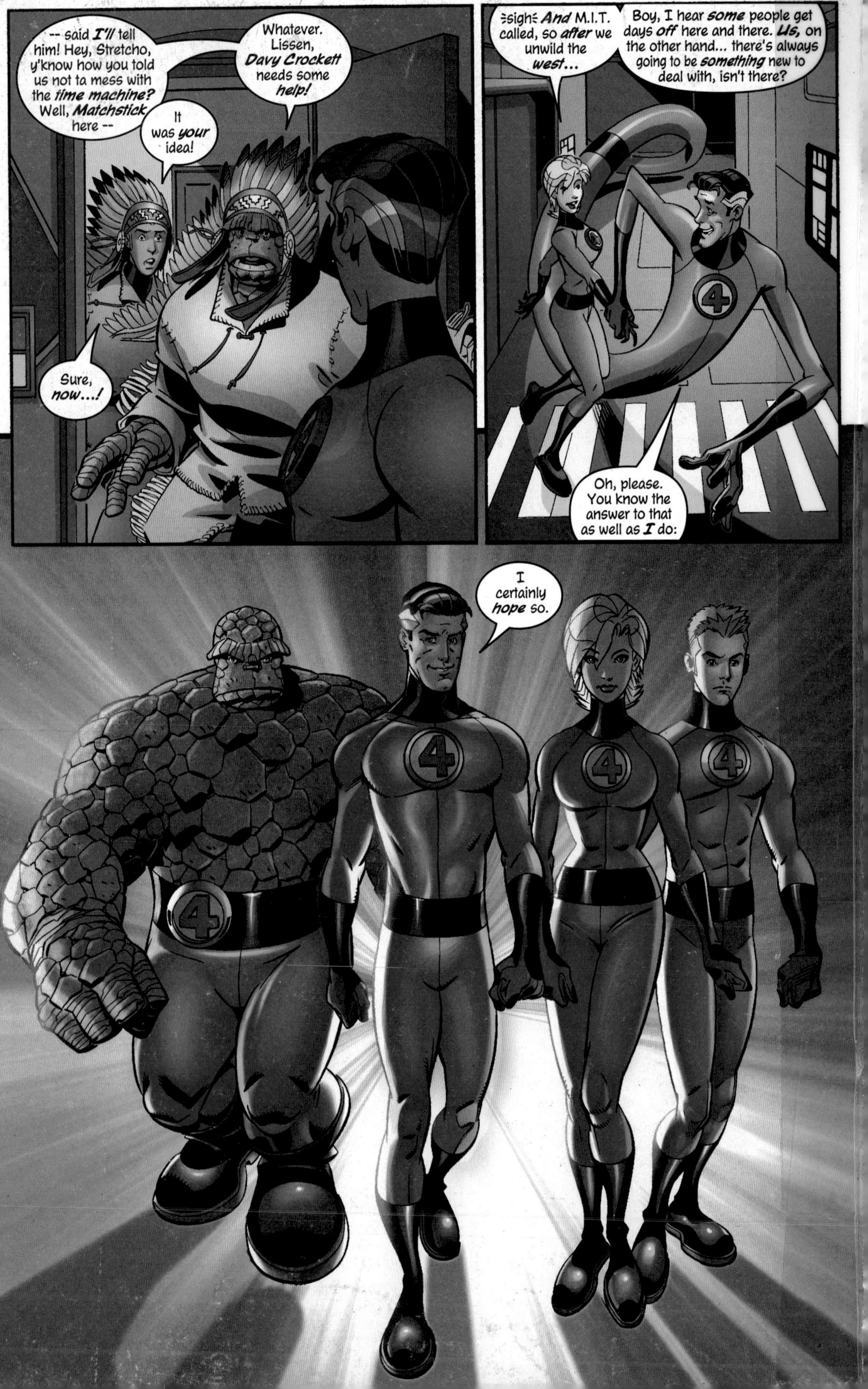
-- said I'll tell him! Hey, Stretcho, y'know how you told us not ta mess with the time machine? Well, Matchstick here --
It was your idea!
Whatever. Lissen, Davy Crockett needs some help!
Sure, now...!
sigh And M.I.T. called, so after we unwild the west...
Boy, I hear some people get days off here and there. Us, on the other hand... there's always going to be something new to deal with, isn't there?
Oh, please. You know the answer to that as well as I do:
I certainly hope so.

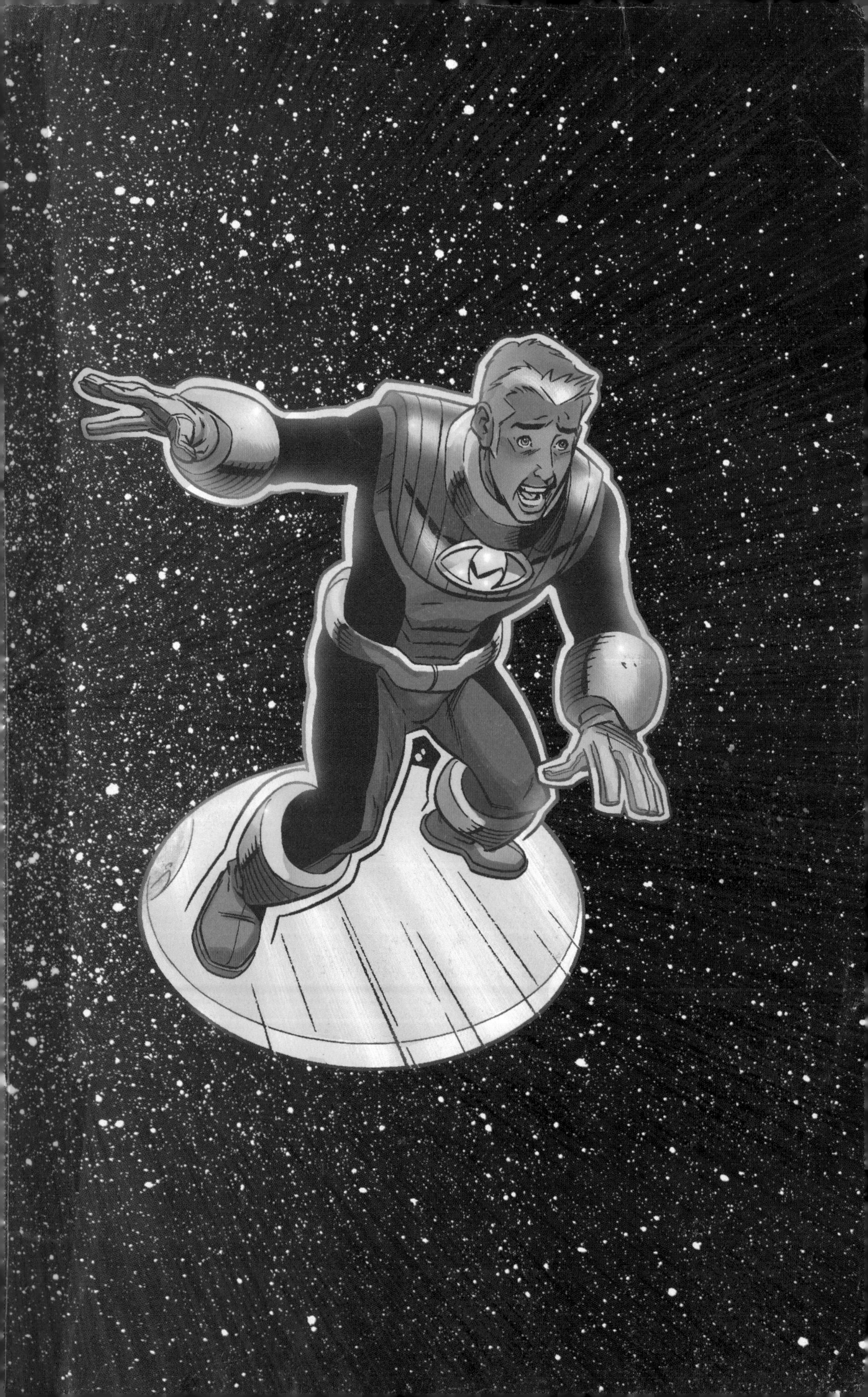

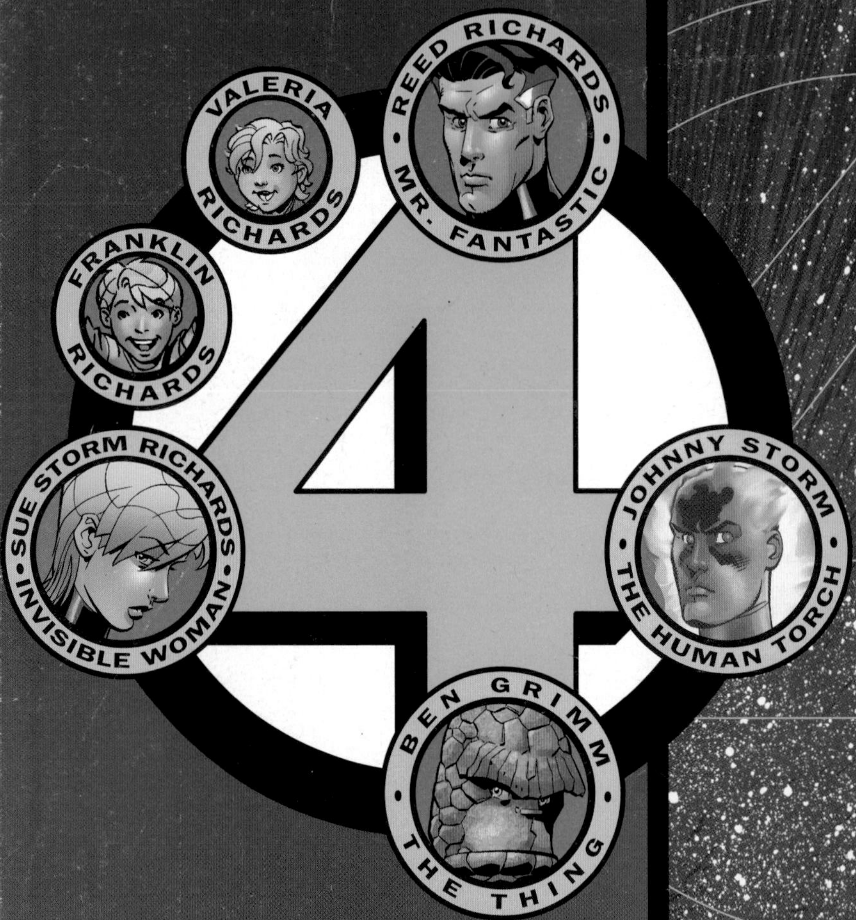
REED RICHARDS
MR. FANTASTIC
VALERIA RICHARDS
FRANKLIN RICHARDS
SUE STORM RICHARDS
INVISIBLE WOMAN
JOHNNY STORM
THE HUMAN TORCH
BEN GRIMM
THE THING

THE FANTASTIC FOUR

4 A team—and a family—of adventurers, explorers and imaginauts, the Fantastic Four lead lives both ordinary—and extraordinary. As of today:

3 An alien being named Zius has been protecting innocents from the world-eating menace known as Galactus. Using advanced science, Zius has developed an "intergalactic shareware" technology capable of rendering entire planets invisible to Galactus's detection.

2 Zius had learned, however, that in this vast universe there is one unique being who has the natural ability to nullify his cloaking shields: Sue Richards, the Invisible Woman. Zius marked her for death before Galactus could someday exploit her power, and only by hiding Sue's abilities in Johnny's body and vice-versa could Reed throw Zius off her trail. All seemed well....

1 ...until Galactus appeared, killed Zius and his crew, and took Johnny instead.